What early readers & medical professionals are saying:

♦ "From one of the bariatric community's thought leaders comes a must read guide for any patient, primary care physician or bariatric surgeon considering bariatric surgery as a treatment for obesity or diabetes. Dr. Sasse takes us through a journey of hope, without sugar-coating the risk involved in this life-changing operation and outlines the key steps to becoming a healthier and happy person through successful preoperative and postoperative treatment plans. Bariatric surgery has been called the most effective tool in the treatment of morbid obesity. This book is the operational manual of that tool."

-- DR. KEVIN HUFFMAN,
MEDICAL DIRECTOR OF THE AMERICAN BARIATRIC CENTERS,
PRESIDENT, AMERICAN BARIATRIC CONSULTANTS

♦ "Dr. Sasse stays at the cutting edge of this technology and offers all of us insight into what the latest innovations are in the newest procedures in safer, and more effective, technology. The newest information on the minimally invasive band with imbrication, and the laparoscopic sleeve procedure are simply a wonder. I am grateful that I no longer have pre-diabetes or high cholesterol, and I am working hard to sustain the new life I have been given. Thank you for writing this book, Dr. Sasse, where do you find the time?"

-- LINDA JONES, WEIGHT-LOSS SURGERY PATIENT,
NOW TRAINING FOR HER FIRST MARATHON

D0896396

♦ "This is an amazing book for the patient or professional who wants to learn about weight-loss surgery. It is the kind of book every surgeon and every surgery center should provide to prospective patients. I learned more about the subject in a couple hours of reading this book than I'd learned in years of anecdotes about bariatric surgery."

--SCOTT BECKER, JD, CPA, HARVARD LAW SCHOOL '89,
PUBLISHER BECKERS ASC REVIEW,
CO-CHAIR, MCGRUIRE WOODS HEALTHCARE PRACTICE

♦ "What an insightful guide for patients seeking to lose weight! But this book is also a highly informative guide for Ambulatory center leaders, health care administrators and personnel who will now understand the coming tied of outpatient procedures for weight loss. One of the best personal health books I have ever read. A unique combination of fascinating technology and powerful inspiration."

--JOHN H. GANSER, MD, FACS

♦ "Dr. Sasse has managed to pull together what is surely to become an international standard. Coupling clear, concise and easy to understand information with real life examples from his own practice, Dr. Sasse pulls together both the clinical and the practical in a style sure to be a hit with patients."

--REGI SCHINDLER, PRESIDENT & CEO, BLIS, INC.

♦ "Dr. Kent Sasse has written the quintessential book on weight-loss surgery. Informative without ever being overwhelming, Dr. Sasse explains the process in an explicit, concise way beneficial to both the mildly curious and those seriously considering this life-changing procedure. Having had the surgery with Dr. Sasse I can truly say that he has laid out the options with all their benefits and risks. Reading his book would give anyone the knowledge and information needed to decide on whether this innovative approach to lifelong health should be in their future."

--KATHY BURKE, WEIGHT-LOSS SURGERY PATIENT

♦ "It took 50 years, but Dr. Sasse has redefined the weight loss standard. He is known for his professionalism and is loved by his patients. His book is the culmination of his work to date in this very important field. A must read for anyone considering their options for weight-loss surgery."

--THOMAS MALLON, CEO, REGENT SURGICAL HEALTH, CHICAGO ILLINOIS

♦ "Not only is his book a help guide and knowledge manual, but it also inspires the reader to see how they CAN DO IT and how they WILL SUCCEED! I will use it to hand out to my Life Coaching clients who are considering both surgical and nonsurgical weight loss."

--RICHARD CUNNINGHAM, PROFESSIONAL LIFE COACH

♦ "An extremely comprehensive look into the most powerful tool for effective long-term weight loss. Dr. Sasse goes far beyond procedural details and provides an all-encompassing look into bariatric weight-loss surgery. Written by one of the foremost experts in the medical weight-loss field, Outpatient Weight-Loss Surgery is an absolutely essential guide for anyone considering weight-loss surgery."

--STEPHEN B. MAYVILLE, PH.D., BCBA
LICENSED CLINICAL PSYCHOLOGIST
DIRECTOR OF PSYCHOLOGICAL SERVICES,
THE INTERNATIONAL METABOLIC INSTITUTE

♦ "Full of practical wisdom and insight, Dr. Sasse's Guide to Outpatient Weight-Loss Surgery provides real-life examples and testimonials plus a careful, experienced surgeon's advice about how to achieve the best results. This book will help many people change their lives for the better."

--COLLEEN COOK, PRESIDENT
BARIATRIC SUPPORT CENTERS INTERNATIONAL,
AUTHOR, THE SUCCESS HABITS OF WEIGHT LOSS SURGERY PATIENTS

Outpatient Weight-Loss Surgery:

The expert guide to minimally invasive weight-loss and the cure for diabetes

Second Edition
A SASSE GUIDE

BY KENT SASSE, MD, MPH, FACS, FACRS

FOREWORD TO THE SECOND EDITION
– SACHIKO T. ST. JEOR, PH.D., R.D.

FOREWORD TO THE FIRST EDITION
– PHILLIP SCHAUER, MD

INTERNATIONAL METABOLIC INSTITUTE, LLC
RENO, NEVADA

Edited by Jennifer R Baumer, INK Communications
Inside pages designed by Hepic Photography, INK Communications
Cover designed by Hep Svadja, Hepic Photography

The author is grateful for permission to include the following previously copyrighted materials and images:
Ethicon EndoSurery, Allergan Corporation, Covidian and EndoGastric Solutions.

Sasse, Kent
Outpatient weight-loss surgery: safe and successful weight loss with modern bariatric surgery, second edition / Kent Sasse.

Includes bibliographical references and index.
ISBN: 978-1-934727-27-0

1. Obesity—Surgery—Popular works. 2. Gastric bypass—Popular works.
3. Weight loss—Popular works. 1. Title.

Dedication

To my family: Cara, Liz, Alexandra, Aden, Olivia and Victoria, who provide life's inspiration.

Acknowledgements

I AM DEEPLY INDEBTED to so many people who have helped to make this book possible and who have helped in its research and writing. First and foremost, I would like to thank my patients, who perform daily miracles of fighting this disease of obesity, and who challenge me and my colleagues to be better caregivers and better people.

I am indebted to so many people for their hard work and dedication to our patients and to the work of combating this disease. To Jared Brandt, Ellen Ackerman, Margo Walker, Sarai Sullivan, Kristine Shoenberger, Gayleen Gott-Anderson, Cindi Lee, Breanna Elrod, Peggy Lugo, Caren Chealander, Donna Wainscoat, Trees Lonis-Muller, Patrick Allen, Curtis Smith, Darolyn Skelton, Laurie McGinley, Marte Lyson, Mason Hermosillo, Dr. Kozar, Dr. Ganser, Dr. Watson, Tracy Visher, Natasha Mulqueen, Deacon Shoenberger, PhD, Stephen Mayville, PhD, Brie Moore, PhD, Mark Conte and Cara Sasse.

Hep Svadja, Jennifer Baumer and Natasha Mulqueen have done an amazing job with editing and designing this book. Dionne Lim and Peggy Lugo have been outstanding research assistants and investigators of facts. I would also like to thank Jason Green, Leah Scherschel and Abbi Whitaker for their hard work, patience, dedication, and sense of humor.

And special thanks to Roy Hill, Norma Seed, Karen Mitchell, Margi Houk, Richard Cunningham, Terry Beauchamp, Carol Bradley, Karen Fisher, Dee Gregory, Eleanor Houk, Beth Devine, Debby Howard, Jonda Jones, Mike Darragh, Nancy Guthery, Sherrill Sundell, Anita Acosta, Kathy Burke and Mary Francis.

Foreword (Second Edition)

I HAVE KNOWN Dr. Sasse for more than 12 years through his work on the faculty at the University of Nevada School of Medicine where he volunteers, teaches and writes. It was clear from his early work in the field of bariatric surgery that he knew something profound about these procedures that most people did not – namely, that they exert a powerful, durable and salutary effect on the body's metabolism, glucose control and appetite. Since the publication of the first edition of this book, so much has emerged from the basic science research laboratory that has confirmed and elucidated his earlier observations: that people can and do succeed at permanently losing weight, improving their quality of life, and curing a host of health conditions – including diabetes. If you or someone you love is overweight or diabetic, this book is an absolute must-read. With over 80 million of us now considered "pre-diabetic," no other book is as important to Americans today, or as timely.

Among the most stunning developments in health and metabolism over the past 25 years are the randomized studies that now clearly place surgery in the forefront of first-line treatment considerations for obese individuals (BMI ≥35 with comorbid conditions, especially Type 2 diabetes). Through Dr. Sasse's clear explanations, we learn how and why these minimally invasive procedures are so effective at reversing the diabetes disease process. This book offers a compelling case for the importance of losing weight as the most critical change a person can make for their health and longevity.

As a Registered Dietitian and nutrition researcher over these past many years, I am thoroughly heartened to see such a lucid and scientifically well-founded expert guide to the nutritional component that is so essential to the long-term success of the procedures. With his delightful writing style, Dr. Sasse presents his clear, specific diet plan in Chapter 6, a plan that will go a long way toward ensuring success as he encourages readers to seek the advice of dietitians and other health professionals.

If you read only one book this year on health, nutrition, weight loss or diabetes, make it this one. It is the only book that effectively describes the latest weight-loss procedures such as the laparoscopic sleeve gastrectomy and the Band with Imbrication. It is the only expert guide written by a practicing bariatric surgeon who works daily on the front lines to deliver the latest science of both surgery and nutrition to his patients for their long-term success. Dr. Sasse stresses that weight loss and the decisions for surgery and other interventions (including diet and exercise) are important, personal decisions. He offers easy to understand information and practical advice that should be considered thoroughly when choosing solutions to a very resistant disease process. Most importantly, he is sincere and through his experience he wishes to share his success, knowledge and the direct practical advice that has helped many of his patients change their lives forever.

– SACHIKO T. ST. JEOR, PH.D., R.D.
PROFESSOR OF INTERNAL MEDICINE EMERITA
CLINICAL PROFESSOR, DEPT. OF FAMILY MEDICINE
UNIVERSITY OF NEVADA SCHOOL OF MEDICINE
RENO AND LAS VEGAS, NEVADA
AND
ADJUNCT PROFESSOR, DIVISION OF NUTRITION
COLLEGE OF HEALTH SCIENCES UNIVERSITY OF UTAH, SALT LAKE CITY, UTAH

4

Foreword (First Edition)

IN RECENT YEARS, pioneering surgeons have applied sophisticated minimally-invasive surgical techniques to the practice of weight-loss surgery, known as bariatric surgery. Long term studies now clearly demonstrate profound improvements in the lives of overweight people who undergo the surgery. The benefits are striking and range from markedly longer lifespan, to improvements in quality of life, to the resolution of diabetes, hypertension, sleep apnea and many other serious diseases. Today, weight gain and obesity adversely affect the lives of a billion people around the world, and solutions that are less invasive and more demonstrably effective are more available now than ever before.

From participating in the initial stages of metabolic and weight-loss surgery, to witnessing the most recent innovations in technical medical gadgetry, it has been immensely gratifying to see my earliest and most optimistic vision of what this surgery could mean to so many people now become manifest. When I authored the widely cited paper, Outcomes After laparoscopic Roux-en-Y gastric bypass for morbid obesity (Annals of Surgery 232(4):515-529, October, 2000), few in the medical community or lay public understood the impact that weight loss surgery could have on an individual person's life, let alone its impact on an overweight society.

That impact is now occurring daily, as over 200,000 people undergo weight loss surgery annually in the U.S. alone. And if this book has the kind of impact I believe it will, that number is likely to rise significantly.

Over the last 40 years I have had the honor of leading the field of weight loss medicine and surgery toward real solutions that work for real people. With great effort and perseverance, and against many obstacles, devoted surgeons discovered techniques that profoundly and favorably affected the lives of overweight people, leading them to dramatically reduce their weight and live longer, healthier lives. These early interventions were invasive, open procedures with higher risks and complications than we would accept today. They led to newer and better procedures, and paved the way for the modern minimally invasive weight loss revolution chronicled in this book.

Dr. Sasse's book, Outpatient Weight Loss Surgery, is stunning not only because the existence of such a book was unthinkable only a few years ago, but also because of the clarity and succinctness with which Dr. Sasse explores the terrain of modern weight loss surgery.

If you or someone you love is overweight or obese, then the book you are holding in your hand is nothing short of essential reading material. This is one of the first books that explains the revolution of modern, minimally invasive, highly effective weight loss surgery and its transition to the outpatient environment. If you or someone you care about has even considered weight loss surgery, I strongly recommend that you read this book for its candid and insightful information and guidance.

What we are witnessing with the publication of this book is a sea-change in the treatment of obesity. As chronicled by Dr. Sasse, long gone are the days when a seriously overweight person had few medical professionals to whom he or she could turn. Long gone are the days when medicine offered little hope for an obese person seeking answers. Forty years ago, surgery was invasive and as yet unproven, and fad diets and dubious injections attracted customers who had few proven alternatives. What is perhaps most striking about the publication of this book is that it marks a turning point to a time in which effective proven, minimally-invasive solutions exist for long term weight loss and health improvement. As this book makes abundantly clear, that time is now.

One of the great tragedies over recent years has been that old stereotypes and the lack of fresh information have deterred many doctors from recommending weight loss surgery and have deterred countless millions of obese patients from seeking it. As numerous studies have now demonstrated, that has led to so much unnecessary suffering, disease and early mortality from obesity.

It is my hope that with the reach of this book, and the greater and more widespread understanding of the impact of obesity on a person's health, that more people who so desperately need it can avail themselves of this valuable medical treatment. Perhaps the move to less and less invasive techniques and the shift to the outpatient arena will inspire more doctors to recommend the procedure and more obese patients to investigate it.

Weight loss surgery is not for everyone and Dr. Sasse's sober and candid discussion of not only the benefits but also the risks and complications associated with weight loss surgery make it valuable reading for anyone considering weight loss treatments or any doctor recommending them.

– PHILLIP SCHAUER, MD
DIRECTOR, BARIATRIC SURGERY PROGRAM CLEVELAND CLINIC
PAST PRESIDENT, AMERICAN SOCIETY FOR METABOLIC AND BARIATRIC SURGEONS

About the Author

Kent Sasse, MD, MPH, FACS, FACRS, is a nationally known surgeon, authority on medically based weight loss, and a leader in the rapidly evolving field of metabolic and bariatric surgery. Google "weight loss expert" and Dr. Sasse usually appears at the very top, worldwide. The distinguished recipient of several awards, including recognition as one of northern Nevada's Healthcare Heroes and membership in the prestigious Alpha Omega Alpha Society for top medical graduates in the country, Dr. Sasse is the founder and medical director of the International Metabolic Institute, or iMetabolic, and nationally recognized medical and surgical weight-loss centers.

Dr. Sasse, a physician and father of five children, has treated thousands of patients seeking to lose weight, listened to their life stories, fought side by side with them in their battles with obesity, and celebrated with them in victories large and small. He founded the Obesity Prevention Foundation, a nonprofit whose mission is to raise awareness of the growing problem of childhood obesity, and to craft community solutions to treat and prevent it. Dr. Sasse has also created an integrated set of books, websites and blog posts covering topics of obesity, weight loss, bariatric surgery and healthy lifestyles. The SasseGuide series currently encompasses three books, *Outpatient Weight-Loss Surgery: Safe and Successful Weight Loss with Modern Bariatric Surgery, Doctor's Orders: 101 Medically Proven Tips for Losing Weight* (winner of the ForeWord Reviews 2009 Book of the Year Bronze Award in the Health category) and *Life-Changing Weight Loss: Feel More Energetic and Live a More Active Life with a Proven, Medically Based Weight-Loss Program.*

The recipient of a bachelor's degree in biochemistry at the University of California San Diego, where he graduated cum laude and Phi Beta Kappa, and two master's degrees, including a master's degree in public health stemming from research related to biostatistics and bioethics, from the University of California Berkeley, Dr. Sasse earned his M.D. from the University of California San Francisco where he was honored as one of its top graduates. He completed residency training in surgery, focusing on Minimally Invasive gastrointestinal surgery, at the University of California San Francisco, as well as fellowship training at the Lahey Clinic in Boston, Massachusetts, before establishing his practice in northern Nevada.

Dedicated to minimally invasive surgical solutions and individualized, state-of-the-art treatment of patients, Dr. Sasse brings a wealth of experience and expertise to the rapidly evolving fields of weight-loss medicine and weight-loss surgery. He has written and continues to pursue research studies regarding metabolism, weight loss, regenerative wound healing, minimally invasive procedures and weight-loss surgery, and he lectures frequently on topics related to obesity and weight reduction at the University of Nevada School of Medicine and to audiences nationally. He authored the widely cited research paper on outpatient weight-loss surgery published in the peer-review medical literature (Outpatient weight loss surgery: initiating a gastric bypass and gastric banding ambulatory weight loss surgery center. JSLS 13(1):50-5 (2009) PMID 19366541). Through his nationally recognized programs, Dr. Sasse and his outstanding staff provide patients the highest level of compassionate medicine, scientific evidence and personalized care in the field of weight reduction.

Dr. Sasse is the author of a number of books:

Outpatient Weight-Loss Surgery: Safe and Successful Weight Loss with Modern Bariatric Surgery, a SasseGuide

Doctor's Orders: 101 Medically Proven Tips for Losing Weight, a SasseGuide.
This book won the ForeWord Reviews 2009 Book of the Year Bronze Award for the Health category.

Life-Changing Weight Loss: Feel More Energetic and Live a More Active Life with a Proven, Medically Based Weight Loss Program

Dr. Sasse has also written a series of e-books focused specifically on special topics which expand the *Outpatient Weight-Loss Surgery* book for certain audiences. Those e-books, available through Amazon Kindle and Smashwords, include:

Seniors and Weight-Loss Surgery
Adolescents and Weight-Loss Surgery
Which Operation is Right for Me? A Guide to Weight-Loss Surgery
After Weight-Loss Surgery: A Guide to Successful Long-Term Weight Loss

Please visit **www.sassesurgical.com** for more information on Dr. Sasse and his programs, publications, including a number of special reports.

Introduction

WEIGHT GAIN REMAINS the most vexing, most widespread, and the most deadly health problem of our time. Since the first edition of Outpatient Weight-Loss Surgery was written, even more of us are overweight and obese, more of us have developed type 2 diabetes as a result, and more of us have seen years of our lives shaved off because of obesity. Yet, while the epidemic of obesity grows unchecked, the minimally invasive solutions for individuals are more effective than ever before.

Today we know that humans and animals exhibit a physiologic "set point" for their weight, and their bodies defend that set point weight. Think of it like a home's thermostat, the heat kicking in when the temperature goes below the set point.1 Our metabolism does the same, kicking in mechanisms that reduce calories burned and increase hunger to drive our weight back up when it falls below the set point. This goes a long way toward explaining the phenomenon of rebound weight gain after a diet. We don't know exactly why everybody's set point weight is going up so much these days – theories mainly blame specific changes in the food supply toward less natural and more calorie-dense foods. It appears we can only minutely lower the set point with exercise and sustained lifestyle changes. But all is not lost – the good news from the world of laboratory research is that weight-loss surgery markedly lowers the body's set point, probably for good. Which goes a long way toward explaining why weight-loss surgery works so well, even for someone who has failed everything else.

Fifteen years ago, this book would have been highly unlikely. Because 15 years ago, it was more than unlikely that the most effective, durable and widely popular surgical weight-loss procedures could be performed as same-day procedures. Fifteen years ago, that was unthinkable.

Today, technology, technique and need have combined so that we stand at a remarkable moment in time when the most successful, proven, life-prolonging and life-changing weight-loss treatments have passed from unproven to the land of the tested, tried and true.

Need alone has greatly advanced the science of bariatric surgery. Unprecedented numbers of people in this country are significantly overweight and looking for ways to help themselves feel better, look better and live longer, healthier lives. I wrote *Outpatient Weight-Loss Surgery: Safe and Successful Weight Loss with Modern Bariatric Surgery* in order to share the revolution taking place in the field of weight-loss treatment.

Since the publication of *Outpatient Weight-Loss Surgery: Safe and Successful Weight Loss with Modern Bariatric Surgery* in 2009, more than 200,000 people in the United States alone have undergone outpatient weight-loss surgical procedures. This means more than 200,000 people have had a life-changing bariatric operation performed in a manner that allowed them to go home the very same day – without staying in the hospital.

The practice of all types of surgery, including weight-loss surgery, continues to shift further and further in the direction of outpatient surgery, which is also called same-day surgery. The majority of all surgical operations performed in the United States are now performed in an outpatient setting.

Today there is growing awareness that opportunities exist for people to undergo surgical weight-loss procedures without invasive open surgery or a hospital stay. In my role as a bariatric surgeon, I have appeared on radio and given media interviews all across the country since the publication of the first edition of *Outpatient Weight-Loss Surgery*. During this time, great interest has grown in every corner of the world as people learn about the minimally invasive solutions available for today's biggest and most dreaded health problem: obesity.

I have had the great pleasure of talking to many readers around the country and have heard from many people who have contacted me through my website and blog, and through Facebook, Twitter and other forms of communication. So many people have asked about new innovations in minimally invasive bariatric surgery that a second edition of this book was needed. After two sold-out printings, it was time to create a second edition with all of the updated information needed for 2014 and beyond.

In this new edition you'll find a great deal of information about fresh new technological advancements in the field of weight-loss surgery. I've included a major sections on laparoscopic Sleeve Gastrectomy (LSG), Mini-Gastric Bypass (MGB), Banding with Imbrication (I-band) and laparoscopic Duodenal Switch (DS), as well as a thorough discussion of the latest innovations in laparoscopic adjustable gastric banding technology including the AP LAP-BAND® from Allergan Corporation. I've also gone into greater detail comparing the two major types of gastric band, the REALIZE™ Band and the LAP-BAND®. A new section of this book discusses emerging and experimental technologies in more detail, and also covers some types of procedures that you, the readers, have asked about. Other sections cover endoscopic revisional procedures, the natural orifice procedure (NOTES surgery), single incision laparoscopy (SILS procedures), and emerging technologies.

This second edition of *Outpatient Weight-Loss Surgery: Safe and Successful Weight Loss with Modern Bariatric Surgery* provides accurate, unbiased, up-to-date information and demystifies the emerging technology of surgical weight-loss procedures. If you are struggling with your weight, or if someone close to you is, this book was written to help you make an informed decision on any weight-loss solution you may be considering. It is both a guide to weight-loss success in the modern era of outpatient treatments and a chronicle of the weight-loss treatment revolution taking place today.

It's time to start living the life you've imagined.

— HENRY JAMES

1

The Outpatient Revolution

A S RECENTLY AS the 1980s, bariatric (or weight-loss) procedures were major, open, full-anesthetic operations performed in the clinical confines of hospital operating rooms. A large incision had to be made, which ran up the abdomen from below the bellybutton to the breastbone and cut through the major abdominal muscles, which are not forgiving of such intrusions and do not heal easily or quickly. Clearly such surgical procedures required a significant stay in the hospital, and complications occurred frequently.

If you first started hearing about bariatric surgery during the 1970s and early 80s, you probably remember it as being a frightening surgical procedure with frequent complications, such as the formation of hernias (or bulges of the muscle incisions), problems that arose from infection, and breathing difficulties. (While any surgical procedure can impair lung function to some degree because of anesthesia, being overweight can stress the lungs even more after an operation, leading to complications such as pneumonia.) In those early days, weight-loss operations were considered less than elective, more often performed because excess weight had put the patient at risk for imminent health complications such as diabetes or heart failure.

Today the news is strikingly different. Minimally invasive laparoscopic surgical techniques have revolutionized surgical weight-loss procedures to the point where the majority of such operations can be performed in outpatient surgery facilities. Data from my own practice, like that from many high volume, high quality surgical centers, has shown a dramatic shift in recent years toward the outpatient arena. What was once a last-chance option in a risky operation is now a 45 minute procedure that can change your life and have you home in time for a protein-shake dinner.

The term "laparoscopic" comes from the term laparos, meaning abdominal, and oscopy meaning using a camera to view what's inside the abdomen. Laparoscopic surgery is performed by inserting a long, thin camera (laparoscope) into the abdomen through tiny keyhole incisions so that complex surgical procedures can be performed without the traditional, larger, open incisions once required for weight-loss operations.

Advances have been made across the fields of surgery (you're probably familiar with the term arthroscopy, which refers to operations performed on the joints using a camera inserted through small incisions). Such procedures cause less trauma to the body than open operations and because the operations are less traumatic for the body, patients can undergo even complex abdominal procedures with only small incisions and minimal pain, discomfort and recovery time.

Another significant factor in the shift of bariatric surgery to outpatient facilities is the evolution toward perfection of surgical weight-loss procedures. Laparoscopic improvements allow surgeons to perform the laparoscopic Roux-en-Y gastric bypass (LRYGB, see Chapter 2), mini-gastric bypass (MGB, see Chapter 2), and the laparoscopic adjustable gastric band (LAGB, made popular by the Lap-Band® from Allergan, Inc.; see Chapter 2). These procedures can be performed by skilled laparoscopic surgeons in about an hour and in many cases require no hospital stay. A fourth procedure, known as laparoscopic sleeve gastrectomy (LSG), has emerged as an effective outpatient weight-loss procedure. The laparoscopic Duodenal Switch (DS) is not truly an outpatient

Types of Surgical Procedures

The top surgical weight-loss procedures are the LAGB, LRYGB, LSG, MGB, DS and Band with Imbrication.

LAGB (the LAP-BAND® Adjustable Banding System or the REALIZE™ Band) involves placement of a flexible silicone band around the upper part of the stomach. The end result? The patient feels less hungry, feels fuller faster, and eats less. A port under the skin allows the surgeon to inject or remove fluid from the band, making it tighter or looser.

LRYGB (laparoscopic Roux-en-Y gastric bypass) is a laparoscopic surgical technique that involves the creation of a small capacity stomach pouch and a small outlet from the pouch directly into the small intestine, where nutrients are absorbed. With the majority of the stomach bypassed, and the pouch able to hold less volume than the stomach could, the person feels satisfied sooner and eats less. Hormonal changes in the body mean the person actually burns more calories too.

LSG (laparoscopic sleeve gastrectomy) removes a large portion of the stomach. The remaining portion of stomach is formed into a long tube that is unable to enlarge or balloon up with food. The restriction reduces the amount a person can eat and causes satiety with less food.

MGB (Mini-Gastric Bypass or Loop Gastric Bypass) is a laparoscopic gastric bypass procedure that involves connecting a loop of the small intestine to a small stomach pouch, thereby creating the same sense of satiety and reduced hunger. It involves one surgical tissue connection instead of two and can be performed on an outpatient basis.

The Duodenal Switch (DS) procedure involves a more complex re-routing of the intestines that results in reduced stomach capacity and reduced nutrient absorption. It is the most invasive of the procedures, and has the most risks, but it may still have a role as a revisional procedure or for people with severe diabetes and a very high BMI.

Band with Imbrication (laparoscopic adjustable gastric band with imbrication of the stomach) is a procedure which adds an imbrication, or surgical in-folding and tightening of the stomach, to the placement of an adjustable gastric band. An outpatient procedure that is still in its infancy, it may improve weight loss and produce faster results over LAGB alone procedure, and it has a limited role in today's environment of the less invasive, highly effective alternatives.

Generally, the LAGB procedure can be performed in 25 to 45 minutes with only 30 to 50 minutes of anesthesia time and a recovery time of only a few hours in an outpatient surgery center. The laparoscopic RYGB usually requires an overnight stay as it is more invasive, with more internal recovery time needed before patients are able to drink liquids (one of the indicators that a patient is ready to be discharged home). Also, there's a greater concern about complications with the laparoscopic Roux-en-Y procedure, which means surgeons prefer to have more patient observation time before discharge. MGB and LSG usually, but don't always, involve an overnight stay.

Twenty-five years ago most surgical procedures were performed in clinical hospital settings. Outpatient surgery centers began in the 1970s and proliferated in the 1980s, and today most U.S. operations are performed at outpatient surgery centers, with inpatient procedures actually on the decline.

There are now over 5,000 Medicare-certified outpatient surgery centers in the U.S., with more being built and coming online every month.

Outpatient surgery centers often have less red tape than full hospitals due to their specialization and expertise. They're also known for more flexibility with scheduling. Better still, outpatient surgery centers have superior safety records when compared to hospitals: an Archives of Surgery paper published in 2004 demonstrated the rate of serious complications and deaths following surgical procedures was significantly lower in outpatient surgical centers than in hospitals.[3] This is because the outpatient environment may have less serious hospital bacteria, because patients who can have procedures in outpatient settings have a lesser incidence of chronic illness, and because procedures performed in an outpatient setting are less invasive than those performed in a full hospital.

Outpatient surgery centers (also known as ASCs, or ambulatory surgery centers) must comply with extensive inspections and certification programs in order to operate. Any outpatient surgery center serving Medicare beneficiaries must be certified by the United States Department of Health and Human Services in order to perform surgical procedures. This process involves compliance with an extensive set of standards and includes inspections and production of records and data. Quality and safety are both factors that continue to drive the growth of outpatient centers, but most people would say the most important change leading to more outpatient weight-loss operations is simply that they work. Numerous long-term studies have shown the success of modern surgical weight-loss procedures in improving health, quality of life and longevity.[4-14]

If you're holding this book in your hands, chances are you or someone you love is or should be considering a surgical weight-loss procedure. It is my sincere hope that this book will help you understand the scope of surgical weight-loss procedures, their pros and cons, and significant health benefits. An informed decision is always the best decision.

What is "Outpatient" Surgery?

Outpatient surgery usually means that the patient is expecting to come to the surgery center or hospital, undergo a surgical procedure, and return home the same day. In recent years, insurance plans and regulators have interpreted this to mean a release from the surgical facility within 24 hours.

As surgery has become less invasive, more procedures are being performed on an outpatient or same-day basis. In fact, more operations of all kinds are performed on an outpatient basis than are performed on an inpatient basis (inpatient meaning there's a hospital stay involved).

With newer, less invasive surgical techniques and technology, even complex procedures such as orthopedic joint operations, spine procedures and even bariatric surgery can be performed with minimal hospital stays.

For most surgeons and to most insurance plans, outpatient surgery means the patient undergoes surgery and returns home within 24 hours. In some cities and states, regulators have expanded the definition of "outpatient" to include certain facilities that allow patients to stay in the facility for up to 72 hours.

With the revolution of effective laparoscopic, the minimally invasive LAGB, MGB and Band-Imbrication weight-loss procedures can usually be performed with a facility stay of a few hours. LSG may be performed with a 24 hour or shorter stay, and laparoscopic RYGB and DS can be performed with a one- to two-night stay.

Trends in Surgical Weight-Loss Procedures

While the dramatic economic downturn of 2008-2009 reduced the number of bariatric procedures performed, the number of weight-loss procedures performed in the United States is expected to be between 200,000 and nearly half a million by the year 2015.[15-18] I believe that may be an underestimate in the long term, and some great technology and grim health statistics support my belief. The obesity epidemic in the U.S. is not letting up. Two-thirds of adult Americans are now considered overweight or obese; one-third of our children also fall into these categories.

We are living at a time when the solutions for serious weight loss are more effective than ever before and also markedly safer and less invasive. Many more people concerned with prevention of disease are considering minimally invasive weight-loss procedures before the onset of health problems that inevitably arise with weight gain.

The ravages of obesity are dramatic. Not only do overweight adults face shortened life spans but overweight children do as well. Excess weight carried over time causes dramatic increases in diabetes, high blood pressure, sleep disturbances, degenerative joint diseases, cancer, heart disease, asthma and a host of other complications.

Some people don't realize that the health problems that stem from the extra pounds occur with even modest weight gain. For example, a study at Harvard shows being even moderately overweight increases the chance of developing type 2 diabetes (diabetes mellitus) sevenfold.[19] Age plays a role, as does genetic makeup, in whether and when people develop problems such as high blood pressure, asthma and diabetes. But even modest weight gain acts as a powerfully detrimental force in bringing about unhealthy conditions.

Simply stated, the number of Americans in need of serious and effective weight-loss solutions easily exceeds 100 million people annually.

Another reason I expect we're going to be seeing an increase in weight-loss

Patient Story: David A.

Procedure: LRYGB
Weight lost: 205 pounds

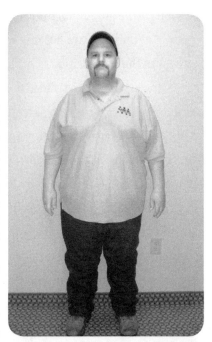

I chose weight-loss surgery for several reasons. I wanted to get my life healthy for my loved ones, friends and especially myself. The process prior to surgery wasn't bad. There were some things I didn't want to do, like blood work; I can't stand the sight of needles. But if you want something bad enough, you'll do anything to get it! There were only good things for the outcome. It's been a great journey, and I wouldn't change anything! I just wish I would have got my health back on track a lot sooner in life!

The only concern I had prior to surgery was if I was going to make it through the procedure. I did, without any complications or problems, thanks to my wonderful surgeon. Since surgery, I've had nothing but success. I've lost about 75 percent of my excess body weight in one year, and life's been great! I enjoy life and look forward to each day. I'm very thankful and grateful for this wonderful new tool and my new life.

operations is the amount of information now getting out to the public from reliable sources. Not only are you holding in your hands a book on outpatient weight-loss surgery, but the information is proliferating in other media as well.

With these highly effective and durable procedures now less invasive and safer than ever before, a high percentage of patients seeking weight-loss operations can undergo effective surgical weight loss with outpatient procedures.[20] And the advent of even newer, even less invasive procedures is going to make getting healthy even more attractive. In 2008 the REALIZE™ Personal Banding Solution (similar to the LAP-BAND®) from Ethicon Endo-Surgery, Inc. (a division of Johnson & Johnson) was marketed for the first time in the United States. The engagement of two laparoscopic gastric band device companies and the continual improvement of ever less invasive and more effective procedures will eventually catapult this type of procedure to new heights. For millions of people who have struggled with weight, these procedures will add years to their lives and remove years of suffering.

The effectiveness of modern bariatric procedures is extraordinary and results in stunning gains in life expectancy and health improvements. The procedures are swiftly moving from inpatient to outpatient settings, where patients experience less pain, more privacy and less time in hospital settings and recovery. I expect to see the frequency of outpatient surgical weight-loss procedures increase sharply as a trend in weight-loss surgery.

Our healthy future in this country depends on getting a grip on surging tides of obesity and weight gain. And until the complex root causes in our food supply, school and social policies, and society behaviors are addressed, the need for effective weight-loss treatment for individuals will remain astronomical and continue to grow.

Weight-Loss Benefits

The first and most obvious benefit following surgical weight-loss procedures is, of course, weight loss. The change in appearance is often dramatic, and the health benefits are apparent almost at once. Weight loss following modern minimally invasive outpatient bariatric surgical procedures is significant and long-lasting in the vast majority of cases.

In order to take a look at modern bariatric surgery, I'd like to examine the most widely performed procedures: the laparoscopic adjustable gastric band (LAGB, such as the LAP-BAND®), the laparoscopic sleeve gastrectomy (LSG), and the laparoscopic Roux-en-Y gastric bypass (LRYGB). Numerous long-term studies have identified the amount of weight lost many years after LRYGB and LAGB, and five or more years after LSG.[7] Most often, the weight lost after the procedure is depicted as the percentage of excess body weight lost.[21] What that means is if you weigh 200 pounds, but your ideal body weight is 150 pounds, then your excess body weight is 50 pounds. If you lost 40 pounds after the procedure, then you would have lost 80 percent of excess body weight (40 is 80 percent of the 50 pounds by which you were over).

Studies have shown that for the first two years post-surgery, average weight loss from LRYGB and LSG is greater than weight loss from LAGB. After the first two years, however, weight-loss outcomes for both procedures can often be similar, according to several studies. For example, a large Australian study examining the outcomes from LRYGB and LAGB procedures found no significant difference in long-term weight loss between the two procedures.[22] Other authors show greater weight loss with LRYGB over the long term, but with more corrective procedures required over those years.[23]

Another study, this one published in 2005 by Maggard and colleagues, showed a consistently greater amount of weight loss observed for LRYGB when compared to LAGB at 12 months postoperative and then again at three years.[24] Both procedures result in profound, sustained, long-term weight loss and profound, well-documented physiological benefits and longevity (people who are healthier are simply apt to live longer).

Long-Term Results

In 2007 two articles appeared in the New England Journal of Medicine describing long-term follow-up studies after surgical weight-loss procedures.[7-8] Both demonstrated dramatic positive results from operations, and both received a level of media coverage I haven't seen in years. The front page of the Wall Street Journal described the studies and the findings, and many other national media outlets covered the news – surgical weight-loss procedures work: they reduce disease and health risks and increase longevity.

One of the studies the Wall Street Journal reported on, the Swedish Obese Subjects study, demonstrated a marked reduction in the 10-year mortality risk when an overweight patient undergoes a surgical weight-loss procedure.[7] In the second study, overweight people in Utah were compared to patients who had undergone LRYGB procedures. The results confirmed again that surgical weight-loss procedures markedly improve long-term survival.[13]

It took a lot of doctors a lot of years to understand that being overweight or obese wasn't simply a matter of vanity or a cosmetic issue, but that being overweight was, in fact, unhealthy. The benefits of losing weight are almost instantaneous. Just as nearly every organ in the body is adversely affected by excessive weight, so is every organ system apt to benefit following weight loss – and all the more quickly following a surgical weight-loss procedure, when the weight is lost rapidly.

Many of the health complications caused by being overweight or obese can be markedly improved, or in some cases even resolved completely, by surgical weight-loss procedures. For younger people, who have not yet been told they have elevated blood sugar or full diabetes or high blood pressure, weight-loss operations can prevent these dreaded health problems from ever beginning.

Following is a discussion of health conditions that can be prevented, significantly altered, improved or even cured following surgical weight-loss procedures. While all of these conditions can develop and exist independent of obesity, all of them can be caused by excessive weight, and all of them are exacerbated by excessive weight (and are therefore considered comorbid conditions). And in the vast majority of cases, these conditions can be improved or even resolved by weight loss.

Asthma and lung disease. Respiratory function, asthma and restrictive lung disease are improved by weight loss.[25]

Obstructive sleep apnea. Many studies have shown an alarming rise in the frequency and deadliness of sleep apnea in the U.S., primarily due to the obesity epidemic. Sleep apnea is a condition marked by snoring and periods when the person actually stops breathing because the soft tissues of the throat obstruct the passage of air. Virtually every study shows an early and profound reduction in sleep apnea in obese patients who undergo bariatric operations.[26-28] In a study in 2004, approximately 83 percent of patients with sleep apnea who underwent bariatric operations resolved the condition entirely without further need of external gear (such as a CPAP or nighttime supplemental oxygen).[28]

Hypertension and heart disease. Cardiac function and hypertension (high blood pressure) improve with weight loss. In one study, approximately 80 percent of patients involved found their high blood pressure either markedly improved or completely resolved after bariatric operations.[29]

Gastroesophageal reflux disease. Both LRYGB and the LAGB effectively separate the lower, acid-producing portion of the stomach from the esophagus so that the acid doesn't travel up into the esophagus and cause symptoms.[30] LSG may not solve this reflux problem as effectively, and in a few cases may exacerbate it.

Diabetes mellitus. No disease is as inextricably linked to obesity as diabetes. Diabetes is currently at epidemic levels in the United States and other countries around the world. In the notably titled article, Who Would Have Thought It? An Operation is the Most Effective Treatment of Diabetes, Walter Poires followed 591 subjects who underwent LRYGB.[31] Of these, 94 had type 2 diabetes mellitus, and all but 11 saw their diabetes resolve completely post-operatively. Numerous other studies have documented the resolution of the condition following surgical weight-loss procedures.

Pre-Diabetes. Chances are that if you are overweight or obese, you already have pre-diabetes. It is the early stage of diabetes, defined by a less severe impairment of the body's metabolic machinery leading to mildly elevated blood glucose levels. The diagnosis can be confirmed by blood testing, and the progression to full-blown diabetes can be stopped in its tracks with bariatric surgery.

Hepatic steatosis. This is a form of severe fatty deposits on the liver, a condition that leads to problems with liver function and the immune system. This leading cause of nonviral, non-alcohol-related cirrhosis improves markedly after surgical bariatric procedures.[34-36]

Polycystic Ovarian Syndrome (PCOS) and infertility. Obesity is a severe adverse factor in infertility, as well as formation of ovarian cysts. Symptoms related to PCOS are improved in people who undergo bariatric operations.[37] Fertility is also markedly increased.

Other physical diseases and disorders. In addition, there exists a body of literature that links weight gain to:

♦ Degenerative joint disease;
♦ Pseudotumor Cerebri (a brain condition that causes severe headaches);
♦ Urinary incontinence; and
♦ Venous stasis disease, a condition causing leg swelling and varicose veins.

Depression and mental illness. A fascinating body of literature has emerged demonstrating that mental illness and obesity are, in fact, linked. A surprising amount of mental illness dissipates and resolves after a weight-loss surgical procedure, confirming that obesity and mental illness feed off each other.[38] This may be especially true of depression, the most common form of mental illness. Being depressed can lead to eating more and gaining weight, but it is also true that being severely overweight can lead to depression. So, once a person begins resolving the obesity, depression often lifts and self-esteem improves.

Quality of life. While difficult to measure in physiological terms, quality of life ranks among the most important measures of the success of any health intervention. If you're debating the value of surgical weight-loss procedures, ask yourself what you're missing in life. Is your weight stopping you from doing the things you want to do, and giving you a sense of loss of energy? Is fear of health complications due to weight causing you anxiety? And are complications from existing health issues taking away from your quality of life?

Numerous studies show the quality of life improves after a bariatric operation.[39, 40] But most people can figure this out for themselves. Experiencing reduction of pain in your joints and spine, watching diabetes melt away and having the doctor say this is the best shape you've been in for years all add up to a definite feeling of well-being.

Doctors tend to focus on cold numbers, such as mortality risk or odds ratios for experiencing a cardiac event. But for people who undergo weight-loss operations, what matters most may be the newfound ability to bend down and tie a shoe or pick up a child or run outside. It may be waking up in the morning without a feeling of dread or pain. For doctors in the field of bariatric surgery, it is probably the numerous and varied stories of improved quality of life that give us the energy and enthusiasm to keep trying to improve the care for our patients.

Survival. And the most important of all the health benefits of weight loss and surgical weight-loss procedures – life. Every study that has set out to measure the impact of bariatric procedures related to long-term survival has shown a striking advantage in favor of patients who undergo bariatric operations. Put as simply as possible: Seriously overweight people who undergo bariatric operations live markedly longer, healthier lives.[41]

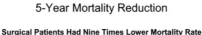

5-Year Mortality Reduction

Surgical Patients Had Nine Times Lower Mortality Rate Within the Study Period

*Includes perioperative (30-day) mortality of 0.4%   p-value 0.001

Christou NV, Sampalis JS, Liberman M, et al. Surgery Decreases Long-Term Mortality, Morbidity, and Health Care Use in Morbidly Obese Patients. Annals of Surgery 2004;240(3):416-424.

Figure 1 shows that patients who underwent bariatric surgical procedures had nine times lower mortality rate than those patients who did not.

THE STUDIES

In 2012, The New England Journal of Medicine published a pair of prospective, randomized, controlled studies on the effects of weight-loss surgery on type 2 diabetes. These studies received a great deal of attention because, while the findings were not news to experts in this field, they were truly randomized and prospective, and published in the most rigorous medical journal in the world. In the first study from the Cleveland Clinic, all the patients had type 2 diabetes mellitus and their BMI ranged from 27-43. On average, each person was taking an average of three diabetic medications and 44 percent of the patients were using insulin. The patients were randomly assigned to one of three treatment groups and underwent either A) intensive medical therapy, B) Roux-en-Y gastric bypass or C) sleeve gastrectomy. After one year, twelve percent of group A patients in the intensive medical therapy group achieved a glycated hemoglobin level of 6 percent or less versus 42 percent in the Roux-en-Y gastric bypass group and 37 percent in the sleeve gastrectomy group.[32]

This study is remarkable – imagine being randomized to medicines vs. undergoing surgery for diabetes! For those of us in the field of metabolic and bariatric surgery, the findings were no surprise whatsoever, but for millions of other readers this may have been their first real exposure to the concept that surgery is the best treatment for diabetes. Now, thanks to this study and others, we see an increasing acceptance among medical providers that surgery is the best treatment for most people with diabetes.

The second study came from Italy and also involved a prospective, randomized methodology comparing standard medical treatment of diabetes to bariatric surgery, in the form of either LRYGB or BPD.[33]

In the two years time frame of the study, zero patients in the medical treatment group achieved complete remission of diabetes. Seventy-five percent of patients in the Roux-en-Y gastric bypass group achieved complete remission of diabetes and 95 percent of patients in the BPD group achieved complete remission of their diabetes.

What These Studies Really Mean

Curing diabetes is a pretty remarkable achievement when compared to conventional medical therapy, which generally focuses on controlling the blood sugar – sometimes referred to as "treating the number," rather than curing the disease. But even more important than the control of the diabetes itself and the freedom from taking medications, including insulin shots and oral pills, is the freedom from the complications of diabetes, the problems with kidney failure, blindness, amputations – the real problems that come from diabetes itself. Ridding individuals of those problems is a monumental achievement.

Resolving Medical Conditions with Newer Procedures

A randomized, controlled, prospective study presented at the International Federation for the Surgery of Obesity and Metabolic Disorders was titled "Sleeve Gastrectomy vs. Mini-Gastric Bypass for the Treatment of Non-Morbid Obese Diabetic Patients." This study brought together 40 patients with a mean body mass index of 29. Patients were randomized to either a laparoscopic sleeve gastrectomy (LSG) or Mini-Gastric Bypass (MGB) with 20 patients in each group, meaning they were chosen at random to undergo either the Mini-Gastric Bypass or the LSG. There were no major complications or deaths, and in short-term follow-up, resolution of type 2 diabetes occurred in 90 percent of patients after Mini-Gastric Bypass and in 50 percent of patients after the sleeve gastrectomy. Both were effective, safe, and minimally invasive, although MGB was considered more effective than sleeve gastrectomy for diabetes in the short term in these patients with a body mass index under 35.

Are You a Candidate for Weight-Loss Surgery?

Surgical weight-loss procedures have come a long way in the last several decades. Not only have the procedures become much safer and much less invasive with the advent of laparoscopic surgery, but the surgical procedures themselves have come to be accepted in the medical field as having real health benefits rather than being viewed as simply cosmetic. The benefits to weight loss have been long-documented, and the benefits from weight-loss operations are now documented as well.

However, weight-loss operations are still surgical procedures, and not to be undertaken lightly. The risks of undergoing an operation must always be weighed against the benefits of that operation. That said, the health risks posed by being seriously overweight usually outweigh the inherent risks of modern surgical weight-loss procedures but every case is different. The criteria used to select appropriate candidates for weight-loss operations were derived from a consensus conference statement put out by the National Institute of Health (NIH) in 1991, and a great deal has emerged and changed in the field since that time. The procedures have become far less invasive and less risky since those early days of open surgery, and are proven far more successful and durable. Little has changed for most centers with respect to their approach to choosing weight-loss operation candidates.

Let's touch briefly on what makes for a good candidate for surgical weight-loss procedures, then, more specifically, for outpatient weight-loss procedures.

The criteria that determine candidates for weight-loss operations depend mainly on the calculation with which readers of this book are probably most familiar: the Body Mass Index (BMI). BMI is calculated from weight and height and is a reliable indicator of body fat for most people.

For adults, BMI is calculated using the following formula:

$$\text{weight (lb) / [height (in)]2 x 703}$$

EXAMPLE: WEIGHT = 150 LBS, HEIGHT = 5'5" (65")
CALCULATION: [150 ÷ (65)2] x 703 = 24.96 OR:
150 ÷ (65 x 65) x 703 = 24.96 OR:

150 ÷ 4225 x 703 = 24.96

If you'd like to avoid doing the math yourself, online BMI calculators (such as mine at www.iMetabolic.com) perform the calculation for you. Or you may choose to use a BMI chart (see Figure 2).

Figure 2. A BMI chart is a simplified way to determine your BMI. Simply find your height on the vertical chart, and then move horizontally until you find the column that expresses your weight.

Weight (lbs)	Height (ft)									
	4'9"	4'11"	5'1"	5'3"	5'5"	5'7"	5'9"	5'11"	6'1"	6'3"
154	33	31	29	27	26	24	23	22	20	19
165	36	33	31	29	28	26	24	23	22	21
176	38	36	33	31	29	28	26	25	23	22
187	40	38	35	33	31	29	28	26	25	24
198	43	40	37	35	33	31	29	28	26	25
209	45	42	40	37	35	33	31	29	28	26
220	48	44	42	39	37	35	33	31	29	28
231	50	47	44	41	39	36	34	32	31	29
243	52	49	46	43	40	38	36	34	32	30
254	55	51	48	45	42	40	38	35	34	32
265	57	53	50	47	44	42	39	37	35	33
276	59	56	52	49	46	43	41	39	37	35
287	62	58	54	51	48	45	42	40	38	36
298	64	60	56	53	50	47	44	42	39	37
309	67	62	58	55	51	48	46	43	41	39
320	69	64	60	57	53	50	47	45	42	40
331	71	67	62	59	55	52	49	46	44	42
342	74	69	65	61	57	54	51	48	45	43
353	76	71	67	63	59	55	52	49	47	44
364	78	73	69	64	61	57	54	51	48	46
375	81	76	71	66	62	59	56	52	50	47
386	83	78	73	68	64	61	57	54	51	48
397	86	80	75	70	66	62	59	56	53	50
408	88	82	77	72	68	64	60	57	54	51
419	90	84	79	74	70	66	62	59	56	53
430	93	87	81	76	72	67	64	60	57	54
441	95	89	83	78	73	69	65	62	59	55
452	98	91	85	80	75	71	67	63	60	57
463	100	93	87	82	77	73	69	65	61	58

Weight Category	BMI
Normal Weight	19 - 24.9
Overweight	25 - 29.9
Obese	30 - 39.9
Extreme Obesity	40 - 58

The Diabetes Solution: Can Bariatric Surgery Cure Diabetes?

The word cure is something physicians use with great caution. We are all too familiar with chronic relapsing and recurring diseases, including cancers and infectious illnesses which may be latent for long periods of time.

Convincing research, including randomized controlled trials, has shown us that laparoscopic Roux-en-Y gastric bypass and laparoscopic sleeve gastrectomy result in a complete remission of diabetes is a high percentage of cases. Should we use the word "cure?"

Let's look at the specifics: Around 85 percent of people with type 2 diabetes who undergo laparoscopic Roux-en-Y gastric bypass will achieve a normal blood sugar and normal hemoglobin A1c level while being entirely off of medication treatment. This generally meets the definition of cure. That is, all traces of the disease are gone while off of any treatment.

33

Yet some questions remain unanswered, such as, how long will this "cure" last? Will the disease recur or resurface? While we don't currently have the full scope of the answers to these questions, we do have some data to guide us. For example, it's known that beyond middle age nearly every adult in the U.S. gains weight steadily every year. This rising body weight correlates with a rising risk of development of type 2 diabetes. We also know that roughly 75 million Americans currently have pre-diabetes, a condition that is likely to lead to type 2 diabetes as the person ages and gains weight. So if the surgical intervention results in substantial weight loss and hormonal and biochemical changes that result in the remission of diabetes, it is likely that as the person gains weight through the aging process that the risk of developing recurrent type 2 diabetes will rise.

So there is reason to believe that for a least a portion of people who undergo gastric bypass or gastric sleeve resection, the diabetes remission may not be permanent. But there's also reason to believe the remission will last many years and the impact will translate into substantial gains in life expectancy.

Studies examining life expectancy specifically demonstrate a marked improvement in life expectancy after gastric bypass surgery when compared with randomized matched controls that did not undergo the surgery. So it's clear from the data that, with respect to both diabetes and overall survival, the risks of not undergoing weight-loss surgery far exceed the risks of having the procedure.

Anecdotally, in our own center, we see that around 85 percent of people who undergo gastric bypass surgery do indeed achieve a full remission or "cure" of the type 2 diabetes and over the years a small percentage of them have developed some recurrence of the disease, usually resulting in a slow rise of blood sugar that is controllable with oral medications. How many years of diabetes-free extended life are achieved for the average person undergoing bariatric surgery? We don't have precise data, but it's clear it's at least several years and maybe more than 10.

This slow-motion disease process of obesity and diabetes linked together plays out over a lifetime. Whether we call laparoscopic bariatric surgery a cure or not, what is clear is that the procedure has a profoundly favorable impact on health, quality of life, remission of diabetes and increased longevity.

While it wasn't intended to do so, the BMI has come to serve as a guideline for physicians in determining if a patient is an appropriate candidate for a weight-loss operation. Generally if your BMI is greater than 30 and you have health problems associated with obesity (such as diabetes or high blood pressure), you are considered a candidate. Even in the absence of such comorbid conditions, if your BMI is greater than 35, you are a candidate. Increasingly, experts believe people with BMIs greater than 28 are also candidates for the less-invasive weight-loss procedures that have emerged as outpatient surgery options described in this book. Studies show a real health benefit even in this mild to moderately obese group.[5]

A growing number of experts believe a bariatric procedure is also advisable for treatment of diabetes even in the absence of obesity. The hormonal changes that stem from gastric bypass in particular can resolve diabetes even in normal weight individuals.[42] This is truly "metabolic" surgery, treating the disease of diabetes.

"Low" BMI

In 2011 the Food and Drug Administration approved the LAP-BAND® for people who have a body mass index of 30 or greater along with an obesity-related health condition, lowering their threshold criterion markedly.

This change by the FDA expanded the number of Americans eligible for LAP-BAND® weight-loss surgery by tens of millions of people in the U.S. The decision reflects the body of data accumulated over the last 20 years showing that outpatient LAP-BAND® weight-loss procedures have become much less invasive and safer at the same time health problems of obesity are more widely recognized.

Some professionals in the medical community refer to this new category of BMI 30 to 35 as a "low BMI" because it's low compared to the previously accepted definitions of morbid obesity, which was a higher BMI. What we're really seeing is a changing medical landscape: minimally invasive weight-loss surgery being used to tackle the serious problem of obesity, which is finally being recognized as a medical problem (rather than a cosmetic problem) and one that deserves medical treatment.

In addition to the change in the attitude of medical professionals, a few insurance companies have also come onboard and are now offering coverage for weight-loss surgery in the lower BMI category. They're starting to understand that addressing the problem sooner rather than waiting for the patient to hit a higher BMI ultimately saves costs and is healthier for their plan members.

Eating Patterns and Eating Disorders

We all eat in different ways. Some of us eat the traditional three square meals a day and never snack. Others graze all day long. There's no single "right" way to eat, but research does identify types of eating behaviors that can lead to unhealthy weight gain.

In addressing problems with your weight, if you choose to undergo a bariatric surgical procedure, you'll first go through an evaluation process with various members of the medical community. While different surgeons have different approaches to preoperative requirements, it's very likely that your process will include evaluations by both a dietitian and a psychologist. Most programs have requirements like these and they can often be very beneficial in helping your bariatric surgeon and other members of your program understand you as an individual. Evaluations can also help you start to understand how you eat and ways in which you can improve your eating routine.

In a large number of studies, not surprisingly, many people who are considering weight loss surgery are "diagnosed" with an eating behavior abnormality or even an eating disorder. Regrettably, in the past this was sometimes used as a reason to exclude a person as a candidate for weight-loss surgery. Excluding people this way was a sad and misguided practice born of a very poor understanding of the problems of obesity and eating disorders, as well as a poor understanding of the fact that people can be successful losing weight and keeping it off with weight-loss surgery whether or not they've been diagnosed with an eating disorder. In fact, very few people who have been diagnosed with eating disorders will lose weight successfully without weight-loss surgery; conversely, most people with an eating disorder can – and will – lose weight after bariatric surgery.

So what are these abnormal eating behaviors and what do they mean for someone considering weight-loss surgery? Different definitions have been used in the past, but here are some commonly used descriptions and how they relate to weight loss surgery success:

1. Binge eating disorder. This is perhaps the most talked about abnormal eating pattern. Binge eating disorder is defined by an over-consumption of food and a sense of a loss of control associated with an emotional state. In numerous studies of pre-surgical obese patients, between 17 and 34 percent of patients exhibited binge eating disorder characteristics. What does this mean? Can a person still lose weight with bariatric surgery if they exhibit binge eating disorder?

    The answer is an emphatic yes. Numerous studies have examined the outcome of weight-loss surgery among patients with binge eating disorder and interesting findings have emerged. The first of these findings is that patients with binge eating disorders lose weight just as well as the patients who do not exhibit binge eating disorder, plain and simple. In my research, I found nine separate studies that confirmed weight-loss results were equivalent between binge eaters and non-binge eaters. Three studies contradict those findings and describe results among bingers to be less successful than results among non-bingers.

A second finding is that after weight-loss surgery most of those patients no longer exhibit the behavior known as binge eating. Very simply, it's much harder to consume large amounts of food after weight-loss surgery. Think about it for a minute: With an adjustable gastric band in position or a small gastric pouch after a bypass, it's pretty difficult to eat a large amount at any one sitting. Therefore, in clinical studies, these patients report much reduced binge eating. This isn't to say a person exhibiting binge eating disorder shouldn't be aware of it and undergo some specific counseling to try to correct the problem. Psychotherapy and, in some cases, medications, have been shown to be effective in reducing binge eating behavior. Certainly the bottom line is that weight-loss surgery is still very much an option and, in fact, it is the recommended option when a person has developed obesity with binge eating disorder and has been unable to successfully lose the weight by other means.

2. Nocturnal eating disorder. A person who eats after 8 p.m., or who wakes up in the middle of the night to eat and feels a great deal of hunger, exhibits features of nocturnal eating disorder. Identifying this problem and working specifically to try to correct it can help people achieve the best weight loss results. Specific psychotherapy and counseling can be helpful if tailored to these issues, and in addition, practicing repeated behaviors over time can help a person to develop new habits and break the cycle of nocturnal eating. Weight-loss surgery results don't appear to be significantly worsened among people with nocturnal eating disorders, so this shouldn't be a reason to exclude anyone from undergoing a weight-loss surgical procedure.

3. Grazing. Grazing has been defined in various ways, but it boils down to a simple concept: some people eat throughout the day in many, many settings and usually in small, frequent amounts. In a recent study by O'Brien and Colleagues, 26 percent of patients seeking to undergo LAP-BAND® surgery were found to fit the definition of grazing.[43] Grazing behavior actually increased somewhat after LAP-BAND® surgery and weight-loss results for people who exhibited grazing behavior were somewhat less in this one study than results for people who did not exhibit grazing behaviors. In two other studies on the subject, no differences in weight loss results were reported when grazers were compared to non-grazers. In one of these studies, the three year outcomes were found to be equal among grazers and non-grazers undergoing gastric banding surgery.

In achieving your goal of successfully losing weight and maintaining a healthy weight, every single bit of help and guidance helps. So if your pre-surgery evaluations turn up unhealthy eating patterns such as these, don't ignore them, face them head-on. Don't imagine that weight-loss surgery cures them; you still have to do that by taking steps that include changing your behavior, changing your habits, attending support groups and possibly undergoing some good therapy. Remember, the most powerful solution to your weight struggle rests with a combination of efforts and treatment: weight-loss surgery plus a comprehensive program that centers on your personal effort and hard work to live a life with long lasting healthy eating habits and exercise.

Surgery Compared to Medical Weight Loss

In one study of the various weight-loss procedures available today, LAGB operations proved far more effective in treating obesity and the health conditions associated with it than multidisciplinary comprehensive medical weight-loss programs (medically supervised weight-loss programs, which included participation from physicians, physical trainers, nutritionists and other experts).[6] However, there is no official guideline or criteria for choosing a surgical weight-loss procedure. If you are considering a weight-loss operation, it will serve you to discuss your needs, wants and possible surgical outcomes with your physician and then make the choice that works for you.

Working with my patients, I like to combine the best of all worlds and bring together the very best elements of medically supervised weight-loss programs and the best techniques from weight-loss surgical procedures. I ask every patient to attend support groups, participate in regular weigh-ins, meet with a dietary coach, exercise, utilize low calorie protein-vitamin shakes, and sometimes take prescription medication. Each of these steps can promote weight loss before surgery and augment the results of the surgical procedure. They work well in helping people lose the weight. In the long term, these efforts are critical to winning the tougher battle of keeping that weight off.

While there are no official criteria, rest assured that every surgeon, every surgical center and every insurance company has its own interpretation of the data available on weight-loss surgery and will apply its own criteria. For the most part, I have found that insurance companies typically require a BMI greater than 40, or a BMI greater than 35 with comorbid conditions, whereas experienced bariatric surgeons look at patients with a BMI of 30 and above as candidates for weight-loss procedures (as the FDA does), all the more so if comorbid conditions are present. Which means there's a gray area between what insurance companies see as warranting a life-changing operation and what physicians and the FDA see as beneficial to a patient's health.

If you meet the surgeon's criteria or the surgery center's criteria but not the criteria your insurance company considers valid, you may want to consider paying out-of-pocket. This is a choice every individual has to make for himself or herself, with the assistance of a physician. (In Chapter 4 we'll take a look at considerations for those candidates for surgical weight-loss procedures who expect to be paying out-of-pocket.)

Inpatient or Outpatient?

The decision to have an outpatient surgical weight-loss procedure is a medical decision, ultimately best made by you and your physician together. Outpatient surgery centers follow different criteria in determining which patients would benefit from outpatient procedures and which patients would be better served in-hospital. Outpatient surgery centers are usually not equipped to handle cases that require an inpatient hospital stay or cases that will involve actively managing complex medical problems.

So, if you have fairly severe medical problems like asthma or heart arrhythmias that require a lot of ongoing treatment and monitoring, and if your BMI is very high (say, greater than 55), and it makes it hard for you to breathe without supplemental oxygen, then you're probably looking at an inpatient hospital setting for your procedure. But it is best to discuss your individual case with your surgeon because sometimes even those conditions are handled effectively in the outpatient setting when the procedure is not very invasive.

Outpatient procedures are a better option for patients expected to undergo procedures with a minimum of complications and a very low chance of hospital admission. While I always hope there will be no complications at all, there is no way to reduce the risk to zero. I always prepare for the worst but plan for the best. Because patients undergoing outpatient weight-loss procedures stay, on average,

Patient Criteria for Outpatient Surgery

Many outpatient centers have devised their own criteria to screen candidates for weight-loss operations, choosing only those in the low-risk categories, which is better for the centers and better for the patients. Choosing to perform procedures in only the low-risk categories is better for the centers because there are then fewer complications and hospital admissions over the course of the year. And since outpatient surgery centers have to report those statistics regularly, they want to show the best safety record possible. And of course the best safety record is exactly what patients want, too.

Following is the list we use, although exceptions do arise. Our criteria have changed over time as we have performed thousands of weight-loss procedures. We have found that specific hard numbers (such as BMI) do not serve well as selection criteria, but rather each individual patient must be considered carefully and approved individually. Similar criteria are in use at other centers.

In order to undergo an outpatient weight-loss operation, a patient must have:

◆ Approval for the outpatient procedure by the bariatric surgeon and anesthesiologist

◆ Approval by the outpatient center medical director (usually also an anesthesiologist)

◆ Approval by case conference committee if the BMI is more than 55

◆ No history of pulmonary hypertension

◆ An anesthesia risk factor classification of ASA III or less (the American Society of Anesthesiology classification system rates an individual's risk of surgical procedures from ASA I – lowest risk – to ASA V – highest risk)

◆ Sleep apnea well-controlled at home with the CPAP system or no sleep apnea present only six hours in the center, they must be healthy enough to undergo the operation and anesthesia and still return home the same day.

If you have serious and active health considerations, especially those made worse by being severely overweight, then you are probably considered high risk for complications from anesthesia and a surgical procedure. The presence of severe sleep apnea, heart failure (or a related severe condition of the heart and lungs called pulmonary hypertension or cor pulmonale) and BMI greater than 55 have all been considered specific conditions that may preclude the outpatient setting. If this is the case, then for safety reasons your surgeon will likely recommend that the procedure be done at the hospital with at least an overnight stay.

Nonsurgical Weight-Loss Alternatives

Nonsurgical options in medical weight loss have evolved more gradually than the surgical options in the past two decades. Perhaps the biggest change has been in the attitude of physicians themselves, who have changed their perspective from that of weight loss being a vain, cosmetic goal that can be safely ignored in the majority of patients asking for medical assistance, to an understanding that weight loss for overweight or obese patients is crucial for improved health, easing of comorbid conditions and increased life spans.

Some of the nonsurgical options that have evolved since the 1980s include incremental improvements in techniques of behavior modification, physician-supervised medical weight-loss programs involving meal replacement bars and shakes, the use of improved and ever-safer prescription weight-loss medications and multidisciplinary weight-loss programs. But keep in mind we can only make a small change the body's "set point" without surgery, so be prepared as your body fights to defend that set point by burning less calories and increasing appetite.

Medical (nonsurgical) weight-loss centers that can deliver multidisciplinary weight-loss programs – those programs that are physician-supervised and bring in other experts (from physical training coaches to life coaches to nutritionists) – have begun to emerge around the country, working with patients to develop state-of-the-art nonsurgical weight-loss techniques and treatment. I founded and serve as medical director of one of these nonsurgical centers, the International Metabolic Institute, or iMetabolic. High-quality medically supervised weight-loss programs do achieve successes, but the successes fall far short of those achieved with surgical weight-loss programs, especially in patients who are more severely overweight. Most studies examining medical (nonsurgical) treatment report that successful patients lose 5 to 10 percent of body weight when they adhere to medical weight-loss programs. Which is good, and even less invasive than the least invasive operation. And for many people with a BMI of 25 to 30, and some with a BMI of more than 30, it is exactly what they need to get healthy and lose weight.

The Set Point

Our body employs complex metabolic regulatory mechanisms to maintain, or "defend" its established weight. Research shows that when we diet and lose pounds, our bodies fight back and actually lower the metabolism so that we burn less calories. And perhaps even more diabolical, hormonal mechanisms lead to an increase in hormones like Ghrelin that make us hungry and a decrease in hormones like Leptin and GLP-1 that make us feel full. It's a powerful physiologic response to defend the set point weight, and as our appetite skyrockets and our metabolism slows, more often than not we re-gain all the weight.

For some people, medical weight-loss programs could be the answer they've been looking for to lose weight, keep it off and experience all the health benefits of doing so. But for many, these programs are only a step in the right direction and not the entire journey. Programs eventually must rely on patients being able to maintain self-control in a bewildering world of brightly lit advertisements for food in every newspaper and magazine, at every commercial break during television shows and in the popcorn-scented lobby of the local movie theater. Many of these programs utilize meal replacement shakes and prescription medicines, which are proven successful strategies in the short to mid-term, but which may not be long-term solutions for weight loss for anyone with a BMI over 30.

Meal replacement bars and shakes work well for rapid weight-loss programs, especially those aimed at helping a patient lose weight before weight-loss surgery (see Chapter 5 for further details). But in a world of dizzying choices for meals virtually at our fingertips, and in a person whose BMI has already climbed to more than 30, it's unlikely meal-replacement bars or shakes are an option that will endure the test of time. More comprehensive medical weight-loss programs work to take that initial success and then build on it with behavior strategies and exercise to bring long-term success to those who are committed to change. This is exactly the strategy we have taken, where the early successful weight loss of our induction programs using meal replacements are then sustained by long-term counseling, behavior change, coaching and support. Losing weight and keeping it off is not easy, though, and we employ a team of psychologists, in addition to life coaches, nutritionists, counselors, fitness trainers and physicians, to bring about the long-term change needed for sustained nonsurgical weight loss.

Unfortunately, few of the studies on nonsurgical medical weight-loss programs stretch beyond one year, at which point patients may well have started experiencing rebound weight gain. Surgical treatment studies normally report markedly greater weight loss and often follow patient progress for 10 or 15 years. Even with this discrepancy, studies that compare surgical and nonsurgical weight-loss treatment have shown that patients lose more weight and experience greater health benefits from surgical treatment.[44-46]

Studies also show weight loss and improved health are more pronounced the heavier the individual was prior to beginning a program, an almost common-sense finding since the more overweight a patient is the more likely the patient is

Patient Story: Anita A.

Procedure: **LRYGB**
Weight lost: **205 pounds**

I didn't have any issues after surgery. In fact, I was very disciplined and committed to my exercise program and my new eating habits.

It was so rewarding to see the changes in my appearance and in my attitude. Each week I pushed myself to do something more challenging in my workout and try new things. I continued to write each day in my journal that I started.

I remember one day after working, driving by my work where there is a walking trail behind it, and it had a hill, and I remember saying to myself, "Wow, wouldn't it be cool to be able to one day climb up that and reach the top?" At that very moment, I made that a goal that within three months I would be climbing that hill, and I did! During this experience, I have discovered goals that I would set for myself and have achieved every one of them.

to be suffering from comorbid conditions and the more weight the patient actually has to lose. And though heavier patients may show better numbers, the findings are well-documented beginning in patients with BMIs as low as 28.

Medically supervised weight-loss programs do not show the dramatic successes of weight-loss surgery, but those of us in the field are trying to improve those numbers as well. A medically supervised program can even be an excellent precursor to a surgical procedure. In fact, n our surgical weight-loss center, all patients lose weight first with medically-supervised programs for four to six weeks right before they undergo their operations. We have found that each patient loses weight, begins to learn better eating and exercise habits and becomes a better, safer surgical candidate with this approach.

Your choices are up to you, and only you can decide the best road for you. At the centers I lead, my staff and I strive to provide the most comprehensive medical weight-loss programs in the world, with a dedicated team of physicians, psychologists, behavior experts, fitness coaches, nutrition experts and life and motivational coaches. For people committed to the long-term hard work involved, I think medically supervised weight loss is a great option, but it gets more difficult when the BMI has already risen to more than 30, and programs like ours are tough to find in every city.

In the end, both nonsurgical and surgical programs play an important role helping overweight patients lose weight and improve their health.

Calculate your BMI at <u>www.iMetabolic.com</u>

We know what we are, but know not what we may be.

– WILLIAM SHAKESPEARE

It Takes Hard Work

This may not be a popular point of view, but it's true: No matter which type of surgery is chosen as a weight-loss solution, surgery is not a magic bullet. You make your own magic, and that takes hard work.

Today there are a variety of surgical weight-loss options, including gastric banding, banding with imbrications, gastric bypass, Mini-Gastric Bypass and sleeve gastrectomy. Everyone's different, and different people have different results from the procedures, but statistics show by and large these procedures work. It is possible to successfully lose weight by undergoing weight-loss surgery, and to keep the weight off. But it takes hard work.

What do I mean by hard work? I don't mean you will have to perform a great deal of physical labor. I don't mean that it's a giant amount of work to sort through the insurance bills and administrative paperwork nonsense (although those things can be hard work, too). And I'm really not talking about a very difficult recovery that requires a lot of hard work, either; most people are back on their feet in a matter of days. What I am talking about is the hard work and determination required for successful weight loss – and this centers squarely on the simple fact that you must put fewer calories into your body every single day. No matter what surgery you undergo, it's not going to be a magic bullet. No surgery provides a magical solution that lets you off the hook – you'll still have to work hard for your weight loss goals.

But the hard work I've mentioned isn't anything you can't handle. Following are some of the key elements of that "hard work":

1. Eat smaller portions.

2. Dramatically cut your carbohydrate intake in both meals and snacks.

48

3. Exercise regularly even if it consists of walking 30 minutes a day.

4. Stay focused on both your short-term and long-term weight-loss goals.

5. Every day, imagine the person you wish to become through your weight-loss efforts.

It takes hard work to reduce calories and to stop eating and drinking the things you've relied on as comfort foods for treats, snacks and favorite meals. It's hard work to break old habits and to ingrain new ones. But this is the price of successful weight loss, better health, more energy and a longer life. We change our lives by first changing our thoughts. If you can imagine it, you can do it!

Using the Medically Supervised Approach to Keep the Weight Off

Most of us are familiar with the dramatic and often temporary results achieved with medically supervised weight-loss programs that use low calorie meal-replacement shakes (think of Oprah). Whether losing weight on such a program is difficult or easy, keeping it off after such dramatic weight loss is tough.

This is one area of great success with weight-loss surgery. Because while willpower may wane, the changes brought about by the surgery are mostly permanent; patients who have undergone weight-loss surgery are simply far less likely to regain the weight. The set point has shifted downward to a healthier weight.

It's not true for everyone. Studies have documented that 10 to 30 percent of people do regain weight after weight-loss surgery when the outcomes of the procedures are examined beyond a 10 year period. (This means 70 to 90 percent of people do keep the weight off beyond 10 years!) So I counsel every single patient that keeping the weight off requires a very high level of commitment to a long-term, daily focus on proper nutrition, reduced calorie intake and regular exercise.

And here is a critical tip to keep in mind: don't ignore weight re-gain. Plan to come in the moment you have re-gained even five pounds. We can intervene in all kinds of ways to stop the backsliding before it becomes more difficult to undo.

What I Do

After I turned 40 I started to find it increasingly difficult to maintain my weight, and I don't mean to keep my weight up. I find it increasingly difficult to keep my weight down where it's been for the last 15 to 20 years. I exercise, I watch my food intake, I even train for and run marathons, but it's not enough. I've discovered, like just about everybody my age and above, that metabolism slows and the tendency to gain weight becomes all the more powerful as we age into the middle years. So what do I do to keep my weight down?

The main tactic I've employed in keeping my weight down is one that has been well demonstrated as successful in clinical studies, and that's the use of a protein-based liquid meal-replacement system – a protein shake. After trying a great many of them, I ultimately designed my own. The basic constituents of this protein powder are whey protein isolate together with vitamins and minerals (no lactose, gluten or artificial sweeteners). I blend one for breakfast every single day. The effect of this is to turn on the metabolism first thing in the day, which increases the body's ability to burn calories rather than storing them (as fat, of course). It also controls appetite.

I also get on the scale every morning, just the same way I advise every single one of my weight-loss patients. If I notice the pounds are starting to creep back on, I increase the number of meals replaced with the protein-based liquid meal-replacement shake and have one for dinner as well as one for breakfast.

The shakes really help control appetite and allow me to avoid consuming a whole lot of calories with a carb-loaded breakfast or a full dinner (with, heaven forbid, dessert!).

The protein shake strategy together with regular walking and running helps me keep my weight down. I fully anticipate as I cross into my 50s that I will have to create an even more aggressive strategy and cut calories even further, likely including even more liquid meal-replacement shakes in my day-to-day regimen.

Change alone is eternal, perpetual, immortal.
~ ARTHUR SCHOPENHAUER

Food for Thought

♦ Weight-loss procedures have evolved since the early 1980s from full open operations to minimally invasive laparoscopic procedures that can often be performed at outpatient surgery centers.

♦ Because of the expertise and experience of surgeons and staff at outpatient surgical centers, weight-loss procedures have become increasingly safe over the last three decades.

♦ In 2007 approximately 200,000 weight-loss operations were performed in the U.S., the majority of which were LAGB or LRYGB procedures.

♦ Medical science now recognizes that the majority of weight-loss procedures are performed because of health risks or health problems rather than vanity.

♦ Medical conditions that can be dramatically improved or even totally reversed by weight-loss operations include asthma and lung disease, obstructive sleep apnea, hypertension and heart disease, gastroesophageal reflux disease, type 2 diabetes, hepatic steatosis, depression and mental illness, Polycystic Ovarian Syndrome and fertility problems.

- Seriously overweight people who undergo bariatric weight-loss operations live longer, healthier lives.

- If you are considering a weight-loss operation, you need to weigh the risks and benefits. Today's minimally invasive weight-loss operations are very safe, but there are always risks involved. The more you know, the better, so ask questions of your surgeon and his or her staff, and talk to anyone you know who has experienced the operation first hand or through the eyes of a loved one.

- Protein shakes serve to control appetite, replace other meals and help maintain long term weight control. Read the labels carefully and avoid those with more than a few grams of carbohydrate per serving.

2

Weighing Your Options

In the last three decades, increasing numbers of complex and invasive operations have moved from the confines of hospitals to the provenance of outpatient surgery settings – from orthopedics, spinal and neurosurgical procedures to gynecological, abdominal and general surgical procedures.

I've seen the changes myself, from both professional and personal points of view. During my training in the 1980s at the University of California, San Francisco, one of the premier university teaching facilities in the world, I witnessed and performed multiple gallbladder operations. At the time, the new laparoscopic techniques with their small incisions were arriving on the scene. Patients underwent two- to three-hour surgical procedures, sometimes with two, three or even four surgeons, all of whom were just learning laparoscopic procedures. The hospital stay was two or three days long, taking the patient away from family and home, during which time a bewildering array of medical students and residents made rounds, poking, prodding and asking questions.

Fast forward to today, when gallbladder surgery is one of the most successful outpatient procedures in the field. Most of my patients scheduled for laparoscopic cholecystectomy (gall bladder removal) have the procedure at an outpatient surgery center. The surgery takes approximately 30 minutes to perform. Recovery room time is two to three hours rather than two to three days, and patients return to their activities and active lives over the space of the next week, many returning to work during that timeframe, though possibly with some

Patient Story: Ignacio V.

Procedure: **LRYGB**

Ignacio recovered very quickly from his LRYGB procedure, and felt healthy enough to start taking long walks within five days of the procedure. He feels healthier than he has in years.

soreness and fatigue and some recovery work still left to do.

From a personal standpoint, when my own father had gallbladder attacks, he underwent a laparoscopic cholecystectomy on a Thursday, went home the same day and returned to work the following Monday, four days after surgery. This was unheard of when I was first learning about surgery.

Weight-loss surgery has changed just as dramatically as gallbladder surgery in the last 30 years. It is now possible to have life-changing surgery that can add years to your life and still return home on the same day.

Hospitals and outpatient surgery centers are only as safe as their employees and systems. This is good news when it comes to outpatient surgery centers where the volume of surgical procedures performed adds an edge of expertise. Working specifically in surgical procedures, these staff members are well-trained and experienced.[47]

But nothing is taken for granted. All outpatient surgery centers are required to have a plan in place for immediate transfer of any patient who develops complications. Many outpatient surgery centers are affiliated with large hospitals and medical centers and, in some cases, connected by underground tunnels, hallways or causeways. Transport, then, occurs instantly and seamlessly, so patients can enjoy the advantages of using an outpatient surgery center with the assurance of instant assistance from a full-service hospital if it becomes necessary.

The smaller size and sharper focus of outpatient surgery centers gives them added safety benefits as well. Outpatient surgery centers provide for less exposure to potential medical errors brought about by a large, overly-busy hospital bureaucracy and less exposure to the drug-resistant bacteria that populate hospitals throughout the United States.

So, knowing that outpatient surgical procedures are quite safe, the next question is:

Can You Really Have an Effective Weight-Loss Operation and be Home in Time for Tea?

Maybe not for tea, but almost undoubtedly in time for a protein-shake dinner. It's hard to imagine an operation as an outpatient procedure, something other than a week in the hospital with medical personnel overseeing and dictating your every move, but medical science has moved surgery to the point where more surgical procedures are performed in outpatient surgery centers than as inpatient procedures in hospitals.[48, 49]

It probably seems strange or incomprehensible, impossible even, to believe that something as life-changing as surgical intervention for weight loss can take place in such a short time and still be effective. Part of this is the feeling that nothing can be attained in life without struggle – nothing comes easy.

An outpatient weight-loss operation is still an operation, an invasive procedure even if it is minimally invasive, with recovery time required, even if the recovery time is much shorter. There may even be the feeling that the weight didn't come on overnight, it came on over a long period of time, most likely over years or even decades – how can such a condition be reversed and changed in a single afternoon?

So, is it really possible to have a life-changing weight-loss procedure and be home the same day? Yes. Decades of research and technological advances have made such dreams reality.

In an early study of outpatient weight-loss surgery, I reported on 194 patients who chose to undergo surgical weight-loss procedures at an outpatient surgery center. Approximately 90 percent of the patients who chose LAP-BAND® operations went home the same day, usually within four to six hours. One-hundred percent of the patients who had laparoscopic RYGB went home in less than 24 hours, after an overnight stay (see Figure 2).

Outpatient Weight-Loss Surgery: Early Study

	LRYGB	LAGB
No. of patients	33	176
Female/Male	32/1	145/31
Mean Age	47	46
OR time (min)	106	75

Figure 3 compares the number of patients, their gender, age and time spent in surgery for both the LRYGB and LAGB procedures.

Is a Surgical Outpatient Weight-Loss Procedure Right for You?

If you've struggled with your weight for years, trying to keep it off or trying to lose it once it's found its way on, you know what a disheartening struggle weight-loss efforts can be. Maybe you've tried all the diets, bought into some fads, "medically proven" and celebrity-endorsed quick fixes. Maybe you've eaten only one food group or avoided another entirely, only to experience rebound weight gain.

And maybe you're tired of being tired, not having enough energy, feeling self-conscious about your weight or experiencing health problems because of it. If so, you are not alone, and you may be on the verge of finding answers to your problems. The answers aren't quick-fix solutions, nor do they involve effortless, instant weight loss. But the combination of modern, state-of-the-art outpatient weight-loss operations, combined with real commitment and quality medical advice is life-changing for most people. The solutions for serious weight loss and long-term health improvement are far more effective, and less invasive, than ever before.

If you've been struggling with your weight, if you're tired of the constant fight and ready to move on to improved health and an improved life with a permanent, proactive solution, you may well be a candidate for a minimally to moderately invasive weight-loss operation. Modern outpatient weight-loss operations are not magical; they still require hard work on your part in order for you to be successful. And as with every procedure in medicine, there are risks and benefits to be weighed. But in most cases, with a minimum of risk, you can turn a losing uphill battle against weight gain into a battle you have proudly won.

Losing the weight and keeping it off is almost certainly the most important thing you can do for your health and longevity. Are you a candidate for outpatient weight-loss surgery?

Current Most-Used Bariatric Techniques

Adjustable Gastric Banding	Vertical Sleeve Gastrectomy	Roux-en-Y Gastric Bypass
Restrictive	Restrictive	Malabsorptive & Restrictive
Place implantable device around upper most part of stomach	Dissect approximately three-fourths of the stomach	Bypass a portion of the small intestine and create a 15-30cc stomach pouch

Figure 4. Comparison of weight-loss surgical techniques.

Long-Term Solutions Require Long-Term Care

If I've learned anything over the 15 years I've spent searching for answers to overweight and obesity, it's that there's no magic wand solution. Being overweight or obese is an unhealthy condition for human beings, and finding a solution to the problem is challenging. In my experience, and based on numerous studies in the field of obesity, weight-loss surgery has proven to be by far the most effective tool in successful weight loss, but it is just that: a tool. What you make with it depends on you.

Embarking on the weight-loss surgery journey with the idea that it's a one-shot "solution" and that the surgeon will look under the hood, rearrange some wiring and send you off on your way as a "skinny person" is starting off with some misconceptions. The surgery, at best, will result in a reduction of hunger, a greater sense of satiety and the willpower to stick to your weight-loss plan with greater success. Think how much easier it would be to avoid the pitfalls of extra calories in the form of snacks, desserts, treats and extras if you're not hungry all the time and when a much smaller portion will satisfy. This is the primary effect of weight-loss surgery: reducing hunger. But it takes someone already committed to reducing calorie intake in order for the surgery to be considered successful. Without commitment and active participation, the surgery isn't going to solve the weight problem.

Surgery isn't a one day event. While the procedure itself may take less than 24 hours from check-in to return home, the effects play out over years and they do not take place in a vacuum. What we've done in my practice and what other successful weight-loss centers around the country have accomplished for committed people who want to lose weight and keep it off goes far beyond successful surgical technique. We've created programs with focus on long-term health, longevity and weight maintenance. The elements of the programs which are supported by clinical evidence as effective tools in the weight-loss project include:

♦ Regular follow-up visits and weigh-ins with the physician-based weight-loss program

♦ Use of meal-replacement liquid protein shakes

♦ Support group attendance with peers who are fighting the same weight-loss battle

♦ Measurement of resting metabolic rate – that information is used for targeting calorie intake numbers in order to lose and then maintain weight.

Weight-loss surgery may not be a magic wand, but it can be the start of a journey to a much healthier life.

A Word About Insurance and BMI

If your BMI is more than 30, you should be able to find a top-notch, highly qualified and skilled bariatric surgeon in the United States to take your case. A BMI of more than 30 means, in the eyes of many experts and the FDA, you are an appropriate candidate, and the risks of surgery are less significant than the risks of continuing to carry the extra weight. If your BMI calculates to 35 or more, you've got very good odds that standard commercial health insurance carriers will even cover the cost of the procedure. Of course, it's up to you, but in the event your health insurance carrier chooses not to cover the surgery, you may want to consider paying out-of-pocket. Take the time to fully understand all the potential costs involved, both short-term and long-term, as described in this book (see Chapter 4 for a discussion of potential costs involved.)

Hormones and Hunger

Hormones are chemicals secreted by the tissues of the body's organs that travel through the bloodstream to exert an effect on another part of the body. For example, adrenaline is a hormone produced by the adrenal glands in response to fear or excitement. Adrenaline travels through the bloodstream causing the heart to beat faster and the blood pressure to rise. Adrenaline even causes our irises to open wider and let in more light to the eyes, to help us flee or fight. We are just beginning to understand the hormones produced by the stomach and other digestive organs, and how these hormones affect our sense of hunger and satiety. We think that after LRYGB, LSG, and to a lesser extent LAGB surgery, changes in these hormones occur, so that the signals traveling to the brain cause a reduction in the level of hunger we experience. Some of the important hormones involved in hunger are ghrelin, insulin, GLP-1 and leptin, but many more are waiting to be discovered and named.

The body communicates from organ to organ using nerves and with hormones that travel through the bloodstream. A complex web of such nerves exists between the brain and the digestive organs of the body. It is believed that some of these nerves carry signals that tell our brains we are full when our stomachs are distended, a phenomenon called "proprioception." Placing the band on the stomach, or performing other weight-loss operations, may induce just this type of signaling that reduces hunger and contributes to the overall, long-term weight loss.

LAGB is a minimally invasive procedure because no gut tissues or organs are removed, stapled or redirected. It is commonly performed as an outpatient procedure, with the patient returning home the same day as surgery.

Laparoscopic Adjustable Gastric Band (LAGB) Procedure

The laparoscopic adjustable gastric band (LAGB, using the LAP-BAND® or REALIZE™ Band) procedure is by far the most common and popular outpatient weight-loss procedure, worldwide, available today. The idea behind LAGB is almost as simple as tightening your belt, only in this instance the belt is internal. During the LAGB procedure a soft silicon polymer band is placed around the upper stomach and positioned so that a medical professional can adjust and tighten the band periodically as weight loss occurs (see Figures 3 and 4).

The technical result is that after the procedure a person with an adjustable gastric band experiences a state of satiety, feeling full through mechanisms that may be hormonal, stimulated by body tissues, or mechanical and psychological.[9] The procedure may trigger weight loss in patients in several different ways: by changing the body's hormones, by direct pressure on the stomach, which signals the brain to eat less, as well as other nerve-assisted mechanisms.

LAGB also has that belt-tightening effect: it produces weight loss through a restrictive mechanism, by making the stomach smaller and unable to hold as much in one sitting, and thereby limits the size of meals and amount of calories that can be consumed. As weight loss occurs, physicians and their assistants can tighten the gastric band through an injection of saline through a small port inserted beneath the skin during the LAGB procedure. The saline makes the band thicker and therefore tighter, which allows patients to continue achieving satiety and weight loss over time.

The LAGB has significant advantages that have made it the procedure of choice in Australia and many countries in Europe. It has taken longer to catch on in the United States because it took longer to go through the FDA approval process. However, while the FDA was doing its job, surgeons in the U.S. continued to do theirs, changing and improving upon other surgical weight-loss techniques, most notably the LRYGB procedure.

LAGB procedures are also reversible, an attractive feature when we consider the pace of change in a field that has seen numerous revolutions toward less invasive and more successful interventions.

Mortality risks for LAGB have generally ranged from 0 to 0.1 percent, lower than that of LRYGB, though experienced centers such as where I work report LRYGB mortality rates of 0.1 to 0.2 percent.[50-53] (About the same as a Cesarean section, another commonly performed procedure, and a fraction of the annual risk of death for an obese person who chooses not to undergo weight-loss surgery.)

In 2007, more than 200,000 Americans underwent weight-loss operations, nearly all of them LAP-BAND® or gastric bypass procedures. (For a discussion on which laparoscopic band might work for you, see Appendix C.) Since then, more people have chosen the sleeve procedure, and lesser-known procedures such as banding with imbrication and Mini-Gastric Bypass have grown in popularity, as we shall soon discuss.

The New Advanced Platform LAP-BAND® System Is It Better?

The LAP-BAND® has been redesigned and the new design has impressed doctors and consumers, but is it better than the bands that came before? Allergen Corporation thinks so and the early data appears to support that belief.

As you can see in the illustrations below, the AP LAP-BAND® looks different from earlier versions mainly because of the new configuration of the internal balloon on the gastric band part. Instead of a smooth, single balloon shaped like a C, the new balloon system is a 360-degree circumferential balloon made up of individual pillows or cushions. One result of this redesign is that there is now no possibility that hard, plastic-type material from the band will be able to rub against the stomach tissues. With the redesign, the only thing in direct contact with the stomach tissues is the balloon system, which is fluid filled and softer than previous bands. It is believed that these changes reduce the possibility of erosion of the stomach tissue.

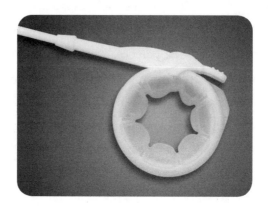

Figure 5. The AP LAP-BAND(R) System.

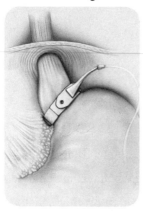

Figure 6 shows detail of laparoscopic banding around the stomach.

In addition, the way the new AP LAP-BAND® is designed means the saline used to fill the band will be distributed more evenly throughout, avoiding any kind of major asymmetry or major creases that the more traditional, single balloon design could have. Detractors of the REALIZE Band™ point out the disadvantages of a band that can crease or become asymmetrical.

Whether the differences inherent in the new design prove significant in the long run is still unknown. However, some surgeons and clinic personnel, as well as the nurse practitioners and physician assistants who have performed band fills in the office, report that they achieve better and more reliable restriction of the stomach with the AP LAP-BAND® than with the other bands.

There are some additional, minor modifications in the design of the AP LAP-BAND® system that are meant to help the surgeon during placement of the band. Smart design features like arrows on the tubing assist the surgeon in determining the direction the tubing is going as he or she is viewing it through the laparoscope. Another improvement is the improved mechanism that locks the band into position.

But ultimately the real question on everyone's mind is does a better band design result in better weight loss? My belief is that most of the weight loss stems from the hard work of the individual who has the band, but clearly the band plays a very important role in helping people reduce portion size, experience satiety sooner and have diminishing hunger hour to hour through the day.

Can a design change of a band really influence those factors enough to see differences in weight loss results? Only time and research will tell, but preliminary data indicates it may be possible. In the illustration below, the weight loss results from an early study with an AP LAP-BAND® are depicted and here the one year weight loss of 47.5 percent exceeds that in the traditional band studies and does appear quite impressive. But it is just one study and it is with selected practices using the new band. In time, longer term studies from multiple centers with comparisons among bands and different population groups will answer the question.

So is the AP LAP-BAND® better than its predecessors? In my view, yes. How much better, only time will tell.

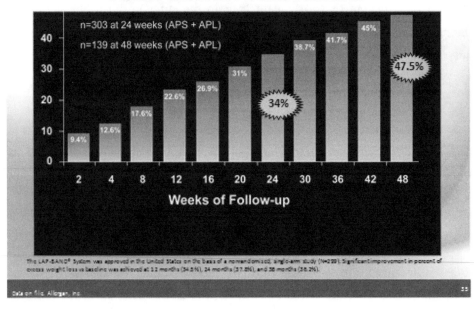

Figure 7. Data results for the new AP LAP-BAND(R) System

Laparoscopic Adjustable Gastric Band with Imbrication (I-band)

Over the long term, studies have proven LAGB to be as successful and almost as effective as LRYGB, but patients who have undergone the procedure are left wanting faster weight loss. The perception among many doctors is that the band is less reliable when it comes to inducing major weight loss than gastric bypass or sleeve. For these reasons, surgeons have combined two techniques: the band plus a surgically stitched in-folding of the stomach, referred to as plication or imbrication. In this procedure, the surgeon shrinks the stomach by progressively folding the stomach wall in upon itself with snug stitches.

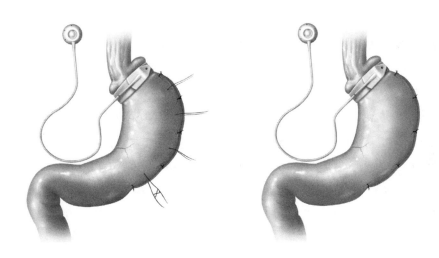

Figure 8 (left) depicts suturing to create Gastric Banding with Imbrication. The image on the right depicts the completed procedure.

Figure 9 depicts the completed Gastric Banding with Imbrication procedure.

The result is the adjustable gastric band wrapped in the usual fashion around the upper stomach with the added feature of a smaller volume of the remainder of the stomach. Many surgeons find that the weight loss tends to occur faster when these two procedures are combined, more like the weight loss induced by the LRYGB procedure, and have given it the nickname of the "supercharged

Lap-Band®."

There are no long-term studies yet to prove whether the addition of the imbrication feature creates consistent or durable advantages, or whether it will result in some as-yet unidentified disadvantages. Early experience in our surgical center, like that of surgeons at other centers, has been very favorable.

Laparoscopic Roux-en-Y Gastric Bypass (LRYGB) Procedure

Laparoscopic Roux-en-Y gastric bypass (LRYGB) is a more complicated procedure than LAGB. It involves creation of a small, 30-cc, stomach pouch, and an outlet from the pouch directly into the upper intestine, where nutrients are absorbed (see Figure 10). By doing this, the majority of the stomach is bypassed, and the pouch, which has less volume than the stomach did, fills more quickly and makes the patient feel full and eat less.

Gastric bypass also intentionally reduces the absorption of some nutrients into the bloodstream. This is because the enzymes that allow our bodies to break down and digest nutrients come from the stomach and the pancreas. After bypass, these enzymes travel downstream and don't come into contact with the food eaten until later in the digestive process. Usually the surgeon creates a length of intestine of around 100 cm, although sometimes we create longer segments for more severely obese patients.

This first part of the intestine is not absorbing nutrients as it would normally because there are no digestive stomach and pancreatic enzymes present over the length of the first 100 cm. After that distance of intestinal length, the enzymes join the digesting food, and normal absorption of nutrients begins in the remaining length of the intestine.

Researchers believe one reason LRYGB works for so many people is that the restrictive nature of the pouch limits the amount of food that can be eaten – there simply isn't room in the stomach any longer to allow the person to overeat. The same kinds of hormonal, psychological and nerve-mediated weight-loss signals are more demonstrably at work as we described for LAGB. In addition, malabsorption causes a few less calories eaten to actually be absorbed into the bloodstream and into the body to be burned or stored as fat. Interestingly, after LRYGB, the body actually burns more calories (per kilogram of body weight) than it did before, and this is a key finding supporting the conclusion that LRYGB changes the set point for weight.[2]

Many patients who undergo LRYGB experience a phenomenon known as "dumping syndrome," which is about as unpleasant as it sounds. Dumping syndrome results in unpleasant flushing, cardiac palpitations and nausea when the patient eats foods rich in carbohydrates (such as desserts). While these side effects are unpleasant and can continue to be present as late as 10 years after the operation, they also work as negative reinforcement, a kind of a behavioral conditioning technique that backs up medical advice to avoid carbohydrates after undergoing the LRYGB procedure. On the plus side, many studies have shown long-term sustained weight loss from 49 to 95 percent of excess preoperative body weight.[54]

A variation on the LRYGB procedure allows for a longer bypass to be created with a 150-cm or 200-cm Roux limb (the part of the intestine brought up and connected to the stomach pouch), which may increase weight loss in patients with higher than average BMI (starting at 50 and above). The greater weight loss probably results from even more hormonal change and possibly more calories passing through the intestine without being absorbed into the bloodstream.

LRYGB is not a new procedure. It's been with us for decades. The name comes from a French surgeon named Roux and the "Y" configuration that results when the intestine is brought up to connect to the stomach pouch.[54] While it's not the newest procedure in our arsenal of weight-loss solutions, the procedure has come a long way since the 1960s and 70s and even since the 1980s and 90s when the operation was still usually performed with an open technique. Some modifications have taken place, such as improved knowledge of the ideal stomach pouch size, ideal length of the Roux limb and better stapling techniques. Now, with the minimally invasive, or laparoscopic, technique, many surgeons favor it as the state-of-the-art weight-loss operation with the best long-term results, especially for more seriously overweight patients.

In my surgery practice, I tend to keep patients overnight if they opt for the LRYGB. A few will need to stay a second night if they are still struggling with postoperative symptoms.

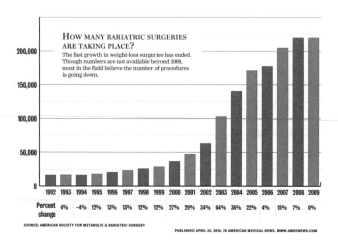

Figure 10. Number of weight-loss procedures by year.

Laparoscopic Sleeve Gastrectomy Procedure

The next procedure that has emerged on the minimally invasive weight-loss surgery scene is called the laparoscopic sleeve gastrectomy (LSG). The procedure can be performed as outpatient surgery and involves removing a large portion – about 75 to 80 percent – of the stomach. The remaining portion of the stomach is formed into a long tube that is unable to enlarge or balloon up with food.

Five year studies show the LSG to be as effective as LRYGB. There's not much longer-term data on this procedure yet, but so far it appears effective in producing weight loss by restricting the amount a person can eat and creating a sense of fullness. It can be performed as an outpatient procedure in selected cases in centers that allow a 23-hour stay. Sleeve gastrectomy has the advantage of being a less complicated or difficult procedure than the LRYGB, with potentially fewer risks.

LSG is becoming recognized as another good outpatient weight-loss surgical procedure for several reasons. First, it can be performed safely in less than an hour with a laparoscopic approach, like the other procedures. Since it doesn't involve an intestinal connection, there's no problem of impaired absorption of vitamins and minerals, or any of the risks caused by the intricate work required in the LRYGB. As a straightforward removal of a portion of the stomach, the LSG offers a simplicity that makes it work well in the outpatient setting. Although concerns persist that patients will have worsened reflux, develop scarring and narrowing of the sleeve, or stretch out the stomach over time, I believe, as do many other experts in this field, that LSG will play a role for many years to come.

Figure 11 depicts stapling to create the sleeve.

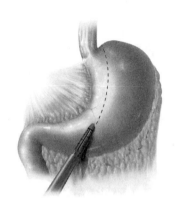

Figure 12 depicts the completed laparoscopic sleeve gastrectomy procedure.

PATIENT STORY: JODY C.

Procedure: **Sleeve Gastrectomy**

I have been heavy my entire life – even as a child. I remember always being the heaviest child on the team. I would work very hard at losing weight only for it to come back.

When I started thinking about having the sleeve gastrectomy I was feeling very uncomfortable and struggling with many different issues. It was when I as diagnosed with Rheumatoid Arthritis that I realized I was going to start feeling older at a much earlier age if I did not do something in order to get my weight under control.

My life after having bariatric surgery is filled with so many new adventures! At four months after surgery I was able to shop for clothes in the Junior section. This is something I never imagined would happen. I have also had a chance to catch up with family members and old friends that I have not seen in a long time and they are stunned at the new me! I am almost unrecognizable for some people that I have known all my life!

Postoperatively I have not had any complications or issues. It really was a very easy process for me. I just wish I would have done this sooner!

The Mini-Gastric Bypass or Loop Gastric Bypass

The concept of a gastric bypass has been around, and been very successful, for several decades. While the most common type of gastric bypass is called the Roux-en-Y, a controversial type of gastric bypass may reduce risks and be simpler to perform.

The Mini-Gastric Bypass (MGB) is a type of gastric bypass operation that can be performed with a laparoscopic technique, using keyhole incisions. The procedure might be more aptly named a Loop Gastric Bypass, and in fact, that term is coming into common usage. The Loop Gastric Bypass name refers to the technique used during the procedure where the surgeon creates a surgical configuration at the top of the small intestine in an area called the jejunum. Part of the small intestine is connected directly to the stomach pouch. For surgeons, a loop gastrojejunostomy (or Loop Gastric Bypass) differs from the Roux-en-Y gastrojejunostomy in that the procedure involves connecting a loop of jejunum instead of creating a "Y" type configuration (see figures 8 and 9).

Mini-Gastric Bypass

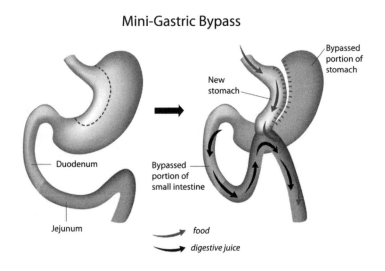

Figure 13. Mini-Gastric B ypass.

Roux-en-Y gastric bypass and Loop or Mini-Gastric Bypass have both been around for several decades. Both have been used frequently for a type of stomach surgery that was widely performed to treat stomach ulcers. With the procedure to treat ulcers, the ulcerated portion of the stomach was removed and afterwards the surgeons reconstructed the area using either Roux-en-Y or Loop Gastric Bypass.

The differences between the two procedures are relatively minor, but debate continues in the medical world over which might offer enough subtle advantages to take the lead, and there are fierce advocates on both sides of the debate. Because the two procedures are so similar and have been used successfully and interchangeably, it stands to reason that the gastric bypass surgery performed today to treat obesity can be performed with either a Roux-en-Y reconstruction or loop reconstruction. And because the procedures are so similar, it should come as no surprise that the results are quite similar and also that there are fierce advocates arguing the advantages of each procedure in the weight-loss surgery realm.

But if the procedures are so similar, what's the point of having both? The rationale behind the MGB is that t he procedure is technically simpler and less risky than the RYGB reconstruction, and the results can be more easily modified or even reversed if there's a need.

Studies have shown weight loss with MGB to be quite comparable to weight-loss success with the RYGB with no change in complication rates.[55]

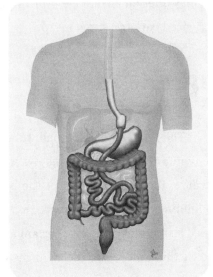

Figure 14. Roux-en-Y Gastric Bypass.

Subsequent studies in several countries have confirmed the procedure appears both safe and effective.[56-59] Some authors believe the MGB procedure offers the advantage of a shorter learning curve and lower complication rates for bariatric surgeons.

With regard to its efficacy as a weight-loss procedure, the MGB has been examined in several studies and shown to have very comparable weight-loss results to RYGB. There hasn't been evidence of increased marginal ulceration, increased gastrointestinal symptoms or difficulties with nausea, vomiting, bloating or other troubles. In fact, recent discussions among surgeons regarding the increased popularity of the sleeve gastrectomy highlight the long, tubularized stomach pouch which is also created with the MGB, and which is well tolerated and rarely has complications of leakage or ulceration.

In my opinion, the MGB causes very similar changes to the digestive process and the appetite, and also similar changes to nutrient absorption as the Roux-en-Y gastric bypass. For some surgeons the technical simplicity of the MGB may offer an advantage over the RYGB, though for most highly skilled and experienced bariatric surgeons, this benefit would be minimal.

The MGB Procedure

The MGB creates a small, tubular-shaped stomach pouch with an outlet directly into the upper intestine, where nutrients are absorbed. Like the RYGB procedure, the pouch is start of the bypass that bypasses most of the stomach, both limiting the amount of space that can be filled up with food so that satiety is reached faster, and creating a certain amount of malabsorption of nutrients. And while we think those two mechanisms help cause the weight loss, newer theories point to hormonal changes caused by bypassing the first section of intestine as the main mechanism by which a lower weight can be reached and become the new set point weight.

Technically speaking, there's one less place in the Loop Gastric Bypass procedure where the surgeon has to reconnect the intestine. There's also often less tension placed on the jejunum as it is connected in the loop fashion to the longer stomach tube pouch than would be the case in the more commonly performed RYGB operation. In my opinion, the overall safety, non-invasiveness and results make the MGB a reasonable option in the battle against obesity.

The Studies

Recent studies have shed additional light on the MGB with studies performed in randomized fashion, meaning patients were actually scheduled to undergo either the LRYGB or the MGB based on the results of a coin flip, to minimize any bias in the study.[58] In one such study the authors found the operative time was significantly less for the MGB procedure. Weight-loss results indicated a trend toward better results with the MGB than the LRYGB at five years. The complication rate was higher for LRYGB (20 percent) vs. the MGB (7.5 percent). Late complication rates and revision rates were similar in the two groups over the five year period.

Like many such studies, this one found the two procedures were both effective and relatively safe. The surgical times might seem long to experienced surgeons – LRYGB was 205 minutes, whereas in the hands of most experienced laparoscopic bariatric surgeons, operative times might be 45 to 70 minutes – however, this is one of the few studies in bariatric surgery that truly represents a randomized trial. Other studies have shown favorable quality of life and weight loss data when compared against LSG and LAGB.

Laparoscopic Duodenal Switch Procedure

The most invasive and complex of the laparo[s] weight-loss procedures is call the Duodenal Switch (DS) procedure, Biliopancreatic Diversion (BPD), and sometimes variations of the procedure are referred as BPD-DS. Basically, this procedure involves the most dramatic

rearrangement of the GI tract. It is not an outpatient procedure. But it does remain an option for some special groups of people battling obesity: individuals who have regained all their weight after previous procedures, and the most severely obese individuals with the most severe diabetes. Most

Figure 15 depicts Duodenal Switch procedure.

surgeons would not recommend DS as a first-line surgical procedure today, as it carries the greatest risks of complications, including severe nutrient deficiencies, when compared to other procedures. But it has shown consistent and impressive weight loss and resolution of diabetes, and for a few individuals in special circumstances, it may be the best option.

Emerging Technologies

We've already examined several common weight-loss surgical procedures, the LAGB, the LAGB with Imbrication, the LRYGB, the MGB and the LSG. In this alphabet soup, the Band, Mini and Sleeve procedures (LAGB, MGB, LSG and LAGB with Imbrication) are performed in outpatient centers, while LRYGB can be outpatient procedure under special circumstances.

New technologies are evolving to meet the needs of society's ongoing search for improved health. Surgeons and surgical technology companies have continued to make advances in surgical instrumentation and techniques, making more procedures available, decreasing the invasiveness of procedures and increasing safety. Laparoscopic techniques moved surgical science light years ahead in increasing safety over the old, open-surgery techniques. Now some researchers believe one day even the minimally invasive laparoscopic procedures could give way to procedures that require no cutting of the organs, no stapling, or even no incisions whatsoever.

IMBRICATION ALONE

Innovative surgeons in many corners of the world have sought to shrink the stomach without removing portions of it or bypassing it. Instead they have folded the stomach in upon itself in a procedure known as gastric imbrication or gastric plication. Others have used the term "wrap" to describe sewing the stomach together upon itself, although it more aptly resembles a "pleat" − like sewing together the folds of a skirt. The data are simply not available to tell us if this strategy will work to induce weight loss. It has some appeal because it is a pretty simple and safe laparoscopic procedure that does not involve using any expensive staplers or bands, and it definitely qualifies as an outpatient procedure. So for economic reasons alone, there is interest in studying this concept further. Most experts doubt that imbrication alone will offer durable weight loss as the stomach seeks to un-do and stretch the plication over time.

ENDOSCOPIC STRATEGIES

Is that still surgery, you ask? Surgery without incisions sounds like magic. It's not. Endoscopic strategies are a form of NOTES surgery, or NOTES procedures (Natural Orifice Transluminal Endoscopic Surgery), meaning there are no external incisions or scars on the body's exterior.

The idea is that with improving technologies, surgeons can perform some procedures by passing instruments down the mouth and esophagus. To accomplish the mission, there must be a sophisticated camera and light for visualization, a flexible endoscope, and some instruments which can pass down the narrow channel of the endoscope. There are several technology companies working on suturing devices and other techniques to shrink the stomach, plicate or fold it internally, and revise previous surgically created stomach pouches. I have used a few of these (the ROSE procedure and the Stomaphyx device) to revise gastric bypass pouches, but none of them is able to offer a primary weight-loss procedure on its own. It remains to be seen whether such strategies will one day offer a successful weight-loss solution. The impressive success of laparoscopic surgery in solving both obesity and diabetes for most people has set the bar very high.

NOTES technology has its fans, among them some U.S. surgeons using novel techniques to remove the appendix through the vagina, and to remove the gallbladder by cutting a hole in the stomach. While there is no doubt that lots of intriguing things can be done using transluminal endoscopic technology, it is less clear that advantages for the patient can be gained. As the technology continues to evolve, we will undoubtedly see some shifts in the way some surgical conditions are handled.

THE INTRAGASTRIC BALLOON

This is another surgery without incisions that sounds like magic, but it's not. The procedure involves passing an endoscope down the mouth and esophagus, into the stomach to plant a large balloon there. The balloon occupies space in the stomach, simulating a feeling of fullness and decreasing hunger. So far, results are disappointing on this endoscopic procedure – patient weight-loss and satisfaction track records aren't as strong as they could be.[60-62] It remains to be seen whether or not the intragastric balloon will come into greater use in the future.

Implantable Gastric Stimulator

Implanting gastric electrical stimulators remains an area of research, but has yet to lead to a clinically effective therapy for obesity.[63-65]

Single Incision Laparoscopic Surgery (SILS)

SILS is the acronym for an emerging technical innovation that allows for some procedures to be performed through a single incision. (Single Incision Laparoscopic Surgery). The minimally invasive surgical companies including Johnson & Johnson, Covidien and Intuitive Health have engineered ways to insert several instruments through a single, if larger, port, rather than placing four or five individual, smaller ports. The result is a single incision, and thus, a single scar, which some people will prefer and consider cosmetically advantageous. While a few surgeons have marketed this novelty successfully, and a subset of younger patients have expressed a preference for this technique, most people find the cosmetic results after laparoscopy to be pretty great already, since the tiny scars often become nearly invisible over time. The tiny standard laparoscopic scars offer some advantages also: they afford the surgeon optimal placement of the instruments, and they very rarely allow hernias to form later in life because the fascial opening is so small. Time will tell whether the compromises the surgeon makes to conduct the procedure with a SILS method – and the increased hernia risk - are worth the perceived cosmetic advantage.

StomaphyX™ and EsophyX™

Two medical devices and procedures from a company called EndoGastric Solutions, based in Seattle. StomaphyX™ showed some initial promise in revising stomach pouches and treating gastroesophageal reflux. They are examples of newer technologies aim to provide surgeons with endoscopic revision options that do not involve any incisions.

Other new, less commonly used weight-loss techniques include gastric imbrication or plication, the intragastric balloon, Apollo's endoscopic suturing device, Ethicon's cinch device (which involves internal stomach sutures) and gastric pacemaking, which involves placing electrodes on the stomach wall and modifying the electrical signaling in the stomach to create a sense of fullness or satiety.

Food for Thought

♦ In the last 30 years, increasing numbers of complex and invasive surgical procedures have changed from open procedures requiring in-hospital stays to minimally invasive laparoscopic procedures performed in outpatient surgery centers, with patients able to return home the same day.

♦ The volume of surgical procedures performed at outpatient surgery centers gives staff there an edge from expertise. Procedures are usually safer, but always do your homework and investigate everything when contemplating undergoing surgery.

♦ Even though most patients undergoing surgical procedures in an outpatient center are healthier than patients who need to be in-hospital, all outpatient centers have a contingency plan for moving patients to a hospital within minutes if complications occur.

♦ It is now possible to have a life-changing weight-loss surgical procedure and be home in time to help the kids with their homework.

◆ The laparoscopic adjustable gastric band (LAGB, using the LAP-BAND®) procedure is by far the most common and popular outpatient weight-loss procedure, worldwide, available today.

◆ The LAGB works essentially like tightening your belt: The soft, flexible silicon band placed around the upper stomach creates a feeling of being full after eating less, encouraging weight loss and preventing overeating.

◆ The laparoscopic Roux-en-Y gastric bypass (LRYGB) involves creation of a small stomach pouch that allows nutrients to bypass the majority of the stomach. The pouch, being smaller than the stomach, creates a feeling of fullness sooner and with less food consumed, and also reduces some of the absorption of nutrients.

◆ The laparoscopic sleeve gastrectomy (LSG) involves removing a portion of the stomach and leaving a long tube that is unable to fill up with large amounts of food.

Change does not necessarily assure progress, but progress implacably requires change. Education is essential to change, for education creates both new wants and the ability to satisfy them.
~ HENRY STEELE COMMAGER

It is not the strongest
of the species that
survives, nor the most
intelligent, but the
one most responsive
to change.

~ CHARLES DARWIN

3

Risk and Reward

Surgical weight-loss procedures are safer today than they ever have been before, but I cannot emphasize enough how important it is to understand the very real risks of undergoing a surgical procedure and the need to compare those to the tremendous benefits and improvements to health and to quality of life that may come from substantial long-term weight loss. Any significant, life-changing decision should include an understanding of the positives and negatives, the upsides and the downsides, the risks and benefits. There is no such thing as too much information when it comes to deciding on whether or not to have a surgical procedure, take a prescription medicine or pursue a health treatment strategy. Read everything you can get your hands on. Talk to everyone you know who may have undergone the same operation or who has a friend or loved one who did. Get second opinions.

Keep in mind there is a body of data showing that, for those patients with significant health risks and a BMI of more than 30 or 35, not undergoing a surgical weight-loss procedure is more dangerous than doing so, even with the attendant risks.

The 1991 NIH Consensus Conference statement on obesity concluded the question came down to risk vs. benefit: Was it riskier in the long term for a person to remain seriously overweight, even morbidly obese, and not undergo a surgical weight-loss procedure, or was it better in the long run and less risky overall to undergo a major open operation? The conclusion at the time took into account data that focused on open operations with all their risks, rather than today's much safer, minimally invasive procedures. At the time the consensus was drafted, the mortality rate as evidenced by major studies from the 1980s exceeded 5 percent for the open procedures. Still, in light of those facts, the consensus was that despite the risks of the weight-loss operations available at that time, the risks of remaining seriously overweight, in fact, exceeded the risks of going through the operation.

It says a lot about the high risks of being seriously overweight that such a conclusion could be reached in an era when the operations being offered were so much less safe and so much more invasive than the procedures available today.

The innovations and technology that have marked the revolution in weight-loss surgery have not changed a simple idea. What has changed is the level of safety. Many of the weight-loss operations performed today are the same in theory as they were in the 1980s and 90s but with modifications that have enhanced effectiveness while reducing risks. For example, the open Roux-en-Y gastric bypass has undergone several minor modifications (changes in stomach pouch size, use of newer staplers, adjustments of the length of the intestine bypassed), and one revolutionary change (the switch to laparoscopic, minimally invasive technique). The long-term weight-loss results are the same or better in magnitude than they were 30 years ago, but the safety record is astronomically improved.

Today, in the hands of a skilled surgeon at a nationally recognized Center of Excellence, or at one of many other high-quality, high-volume centers, the mortality risk for undergoing a minimally invasive bariatric operation ought to be less than one in 1,000. Think of it: Only 20 years ago that same operation carried a mortality risk perhaps as great as one in 20 and now the risk is less than one in

1,000, and, in some cases, published risks from high volume centers such as where I work are below even that.[68-70]

THE EVOLUTION OF GASTRIC BANDING

Open vertical banded gastroplasty gained popularity in the 1970s as an open abdominal procedure involving placement of a nonadjustable, firm silicon band around the upper stomach. It was successful in producing weight loss, and was still being recommended at the time of the NIH Consensus Conference in 1991. However, some problems arose with band erosion into the stomach tissues, and the long-term weight-loss results were disappointing.[66, 67]

Beginning with the Swedish band (now being released in the U.S. as the REALIZE™ Band), and continuing to the LAP-BAND®, surgeons and engineers created a softer, adjustable band that had fewer problems and could be placed laparoscopically. The new generation of bands can be adjusted over time, and the long-term weight loss, as a result, is markedly better.

Experience Matters

Before we go into detail about the types of risks associated with each type of surgical weight-loss procedure, I want to emphasize that these risk percentages apply only to people undergoing procedures performed by experienced, well-trained bariatric surgeons. I can't emphasize enough how important it is to seek out an experienced, well-trained surgeon with a proven track record before undergoing such an important step.

Data on many types of complex surgical procedures, such as cardiac bypass and pancreatic resections, shows that complication and mortality risks are far lower and results far better in the hands of well-trained, experienced surgeons. Just as an outpatient surgery center will often have a better track record for safety due to its focus on one thing – surgery – than a general hospital tasked with caring for any and every contingency, so a surgeon who focuses on specific operations and has trained for and performed many of the same operations will have a better safety and results record (results are measured by the lack of complications from procedures performed and success of weight loss following the procedure).

Risks of Outpatient Surgical Weight-Loss Procedures

The increase in the number of bariatric surgical procedures performed in the United States has risen at the same time obesity rates have risen among the population.

During the same period of time the related risks of outpatient weight-loss operations have fallen in proportion to the numbers of procedures performed. The more experienced surgeons become and the more weight-loss operations are performed, the safer the procedures become.

Mortality risk for bariatric surgical procedures has declined sharply since the 1970s and 80s. If you're remembering all the risks related to weight-loss operations, likely you're remembering the early days of the procedures, when mortality rates of 10 percent were not uncommon. Bariatric operations are much less dangerous now. Studies have appeared over the last two decades that chronicle the falling risk and mortality rates. A study covering the years 1987 to 2001 and including more than 3,300 bariatric procedures in Washington State showed an overall 30-day mortality rate of 1.9 percent.[71] A separate study of more than 16,000 LRYGB procedures in California showed a mortality rate of 0.3 percent.[72] As the years have passed, the reported mortality rates have continued to drop.

For LAGB procedures, the risk of death varies from 0 to 0.3 percent depending on the study, though most large studies report rates well below 0.1 percent. A systematic review in Australia found LAGB approximately tenfold safer than gastric bypass in terms of the 30-day mortality risk.[73, 74]

Other studies have contradicted this wide disparity in safety between the two procedures. For while both procedures have become very safe and effective with experienced surgeons, there exists a certain low level of baseline risk that stems from a seriously overweight patient undergoing an operation of any kind.

What this means in human terms, rather than in stark numbers of mortality, is this: For every 1,000 patients who undergo LAGB surgical procedures, one may face complications that result in death.

Consider this fact for the sake of comparison: In any given year, a person with a BMI of more than 40 faces a substantially higher risk of death, around a 1 to 2 percent chance, just from the strain on the heart and lungs and the complications of diabetes, blood clots and other conditions created or exacerbated by the extra pounds.[75, 76]

The American meta-analysis (a study that combines and analyzes results from many studies, performed to reach broader conclusions than individual studies alone) found no significant difference in mortality between the gastric bypass and the LAGB procedures.[24] What studies did show was that the more experienced the surgeon, the lower the risk of mortality and serious complications.[70]

Another study also noted that the percentage of risk drops with the experience of the surgeon: Surgeons who have performed 20 procedures operate with a 6 percent mortality risk; surgeons who have performed more than 250 procedures have a risk of virtually zero percent.[30]

In our center, we've seen our own data confirm these findings. Among our more than 4,000 cases, the overall 30-day mortality risk since the practice was started is less than 0.2 percent. In our practice we perform roughly equal numbers of LRYGB procedures, LAGB procedures, and Sleeves. The statistics at our center corroborate what is reported in the literature. The drop in mortality rates is occurring for many reasons: better systems in place to prevent errors, better patient selection and evaluation prior to surgery, preoperative weight loss and risk reduction, improved experience of the nursing, anesthesia and surgical staff, better patient education, and surgeon experience.

POSTOPERATIVE NAUSEA AND VOMITING

Probably the most frequent adverse event reported by patients undergoing any kind of operation, including a bariatric procedure, is postoperative nausea and vomiting. Whether it is caused by the combination of the anesthetic drugs used during operations or the laparoscopy or the manipulation of the stomach itself, the result is a significant number of people with some postoperative nausea.

For many people, this is fairly mild and goes away within a few hours to a day. In other people it is not present at all. In very rare cases there may be some more serious cause for postoperative nausea and vomiting, such as a blockage of the intestine. Generally if the symptoms persist more than a few days the surgeon will begin looking for other potential causes with X-ray studies, but generally speaking, surgeons look first at the narcotic pain medications, anesthetics and other drugs, including antibiotics, which can cause nausea for some people.

Vomiting is not usually dangerous and will almost never harm the incisions of a laparoscopic procedure. But it is unpleasant, even painful, and therefore my staff and I work to avoid it in all our patients.

Sometimes when the gastric pouch is fairly small and the anastomosis (where the stomach is connected to the intestine) is fairly snug, people experience some nausea and regurgitation or vomiting early in the first few days or weeks after the procedure as they begin eating and drinking again. This is reasonably common and is nothing to be alarmed about as long as you are able to continue drinking and stay hydrated. The condition, in general, should improve over time. If symptoms appear to be worsening instead of improving over the course of two or three days, or if other, more serious, symptoms (such as high fevers and shaking or chills) and serious pain occur, a call to the surgeon and a trip to the physician's office or hospital will be required.

CENTERS OF EXCELLENCE

The American Society of Metabolic and Bariatric Surgery acknowledges Centers of Excellence in bariatric surgery. It has undertaken the noble process of certifying programs throughout the country by meticulously reviewing data submitted by the programs and the hospitals or surgery centers and then by performing site visits and inspections. The effort is meant to provide standards of reporting and standards of quality that anyone can rely upon when selecting a bariatric surgeon. The ASMBS effort recently joined forces with another surgical organization, the American College of Surgeons, in its certification process for bariatric Centers of Excellence, with much the same objectives.

Even more confusing and, from some points of view, bizarre, some insurance plans, such as Blue Cross of California, have undertaken their own effort to certify programs they call Centers of Expertise, which of course do not recognize the Centers of Excellence identified by the above two surgical organizations.

Are the COEs really excellent or expert? Probably. Are there excellent bariatric surgeons who are not members of COEs? Undoubtedly.

For the surgeon and the surgeon's practice, COE designation in the past proved expensive, time-consuming and cumbersome to apply for from even one of these entities, let alone three or more. The process systematically favors larger institutional programs that are usually university-based because of the unusually large investment of time and resources to comply with the application process and the data-reporting requirements. These do not necessarily guarantee the best surgeons or the best programs; these entities may simply have the staff and budget to undertake the bureaucratic effort. Going forward, more of the burden has been shifted to hospitals, but the redundant processes put forward by insurers are unhelpful.

For my part, I spear-headed an effort to obtain COE designations and found the process expensive and time-consuming. The most exciting and valuable feature of the effort is sharing of outcomes data in what is one of the most comprehensive and well-organized efforts at quality improvement.

In the future, COEs may be the only centers that insurers will reimburse. On the other hand, surgical practices that find the process expensive and cumbersome may opt out and appeal directly to consumers based on their local excellent track records. Hopefully, the COE process will serve patients well by raising the standards of the field so that safety and weight-loss success will be maximized.

HEART, LUNG, KIDNEY AND OTHER ORGAN DYSFUNCTION AND

COMPLICATIONS

Complications that arise with the major organs either during or after operations are generally due to underlying conditions, from which seriously overweight people may suffer.

For example, it is quite common for a person to have suffered the effects of hypertension with slow but steady damage to the heart, arteries and blood vessels, and brain for years prior to coming in for a weight-loss procedure. The same can be said for damage to the kidneys and lungs. Just as a long-term smoker can often have undiagnosed or unrecognized emphysema, a person with long-term obesity can have unrecognized damage or dysfunction of the lungs, kidneys and other organs simply as a result of the years of extra weight.

Previously undetected damage to the organs can become a problem postoperatively when a patient is in a weakened. Experienced bariatric staff are aware of these potential issues and are always on the lookout for some kind of organ dysfunction during the postoperative period. Normally, my staff and I test for these types of events with laboratory tests before and after weight-loss surgery.

Cardiac arrhythmias (irregular heartbeat) and postoperative hypoxia (low levels of oxygen in the blood) are two of the most common postoperative problems.

Usually, my staff and I are able to anticipate undiagnosed serious heart disease, and we test for this in the preoperative stage, so we don't often get many surprises of serious postoperative heart problems. However, even a person who has passed a preoperative stress test with flying colors can, on rare occasion, experience a serious postoperative heart attack. Likewise, a person who generally doesn't have exceptional shortness of breath during everyday life may experience serious shortness of breath or even develop postoperative pneumonia or hypoxia after undergoing an operation.

These complications are more common after open procedures than they are following laparoscopic procedures. In particular, pulmonary (lung) complications

94

are much less apt to occur after a laparoscopic procedure than an open procedure because the pain and the cutting of the abdominal wall in open procedures is so much less invasive in the laparoscopy procedures.[77-79]

BLOOD CLOTS

Blood clots remain an important potential complication after any type of surgical procedure, including those used for weight loss. People who are seriously overweight are – you guessed it – at an increased risk of developing blood clots over and above that of the standard normal-weight patient.

Blood clots can form during surgical procedures because a person is lying flat on the operating table without moving. Normally, regular muscular contractions of the legs propel the blood back up through the legs and body to the heart. If a person is simply lying flat and not moving at all for a significant period of time, the blood can stagnate or pool in the veins and a blood clot can form. While this is true of anyone who is still for extensive periods of time, it is more of a problem in the overweight population in whom the added fat further slows the return of venous blood. So this is one of the big reasons we insist on patients getting up and walking the same day as their surgery.

Another group of people who are at increased risk above and beyond that of the average overweight population are those people who have a kind of metabolic or genetic clotting disorder. Such disorders can be very subtle and can occasionally remain undiagnosed prior to an operation.

One way surgeons and patients can combat unexpected clotting problems is for an experienced weight-loss center to have a clear-cut repeated policy and mechanisms in place to prevent blood clots. Today nearly every patient wears pneumatic sequential compression stockings during operations. These stockings, which look like something out of a science fiction movie, squeeze the legs, ankles and feet and serve to propel the blood up the veins and back to the heart, in close to the same manner normal muscle contractions would. We put the stockings on the patient and start the stockings squeezing before the procedure begins. This results in a dramatic reduction of the risk of blood clotting, even in those patients who have a metabolic or genetic clotting disorder.

The more experienced the surgeon, the better the chances of avoiding blood clots. This is because of the length of time it takes for the procedure. A less-experienced surgeon may take two, three or even four hours performing the LRYGB, for example, whereas an experienced surgeon, will typically do the operation in about an hour. It's not a race – speed alone isn't the important thing, it's that the less time the patient spends on the operating table, flat and without normal movement and muscular contractions that move the blood through the veins, the better. So, in the end, performing the surgery quickly reduces the risk of blood clots.

One more way to reduce the risk of blood clots is to use a low-dose blood thinner, such as heparin or enoxeparin. This kind of medication is often given by injection before or after an operation. Blood-thinning medications reduce the risk of blood clots even further, but they can also elevate the risk of bleeding slightly. As with many challenging decisions regarding the care of surgical patients, the decision to employ a blood-thinning medication requires a careful balancing of the risks of bleeding versus the risks of clotting.

Finally, a last method that can be employed to prevent blood clots involves the placement of a type of filter in the large veins that bring the returning blood from the legs back to the heart, the inferior vena cava. Inferior vena cava filters (also called Greenfield filters) are very successful at preventing blood clots from traveling from the legs to the heart. While they don't prevent blood clots, per se, they do in fact result in a significantly decreased risk for developing serious consequences or complications from blood clots.

INFECTION

Infection occurs in approximately 1 percent of all surgical incisions regardless of the type of surgery, primarily as a result of gram-positive bacteria that live on skin and throughout the body. Modern antibiotics and preoperative scrubs have dramatically reduced the risks of these types of infections from the days when it was 10 or 20 percent to the standard of perhaps 1 percent.

In most cases, this type of infection isn't a serious complication. It may result in the need for postoperative antibiotics or incising and draining a small abscess at the surgical site, but this is not considered life-threatening, except in very rare cases.

In recent years media attention has focused on some aggressive hospital bacteria that have resulted in serious infections and death. The most common of these is called methicillin-resistant staphylococcus aureus or MRSA. The prevalence of these drug-resistant bacteria has increased in recent years, and infections can be more serious. Some patients are particularly susceptible to staph infections, and may have a history of them occurring in the groin, back or other skin and soft tissues. And obesity is a major risk factor.[80] This is due in part to the impaired blood supply through the extensive subcutaneous fat. The infection-fighting and infection-preventing cells of the body have to travel to the skin to counter these kinds of infections. Obesity makes that process more difficult because the cells have to travel through extensive fat to get to the skin.

We have seen a few such infection cases in our region, but none that required extraordinary treatments to resolve. Some centers and regions of the country have not been so lucky – so it may be worth asking your surgeon if this has been a frequent problem at your hospital or center.

If you have a history of repeated staph infections, you can take steps to avoid another occurring at the time of your weight-loss surgery by doing the following:

- Inform your surgeon
- Consider a preoperative scrub at home with Hibiclens or other antibacterial products
- Lose weight preoperatively
- Ask about the prevalence of MRSA at the facility

Another type of infection can be considerably more serious. This type occurs internally and results in either peritonitis (inflammation of the thin membrane that lines the abdominal wall and covers most of the organs of the body) or an abscess (a round pocket of fluid with infection) within the abdomen. Such infections are generally caused by microorganisms that escape from the inner lining of the intestine or stomach and travel outside these organs into the peritoneal cavity (the space inside the abdomen where the intestines are). Modern antibiotics and, possibly in some cases, bowel preparations (an oral laxative that reduces the amount of waste, and bacteria, within the intestines the day before surgery) have contributed to the reduction of this type of infection but have not eliminated them.

Types of Procedures, Types of Risks

When you're contemplating an operation, you need to consider the risks. With modern minimally invasive weight-loss procedures, the risks have been reduced considerably as the science has expanded and more and more surgeons have improved expertise. The best understanding of your own risk will come from a discussion between you and your surgeon of your own health status and the specific procedure planned.

Risks with outpatient weight-loss operations are different for each procedure, so each should be considered separately.

LAGB Risks

Short-term complications for the LAGB procedure include infection, bleeding and complications around the site of the port. Longer term complications include band slippage (movement of the band within the body), dysphagia (difficulty swallowing), band erosion and problems of dislodgement or flipping of the access port.

There have been a limited number of cases in which the gastric band has had to be removed. In an extensive series of more than 2,700 bariatric surgeries performed by a single center, the band was removed in 3.7 percent of patients over a period of 10 years, largely because of complications from erosions and slippage.[81-83] This amounts to three to four people out of 100. Most surgeons in this field believe the risks of these types of problems have fallen further since this study, due to improvements in the design of the bands and the techniques of the surgeons implanting them.

There are also issues of how tight to make the band. A band could be too tight, producing a sensation of very tight restriction and making it difficult for the patient to drink liquids. A band producing tightness or near complete restriction is a complication that occurs in as many as 1 to 3 percent of procedures. It is a frustrating problem and can take days to resolve as the postoperative swelling goes down. During that time the patient will probably have to remain in a hospital on an IV drip for hydration. While it is not an unusual complication, the odds of experiencing such a complication are considerably reduced by choosing an experienced bariatric surgeon. And a tight band is not regarded as a serious complication, more like an inconvenience, as the patient has to wait around in the hospital for swelling to go down.

Conversion to an open incision could become necessary due to a number of causes, but may occur because of technical difficulties during the procedure or because of excessive bleeding. But again excessive bleeding occurs in less than 1 percent of operations performed by experienced surgeons. If an open incision becomes necessary, then the patient would probably require admission to a hospital.

LRYGB Risks

The laparoscopic RYGB procedure is a technically more complex and advanced procedure than the LAGB and requires a bariatric surgeon with specialized skill and training in that specific procedure. It isn't a procedure that's right for every surgeon to handle in an outpatient setting.

Most of the patients undergoing the laparoscopic RYGB procedure have a hospital stay of between 24 and 40 hours. So, while this book is focused on the changing landscape of weight-loss surgery, which has led to the dramatic revolution from major invasive open procedures to modern minimally invasive outpatient procedures, be aware that the state-of-the-art LRYGB weight-loss surgery for many patients in most states will still require a short hospital stay, and the procedure at most practices is considered not quite outpatient surgery.

LRYGB can be performed in about an hour, and patients generally can be discharged from the hospital in less than 24 hours. Once a surgeon has performed perhaps 500 to 1,000 of the LRYGB procedures in the hospital setting, it is possible to perform LRYGB in an outpatient setting, in selected patients who don't have excessive health risks or high BMIs.

Outpatient centers usually don't allow patients to stay more than 23 hours, so the patient must be extra motivated to head home within that time frame. Sometimes this motivation stems from a desire to be away from the hospital setting, a desire to return to the comforts of home or the desire to minimize costs. A motivated patient will generally do the preop work and be prepared, having stuck to a meal-replacement diet, lost the preoperative weight and attended classes so as to know what to expect.

Properly prepared, a motivated patient who wants to recover faster and get back home is a good thing. But statistics show the sooner you leave the facility, the higher the chance you'll return with complications after some types of weight-loss surgery. A patient who leaves after only five hours might return with nausea and vomiting. The concerns about leaving the surgical facility too quickly need to be weighed against the risks of remaining in the facility, exposed to bacteria and discomfort.

In some geographic areas, regulations allow outpatient surgery centers to permit patients to stay up to 72 hours. So, in such a facility, almost every LRYGB procedure would be considered "outpatient."

In nearly all cases, the gastric bypass procedure can be performed with a laparoscopic or minimally invasive approach. For outpatient LRYGB surgery, we carefully select motivated, low-risk candidates who can be safely discharged home within the 23-hour time window. This is still a difference of hours – not days.

Today, in my practice, 99 percent of RYGB procedures are performed laparoscopically, making it more likely the patient can be released at less than 23 hours in the surgical facility, and thus making LRYGB an outpatient procedure.

According to our data at my practice, most people who truly want an outpatient procedure choose LAGB or LSG. I generally counsel my LRYGB patients that they will stay in the hospital one or two nights and experience home recovery times of one to two weeks. Nearly everyone has responsibilities in daily life, from regular jobs to families and kids; because of the nature of the operation I recommend patients plan for two weeks off from these activities before returning full-bore. This allows most people plenty of time to recover and prepare to move forward with their lives.

For most people, this short hospital stay is easily accomplished and reimbursed without financial strain. In fact, in many cases, this rather short hospital stay is unexpectedly welcome news for the insurance companies who were expecting to get hit for a full four-, five-, six- or seven-night hospital stay.

Nowadays, the surgeon's office obtains pre-authorization from insurance plans for weight-loss surgery. Sometimes this authorization indicates the number of days expected for hospitalization, and, while we generally have patients in the hospital one to two days, it is not surprising to see authorizations returned for five to six days. The reasons for this often stem from outdated systems used by the insurers, who are using their experience from open abdominal operations to plan the hospital stays.

For patients undergoing LRYGB at our outpatient facility, I usually keep patients in the facility overnight for observation; the patients are discharged early the next morning. In the rare event that complications arise and hospital admission becomes necessary, there's already a plan in place for the patient to be admitted to the hospital for further evaluation or treatment.

Beyond mortality risk, the main short-term complications for LRYGB procedures stem from potential problems associated with the tissue connection of the stomach pouch to the intestine or between two parts of the intestine. Among the most serious complications, the most common are:

♦ Leaking at the anastamosis site
♦ Bleeding
♦ Bowel obstruction
♦ Pulmonary embolus (blood clot in the lungs)

These potentially life-threatening complications can be corrected by early recognition of the problem and proper intervention. In the case of leaks, serious bleeding or bowel obstruction, surgery is often needed to correct the problem. In the case of a blood clot, medication is given to thin the blood and dissolve the clot.

Complications that can occur later (over weeks to months) include anastamotic stricture (narrowing of the tissue connecting the stomach pouch to the intestine), marginal ulcer (formation of an ulcer or sore on the inside lining of the stomach pouch), vitamin deficiency caused by lack of vitamin supplementation and bowel obstruction. Each of these complications can be corrected by accurate diagnosis and medical treatment, and there's time to sort them out, usually with office visits and tests.

Patient Story: Heather T.

Procedure: **LRYGB**
Weight lost: **127 pounds**

I know that this surgery is not for everyone, but this was the surgery for me! The reason why I wanted the surgery was because I had two small boys, bad health and bad eating habits. My surgeon and his awesome office staff gave me the power to re-invent my life. The very same day I got out of the hospital from having surgery, I started walking. At two weeks, swimming and working out. I don't need plastic surgery; my body is beautiful and healthy. You will always want to take care of yourself because it is so much easier now. Why would you go through such a major surgery and waste it? I needed to learn about what was good for me to eat and drink. Almost two years out, I can eat well, but I learned meals, portions, protein, low carb. This surgery gave me the confidence in so many ways to become what I always wanted to be.

BLEEDING

Bleeding is a fairly rare complication occurring in less than 1 percent of weight-loss operations. The literature, across the board, shows that minimally invasive operations have consistently had a lower risk of bleeding than open procedures.

It's not entirely clear why this is the case. It could be the magnification of the camera system on the surgical site during laparoscopy allows a surgeon to stem bleeding where it wouldn't be possible during open procedures. For whatever reason, the risk of bleeding with laparoscopic RYGB is quite low, a portion of 1 percent, meaning there's less than one in 100 chances you'll experience significant bleeding, require a blood transfusion or a return trip to the operating room to correct bleeding if you choose LRYGB and an experienced surgeon.

Bleeding from staple lines after surgery can sometimes occur. Both bleeding during the operation and bleeding from staple lines after surgery are risks more common in people taking blood-thinning medicines such as Coumadin or heparin and its derivatives. In addition, patients who take aspirin, Plavix and ibuprofen, as well as other medications that may affect the aggravation of platelets (an important part of forming a blood clot), may experience elevated risks of postoperative hemorrhage. In most cases, the bleeding will stop on its own without any special treatment other than possibly reversing the effects of an anticoagulant (with additional medication). Generally, bleeding from the staple lines or bleeding from the operation would occur in the hours directly following surgery while the patient was still in the hospital or surgery center. It is possible that slow or steady bleeding could result in light-headedness, pallor and racing heart rate after return home, making a call to the doctor necessary.

Even given how low the odds are, it is still possible a person could end up needing a blood transfusion, an endoscopy (a nonsurgical procedure to examine and cauterize an organ using a flexible fiber optic tube passed down the esophagus) or even further surgery to stop excessive or persistent bleeding.

It is always important to tell your surgeon if you have a propensity to bleed more than what is considered normal during surgical procedures (for example, if you have received multiple blood transfusions during routine operations) or if you are taking any medications, especially those that thin the blood. In addition, if you have a personal history of blood clots (called thromboembolism) either in the legs or those that have traveled to the lungs, make sure to tell your surgeon about this so your risks can be better assessed.

ANASTOMOTIC LEAK

The most important determinant of the risk of intra-abdominal infection is the risk of anastomotic leak. In LRYGB surgery there are two sets of connections (anastamoses) created. The first of these occurs from the small stomach pouch to the Roux limb of the intestine, and the second of these occurs from the Roux limb of the intestine to the rest of the intestinal stream.

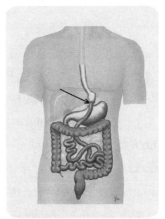

Figure 16 shows the LRYGB procedure. The arrow indicates the connection point the surgeon forms to the stomach pouch.

Either of these sites of tissue connection can result in a leak, which can be quite dangerous and lead to peritonitis or intra-abdominal abscess. While the risk of these complications is about 1 percent, that does not mean that 1 percent of all patients undergoing gastric bypass surgery will develop peritonitis and serious infection. An experienced and careful bariatric surgeon will have had several, if not many, leaks occur in patients in the past.

The surgeon will know the signs and symptoms of a leak and be able to make the diagnosis of a leak early before serious infection or peritonitis can set in.

In our practice, in the first 1,000 operations the risk of anastamotic leak was approximately 3 percent. In the second 1,000 operations the risk of anastomotic leak was 0.3 percent. In the third 1,000 cases the risk of leak was 0.2 percent. The experience of having performed many hundreds of LRYGB procedures has led to some important conscious and subconscious learning about the ideal way to form the stomach pouch and the ideal way to form the stomach-intestinal connection.

What we've learned is that subtle critical differences exist from one operation to the next, caused by the different anatomy of individual patients and the tissue quality of each individual. Experience allows the surgeon to adapt to many unexpected findings and anatomies and create healthy, safe, solid, non-leaking anastomoses.

The vast majority of leaks that do happen occur between the stomach pouch and the small intestine. It is much less common for the downstream intestine-to-intestine connection to result in a leak. And despite the levels of safety attained in today's weight-loss operations, the anastomotic leak remains the most serious complication of the LRYGB procedure and is probably the cause of the majority of deaths reported in the 30 days directly following surgery.

In the longer term after LRYGB, a few people may experience trouble from some largely preventable conditions: vitamin deficiencies, gastritis and stomach ulcers. By following your surgeon's advice on proper vitamin intake, and regularly monitoring blood levels, the vitamin problem can be avoided. Ibuprofen and all of its NSAID cousins cause most of the gastritis and stomach ulcer, so avoiding those drugs eliminates most of that problem.

Any operation can lead to some unwanted scar tissue, and intestinal blockages have been known to occur as a result. Another kind of blockage can stem from something called an internal hernia, in which some of the intestine gets trapped inside the tight spaces in the abdomen. There is nothing special that can be done to avoid these last two problems; fortunately they are uncommon, but I mention them here to raise awareness and know to seek expert help if a problem does arise.

Tissues and Leaks

There's been a great deal of research into the cause of these leaks. During surgery most bariatric surgeons employ a variety of endoscopic stapling techniques to create the anastomosis. In order to create a connection where one hasn't been before, the surgeon must first make incisions to free the tissue that will be moved and then staple or suture the tissue to create the new connection (a procedure also often used to remove a segment of the intestine and re-connect the ends, to treat benign diseases such as polyps, diverticulosis, growths, masses, ulcers or unusual bleeding, and for cancers and lymphoma of the stomach or intestines).

Whether the surgery being performed is for direct treatment of disease or for weight loss, the surgeon is creating connections between two sets of tissues that were not previously connected. In general, it is believed that when a leak occurs, it is because the cells of the tissues that have been connected fail to adequately mesh together and form a natural biological connection. (You can picture this basically as a cut on the finger that removes a section of flesh. The two sides of the cut need to be brought together in order to heal. Healing may take longer if the tissues on the two sides don't mesh together to form the missing flesh.)

In order to form the best, strongest possible connection when the tissues are connected to form the anastomosis, certain conditions need to be present. There needs to be a good, healthy supply of blood to the tissues involved, which requires the patient to be healthy and not suffering from anemia or a compromised immune system. There also needs to be an absence of tension at the site where the connection is created – the tissue needs to not be straining to make the connection; a strain can cause a tear and therefore a leak.

These two factors alone are probably the most important issues with any type of gastrointestinal connection, but there are additional factors that can complicate a procedure. Chronic steroid use, a compromised immune system from liver disease, poor nutrition, cancer or severe circulatory problems may affect the adequacy of the blood supply to the tissues, making it difficult for the connection to hold without leaks. A young, healthy patient with no problems other than weight would be the ideal candidate for an LRYGB procedure (or any surgical procedure, for that matter), But don't worry; all the studies we cite here, including our own data of more than 4,000 weight-loss operations, involve people of all ages, many with substantial medical problems, just like the medical problems listed above.

A patient is at risk for a leak usually only for the first 24 to 48 hours after surgery. In fact, the vast majority of leaks will occur within eight hours of surgery. Very, very rarely, can a leak occur several days after surgery.

DETECTING LEAKS

The signs and symptoms of a leak vary between individuals, but most often involve rapid heart rate, then rapid breathing, fever and increased pain. The first thing a surgeon does when it is believed a leak has occurred is immediately confirm the diagnosis and act to repair it.

Some surgeons use imaging studies, such as an upper gastrointestinal contrast study or CT scan (the traditional CAT scan we've all heard of) to determine if a leak has in fact occurred. Such tests aren't perfect but can help a surgeon pinpoint trouble. Often, if it is believed a patient's anastomosis has developed a leak, the surgeon will return the patient to the operating room for a re-exploration, either laparoscopically or, at this point, through an open abdominal incision. In my own practice the test employed depends on the level of likelihood that there may be a leak. As with other experienced surgeons in this field, we have tried all of the above tests and procedures. We've even performed exploratory open surgery and discovered patients who didn't have leaks at all but rather some other processes mimicking symptoms of leaks. (For example, a patient with extreme anxiety reported abnormally high levels of pain and elevated heart rate. What seemed a very high possibility of a leak proved to be a healthy, normal anastamosis at laparoscopy.)

An Ounce of Prevention

One of the ways we've found to protect against the possibility of anastomotic leaks at my practice has been to perform a pressure test of the gastrojejunal anastomosis while the patient is still in the operating room. We test the tenacity of the pouch before ending the operation. So, once the operation is finished, and we're sure the results are excellent, and there's little chance of leaks, we test the anastomosis. We pass a soft tube down the esophagus to the point of the anastomosis, prevent intestinal outflow from the anastomosis, and fill the stomach pouch with a blue-dyed saline. This puts pressure on the stomach pouch and on the new connection and allows us to make certain there are no leaks. If there are, we can make repairs, revisions or reinforcements right then and there, making sure we've got a tight seal with no chance of leaks.

Now that we've done some 3,000 leak tests, it's become increasingly uncommon for us to find any leaks during the operation. I'd estimate we find subtle leakage in one out of every 100 cases. Even then it's not certain those cases would have lead to clinical leak and infection, but testing for leaks during the actual operation gives us an extra edge in achieving a high degree of safety and security.

Detected early, a leak usually creates no long-term complications or consequences, but when a leak isn't discovered promptly it can result in severe complications.

Whatever test is used to check for a leak, usually the follow-up treatment by a savvy team of surgeons and nurses that employs early and aggressive detection and intervention will successfully mitigate the consequences of a leak.

PATIENT STORY: JUDITH D.

Procedure: **Sleeve gastrectomy**

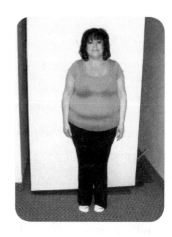

I struggled with being overweight my entire life. I was always the fat one among my friends. I had tried every single diet with little, or short-term, success. It wasn't until I reached menopause that my weight became unbearable.

The one thing I really struggled with prior to having the sleeve gastrectomy was depression. I used to have such difficulty getting out of bed. I became too embarrassed to even go grocery shopping because I just wanted to hide. I wanted to hide from myself and from the world.

I had always thought that bariatric surgery would be a very traumatic experience. Once I got started in the process I realized that it was not. I did not have any complications and I was back to my normal routine sooner than expected.

My life after bariatric surgery is drastically different. Now want to get out of bed and enjoy the time with my family. I love to go walking, quad riding, and enjoying the time with my family that weight had once robbed. Bariatric surgery may not be the answer, it's a tool – but it works!

Loop Gastric Bypass Risks

LEAKS

In recent years the treatment of anastomotic leaks has improved by employing expandable, metallic stents – long tubes that are placed inside the esophagus and stomach area and which can extend across the area where the tissue connection has become disrupted and a leak has occurred. Basically this means the new tube (the stent) is placed right inside the other tube (the stomach). The stents can be placed with an endoscopic procedure in which a flexible endoscope is passed down through the mouth and esophagus. This means that in most cases placement of a stent does not require surgery. The stents allow the leak to seal – the leak simply heals around the stent all by itself. When everything goes well, stents allow the tissues to heal so that the patient can resume taking in liquids and even solids by mouth. Stents can occasionally cause minor problems themselves, either causing nausea by migrating downstream into the lower stomach, or they may cause some (usually minor) bleeding from irritation of the walls of the stomach.

Quite a few studies have now described successful use of stents in the treatment of potentially life-threatening leaks. Some of these studies have reported placing the stents in combination with surgically washing out the abdomen and cleaning up any infection that might have occurred as a result of the leak. Others have described placement of the stents endoscopically without any re-operative surgery. I have gained some experience with stents over the last few years and have seen them successfully utilized to control an otherwise difficult leak. In one particularly challenging case, a patient developed a leak after a sleeve gastrectomy procedure and our efforts to close the leaking stomach edge with open re-operative surgery failed because of poor tissue quality. We really had very few good options and the placement of the stent allowed the leak to seal and be controlled. The patient went on to recover fully.

One of the problems that can occur with the use of stents is that stents placed within the stomach can sometimes migrate and result in a blockage of the stomach. This can make it impossible for the patient to resume eating and is very uncomfortable. In other cases, the stent may not successfully enable closure of the leak and further surgery can be required.

Because the possibility of a leak after gastric bypass surgery or sleeve gastrectomy remains such a potentially serious and life-threatening complication, it is imperative that the bariatric surgeon apply all of the skill and expertise available to address the problem as effectively as possible and as early as possible. Techniques to manage leaks continue to evolve, and the use of endoscopic stents appears to offer promising advantages, becoming part of the armamentarium of many of the best surgeons.

LSG Risks

Laparoscopic sleeve gastrectomy (LSG) involves removing a significant portion of the stomach, permanently reducing the size of the stomach overall. The level of invasiveness and complexity is in between that of the LAGB (less invasive/complex) and the LRYGB (more invasive/complex). Because of this, the mortality risk is quite low.[84-87]

As with the LAGB and the LRYGB, LSG involves a laparoscopic procedure on the stomach with general anesthesia. Because general anesthesia is involved, there are some risks to be considered. The procedure can be performed in the outpatient setting, often with discharge within the 23-hour window. The chief complications seen with LSG are:

- Vomiting
- Leaking at the cut edge of the stomach
- Bleeding
- Conversion to open procedure

In LSG, part of the stomach is removed, leaving the remaining stomach smaller, narrower and more tube-like.

The result is a form of restriction of the stomach and on how much the patient can eat. Sometimes in the immediate postoperative period, the surgery can result in nausea and vomiting that can take days to resolve. Usually, with preparation, anti-nausea medications and a liquid diet, patients can avoid this and still go home after the overnight stay, but not always. Occasionally patients need to stay in the hospital for intravenous hydration and wait until the swelling goes down and the newly reduced stomach settles down before going home.

LSG doesn't involve an anastamosis, but it does involve a long staple line along the edge of the newly-shrunken stomach. So, while it is quite rare, a leak could potentially occur anywhere along the edge of the stomach where it was cut and stapled or sutured. The detection and consequences would be the same as those discussed above for leaks after LRYGB operations.

Other complications, such as conversion to open surgery and bleeding, can occur in rare cases. Overall the risks of developing problems after an LSG procedure appear to fall in between those of the LAGB and the LRYGB, and are rare overall.

What we don't know is whether more patients with LSG will, over the long term, develop some nutritional abnormalities or problems with gastroesophageal reflux (heartburn). And perhaps the most important thing we don't know is whether or not, over the long term, the LSG will remain durable and not lead to stretching out of the stomach pouch or tube. Based on what I know about LRYGB and other types of surgery, it seems likely to me that some people will develop dilation of the new stomach tube over time, but whether this will occur in many of the patients undergoing this procedure or only a few, only time will tell.

TISSUES AND LEAKS

LSG tissue healing and staple line leaks are a concern, but the potential problems tend to occur much later than is the case for almost any other procedure surgeons commonly perform. In LSG, the most common time for leaks to occur is several weeks after surgery, not within 24 hours as is the case with LRYGB.

These so-called "delayed leaks" tend to be very small "micro leaks" that produce somewhat more subtle symptoms than after LRYGB. The symptoms are most commonly pain and fever, but since it occurs in this delayed fashion, it is important that each person involved know that a delayed leak is a possibility and that even fairly mild symptoms during the first six weeks after surgery deserve investigation.

Dealing with Complications

With obesity, undergoing weight-loss surgery today is statistically a lot safer than NOT having weight-loss surgery. But if complications do occur after your bariatric surgery, you and your surgeon need to be prepared to do whatever it takes to resolve the problem. Complications are a statistical reality just like plane crashes and other adverse events that occur in complex systems and endeavors. But just as flying is still statistically markedly safer than driving, undergoing a weight-loss surgical procedure is still safer than living with the health complications and threats posed by being overweight or obese. To put it simply, if you're overweight or obese, your health risks are already greater than the health risks posed by having a weight-loss operation.

If you have followed the advice in this book, then you have researched well and chosen an experienced and capable surgeon who is well-qualified to help resolve potential complications. Now you must adopt the best possible attitude and move forward to resolve the situation as quickly and completely as possible. It can be very difficult, both physically and emotionally, to deal with a complication from surgery. Complications can often mean a much-prolonged course of illness and recovery, delayed plans for returning to work, and to social and family life. Complications can mean facing frightening experiences like re-operative or open surgery with still more risks at every turn. In the vast majority of cases, however, even serious complications are safely resolved, and the surgeon and the patient can fight through them together to achieve a successful result.

It doesn't help your recovery or your health to become angry and to focus on what might have been, or who did what wrong. If something was done "wrong," there will be plenty of time for you to sort that out when you are recovered and well. The key thing to focus on now is recovery, and finding the shortest, safest and best path to achieve the best recovery possible.

Sometimes when people experience complications they want to change surgeons. Sometimes the complication brings to light concerns that a patient or the patient's family already had about a surgeon or the surgical team. And it is occasionally best to change surgeons; just try to be objective and make sure you are changing to a highly skilled and experienced bariatric surgeon who has tackled this type of complication previously – don't change to someone who is less capable of helping you when you most need help. No surgeon who is performing high numbers of complex surgical procedures does so without experiencing complications of those procedures over the years. The very best surgeons in any field have learned how to fight through some very serious complications and achieve the best results for their patients. After all, that's why you chose them in the first place.

Risks of Not Undergoing Surgical Weight Loss

Obesity is one of those situations in which not taking action is the riskiest choice. Numerous studies have compared the risks of not undergoing weight-loss surgery to those of undergoing surgery, and every study shows markedly higher risks and fatalities from standing pat and not having a procedure.[41]

The risks of weight-loss operations must also be held up and compared to the risks of not having a surgical weight-loss procedure. Consider the risks faced by the decision not to undergo a modern weight-loss operation and choosing instead to either work through a nonsurgical weight-loss program (there are several excellent programs, as well as other not-so-excellent programs) or to simply ignore the whole problem of being overweight.

Several studies have shown that the risks of not undergoing weight-loss operations for the seriously overweight are substantial.[71] Studies that provide a nonsurgical control group of overweight patients indicate a much greater risk of heart disease, diabetes and mortality over the years following the studies compared to those patients who underwent weight-loss surgery.

A study that compared the surgical group to a group of seriously overweight people undergoing an extensive medically supervised (nonsurgical) weight-loss program (something very few people actually do), found the medical group fared far worse in terms of weight loss and health outcomes.[43] This is not to say you should not enroll in a high quality nonsurgical, medically supervised weight-loss program. In fact, it may be the best first step you can take if you are serious about losing the weight.

Many people, especially those with a lower BMI (say, less than 30) can enjoy success with a medically supervised weight-loss program that employs counseling, dietary coaching, meal replacements, exercise, prescription drugs and consultation with doctors and psychologists. However, it's difficult to find programs that can combine all these elements, along with support groups and motivational challenges for patients, under one roof.

Most health insurance plans won't pay for medically supervised nonsurgical weight-loss programs, although Medicare has recently changed its rules to do so. In addition, people with BMIs of more than 30 have a harder time achieving their weight-loss and health goals without operations.

The bottom line is that with or without surgery, losing the weight and keeping it off requires commitment, support and the right tools. The ideal approach rests with integrating both surgery and a great medically supervised plan into your long-term approach to lose the weight, keep it off and stay healthy. The key is to understand that every month of living with the extra weight incurs risks, so calculate those carefully into your analysis of the risks of outpatient weight-loss surgery.

Considering that weight gain is the primary risk factor for elevations of cholesterol and lipids, high blood pressure, diabetes, heart disease and shortened life expectancy, it stands to reason that the risks of not aggressively bringing the weight down are pretty substantial.

I know the price of success: dedication, hard work, and an unremitting devotion to the things you want to see happen.

~ FRANK LLOYD WRIGHT

Food for Thought

◆ Today's minimally invasive weight-loss operations are significant and life changing, and a body of data shows that for patients with a BMI of more than 35, not undergoing a surgical weight-loss procedure is more risky than doing so.

◆ The 1991 National Institutes of Health Consensus Conference statement on obesity addressed the topic of weight-loss procedures. At the time, the mortality rate for the open procedures exceeded 5 percent. Despite this, the statement indicated that the risks of remaining seriously overweight exceeded the risks of having the operations.

◆ Many weight-loss procedures performed today are the same in theory as they were in the 1980s and 90s but modifications have enhanced their effectiveness while drastically cutting the risks.

◆ The best way to minimize any risks associated with undergoing bariatric or weight-loss surgery is to seek out an experienced, well-trained surgeon with a proven track record.

♦ Surgeons who have performed 20 procedures operate with a 6 percent mortality risk. Surgeons who have performed more than 250 procedures operate with virtually 0 percent risk.

♦ Without surgery, losing the weight and keeping it off requires commitment, support and the right tools. For some people a medically supervised program combining counseling, dietary coaching, meal replacements, exercise, prescription drugs and consultation with doctors and psychologists can help, but finding a program with all the right components can be challenging.

♦ Weight gain is the primary risk factor for the elevation of cholesterol and lipids, high blood pressure, diabetes, heart disease and shortened life expectancy. The risks for not aggressively bringing down the weight are substantial.

Always bear in
mind that your
own resolution
to succeed
is more important
than any other
one thing.

~ ABRAHAM LINCOLN

4

Choice

Today's surgical weight-loss procedures offer a variety of choices. If you decide to undergo a weight-loss operation, many of the choices will be up to you. There are choices in procedure and choices in what experienced, well-trained bariatric surgeon you choose to perform your procedure. You'll need to choose which outpatient surgery center to use or which hospital if you choose to have the operation performed in a traditional hospital setting.

Every choice is important when it comes to your health and well-being, and before making any decisions you should research your options as thoroughly as possible and understand the pros and cons of each choice. Reading this book is a great start, but don't stop here! (See the Resources section at the end for more sources of information.)

Choosing a Bariatric Surgeon

When you've made the decision to move ahead with a weight-loss operation, LAGB, LRYGB, LSG or perhaps a different procedure, it is time to select the right program and the right surgeon.

You can start with your friends and colleagues who have had successful weight-loss procedures and ask them who they recommend. Then I'd compare notes with your own doctors, both primary care docs and specialists. Then, continue your research with the specialty societies: the American College of Surgeons (ACS) and the American Society of Metabolic and Bariatric Surgery (ASMBS). The surgeons you can find at the ASMBS site (www.ASBS.org) are a good place to start in selecting the right program and the right surgeon.

It's always important to talk to as many people and get as many recommendations as possible from people both within the health care industry and without. Talk to everyone you can and try to gain as much information as possible about the surgeon and the program. And then compare. Talk to people involved with competing programs and centers, go online and take a look at the various programs available.

The Web is one place where people have given lots of feedback about various programs, and it's easy to access this information (Appendix C should help). By reading through the comments from past and present patients, you may gain further insight. You might also check out my blog and read comments (www. sasseguide.com), or leave one yourself on our Facebook page (www.Facebook. com/Dr.Sasse).

Not every piece of the puzzle that you find will create a full picture in and of itself, but each will give you a little bit more information and help you feel a little bit more comfortable about your decision.

Choosing an Outpatient Surgery Center

When it comes to choosing the facility at which you will undergo a weight-loss operation, you have many choices. You may have an established relationship with a hospital in your community. Your insurance plan likely has a list of contracted facilities that are approved for "in network" reimbursement, and these facilities may include hospitals and outpatient surgery centers. Your surgeon may also have a relationship with a specific outpatient surgery center. One of your considerations will be whether or not to investigate and choose any of these different options.

What should you look for?

Your top consideration should be that the center provides a safe, comfortable and professional environment for your surgical experience. Some people find the hospital environment too clinical or sterile and cold. Others feel more comfortable in the larger, standard hospital environment.

Some people may prefer the security of knowing that a full hospital apparatus is available should any problems arise and that an intensive care unit and complex radiology department are available if there are complications following surgery. However, since all outpatient surgery centers have contingency plans in case complications arise, and since many are associated or even physically attached to major hospitals, more and more patients are comfortable with outpatient surgery centers. And for the most part, other hospital features won't be necessary for the vast majority of patients undergoing minimally invasive weight-loss surgery.

You should also factor in the convenience of scheduling at an outpatient surgical center, which is usually easier than scheduling through a hospital. This means you have more options for scheduling the time and date of your operation, which may make it easier for friends and family to arrange your transport to and from the center and arrange for your care after you return home.

Lastly, you'll want to visit the facility and see the kind of environment provided and determine whether it provides a comfort level that is acceptable to you. Many outpatient surgery centers make an effort to provide a warm and pleasant experience for both patient and visitors, who may be spending time in the waiting room.

Making a choice of where to have surgery may seem intimidating, but really you're making the decision the same way you make other important decisions in your life – by gathering the facts and comparing your options. I suggest you start with the surgeon you're interviewing for your weight-loss surgery. Ask where the surgeon prefers to perform procedures and then go and visit the facilities. You can learn a great deal by walking through a facility or asking for a tour. You can gain a sense of the professionalism at the center and gauge the cleanliness with your own eyes. Ask the surgeon why he or she prefers one center over another. Ask the surgeon how many weight-loss surgical procedures have been performed at the facility.

When interviewing the surgeon, here's a list of questions you can start with:

1. How many weight-loss procedures has the surgeon performed?
2. How many of them were performed in an outpatient center or outpatient setting?
3. Which procedures does the surgeon perform?
4. Is the surgeon a Board-Certified surgeon, a Fellow of the American College of Surgeons?
5. Is the surgeon a member of the American Society of Metabolic and Bariatric Surgery?
6. How many years has the surgeon been performing bariatric surgery?
7. What preoperative diet and weight-loss strategies are recommended? (See Chapter 5 for more information about what sort of preoperative diets are standard.)
8. What postoperative education and support is provided?
9. How often do support groups meet? (See Chapter 5 for more information on support groups.)
10. What testing and preoperative evaluation (see Chapter 5 for more information) does the surgeon require?

A lot of surgeons and centers make all this type of information available on their websites and in patient materials. You may be able to obtain all the facts without taking up all your time with the surgeon focusing on these topics. Instead you may want to spend some of that time talking about you, about the uniqueness of your case, and how the surgeon feels he or she can best help you achieve your goals.

PATIENT STORY: STEVEN "RICHARD" D.

Procedure: **LRYGB**

My weight topped out at 308 pounds. I had difficultly getting out of bed. I was out of breath all of the time. I could no longer take my dog around the block for a walk. Not only that, I was stating to deal with major health issues that were becoming cumbersome.

My breaking point was when I realized that I was no longer able to take care of my own personal hygiene. I also realized that my time on earth was getting shorter and shorter. I had to do something and it needed to be done quickly.

I had the gastric bypass on July 27, 2011. In nine months I lost 190 pounds. It was so fast, and so exciting at the same time.

My life now is spent living instead of dying. I am almost never home. I am always out riding my motorcycle, and actually enjoying time at the gym. I am now full of energy. My only regret is that I didn't do this sooner. I feel like I wasted 20 years being miserable, when I could have been living free!

No Quick Fix

One thing that every bariatric expert can agree on is that weight-loss operations are not quick fixes. Success after weight-loss surgery comes to those who commit – mind, body and soul – to long-term behavior change, exercise and good food choices. It is hard work. For many people, weight-loss operations change nearly impossible battles into very winnable battles. But no matter what media coverage depicts weight-loss surgery as an easy fix, it most certainly is not. Anyone undergoing a weight loss operation must take advantage of every bit of the counseling available and utilize support groups and establish long-term, positive habits for success.

Adolescents and Outpatient Weight-Loss Surgery

Adolescents and children present a particularly challenging subgroup for health care providers, surgeons, parents and families. As surgeons, we want to help, but we are also aware of the complexity of obesity as a disease and its relationship to both the developing psyche and body of a child or adolescent. There has been a good deal of research directed at the topic of weight-loss surgery for adolescents, and the topic remains controversial.[88-91]

On the one hand, people who emphasize the psychosocial aspects of weight gain and unhealthy habits, decision-making and behavioral aspects of this problem point out that children and adolescents have developing brains and have a greater likelihood of changing their lives and resolving weight problems without resorting to surgical procedures. On the other hand, advocates for overweight adolescents point out that it can be considered cruel to withhold valuable treatment for such a devastating problem. They emphasize that the important years of adolescence – high school and college years – are critical for the formation of healthy relationships, self-esteem and career paths and that these formative years set the compass for the direction of these young people's lives.

Adolescent weight-loss surgery will probably continue to be a debated topic for years to come, but I think the most important consideration must be the health of the adolescent. In unusual cases where a young person is developing high blood pressure, liver disease and takes insulin for diabetes, we are talking about life-threatening conditions. For other adolescents, the problem of obesity is intertwined with social, behavioral and mood problems and a terrible lack of knowledge about nutrition and health.

Physically, adolescents are usually excellent surgical candidates for medical procedures because they tend to be healthier by virtue of being young. They have not had all the extra years to carry around or develop all the extra weight and generally have not developed conditions such as diabetes and heart disease.

The decision for a weight-loss procedure extends beyond cosmetic considerations. With adolescents, a weight-loss operation is often proactive – a procedure meant to pre-empt the deleterious physical effects of being overweight that will most likely develop as the child enters adulthood.

Our approach at my practice has been to perform LAP-BAND® surgery for adolescents under the auspices of a research study protocol.[92] It requires that adolescents be seen, evaluated and approved by a psychologist and pediatrician, as well as a parent, prior to entering the program. Only the LAGB is offered, because I feel the fact that the procedure can be reversed is important when the decision for surgery is made for a minor.

In the past when the only surgical options available were more invasive and more permanent procedures such as biliopancreatic diversion and gastric bypass, it made less sense to offer weight-loss surgery to a wide population of overweight adolescents. There would almost definitely be complications to answer for, and the permanence of the surgical intervention could certainly be questioned by those who point out that minors do not have the same level of decision-making capability as adults.

Some opponents of adolescent weight-loss surgery would also contend that successful weight-loss surgery requires a high level of commitment on the part of the patient. And since adolescents often lack the experience and

ADOLESCENT SUCCESS

I have performed LAGB surgery on a number of adolescents with strong support of their parents, pediatricians and psychologists. In each case, these adolescents had tried everything to lose weight and understood the seriousness of their decisions. One young man whose parents were both severely overweight felt that he had no chance of attaining a healthy weight in high school without help. Following the LAP-BAND® procedure he lost 70 pounds and moved into his senior year with a much healthier body and much healthier self-image. And he went on the attend college and has maintained his weight loss.

It is also important to note that the entire recovery process for the outpatient procedure takes about a week. For the young man in question, he was able to have the operation during a break from school and not have to face probing questions about taking a medical leave. The LAGB option allowed him and his family to keep the decision private.

maturity to make such a deep commitment to lifestyle changes and healthier habits, they should be made to wait a few years until they reach adulthood.

Because the LAGB procedure has a track record of success, a compelling case can be made to make it more available to adolescents. Just as for adults, LAGB surgery is minimally invasive, requiring only a 30- to 40-minute procedure, and is reversible with another fairly minimal procedure and few adverse consequences. There are currently no standard criteria for selecting adolescents for weight-loss surgery. Most centers that perform adolescent weight-loss surgery will consider candidates with a BMI of 35 or greater, as long as the parent and the child are committed to long-term success, and the patient passes the psychological screening.

Aging Individuals and Outpatient Weight-Loss Procedures

Strikingly few seriously overweight individuals live late into life. The medical and health implications and consequences are simply too much as we age. But there are a large number of individuals in their 50s, 60s and 70s who are moderately overweight or even seriously obese but lack the tools to successfully lose weight and regain a more active lifestyle. These individuals are at high risk for serious health problems and early death.

We don't hear as often about the potential benefits of minimally invasive weight-loss procedures for people in their 60s and older, but not only are the benefits considerable, the procedures are now available as outpatient operations for older patients who might not previously have been surgical candidates at all.

All four of the main procedures discussed – the LAGB, LRYGB, LSG and MGB – are usually tolerated well by older patients. Many of us working in the field have observed that seniors often tolerate the discomfort and inconvenience of weight-loss procedures and anesthesia with greater aplomb and less pain and suffering than their younger counterparts.

Reversibility is not as crucial a concern in this population as it is with adolescents, but the minimal invasiveness of the procedure is critical. It allows older patients with potentially serious health problems to undergo weight-loss procedures that can move them light years closer to solving problems caused by being overweight.

Studies have demonstrated that older patients do well after LAGB, LSG and LRYGB surgery and lose weight (though weight loss may be somewhat harder for them to achieve with the same magnitude of dramatic results than it is for middle-aged and younger patients).[93-96] I know that the odds of making the needed changes at this stage of life without surgical intervention are often very slim indeed. I have performed LAGB, LSG and LRYGB surgery on a large number of patients in their 60s and 70s and have been very pleased to watch them prove they can make good use of their new weapons in the weight-loss war. These patients have been able to lose weight, improve their health, increase their activities and elevate their quality of life.

So which procedure is "the best" for seniors? No one knows for certain, but I believe a case can be made for the sleeve gastrectomy (LSG) for many individuals. I say this for a number of reasons. First, it is minimally invasive and well-tolerated in seniors. Next, the LSG nearly always produces immediate positive results – the weight loss is almost always faster that with the LAGB. In seniors, the time horizon demands somewhat faster results so years of quality of life can be added. Additionally, the Sleeve procedure avoids the intestinal portion of the LRYGB procedure and thus avoids the risks, such as vitamin malabsorbtion, from that portion of the procedure. I have had many, many seniors do well in losing weight with all of the procedures, so in the end, it is best to talk it over with a well-qualified bariatric surgeon and choose the best fit for you individually.

Unfortunate Financial Realities

Seniors face an additional battle in weight loss: that of getting their weight-loss procedures covered by insurance. Although more and more conventional insurance plans are covering weight-loss operations, and so is Medicare, that doesn't mean seniors are going to have financial access to surgical procedures. Once a person turns 65 and becomes automatically covered under Medicare, most surgeons will not accept that patient as a candidate for weight-loss surgery.

Why not? Because insurance companies don't seem to understand that a successful weight-loss operation takes more than a scalpel and some anesthesia. Medicare "covers" the service and pays the facility and the surgeon at a rate usually insufficient to cover costs for the surgical practice to perform the procedure, let alone provide education and follow-up to the patient – important components to successful surgical weight-loss programs.

As a result, most practices quickly close their doors to patients on Medicare. My own practice was, until fairly recently, the only Center of Excellence program west of the Mississippi River to accept new Medicare patients, and now even we have had to limit the number of these cases each year, performed as a type of community service.

The problem is compounded by the fact that surgeons, by virtue of being

"Medicare providers," are not allowed to accept fees other than the standard Medicare fee schedule for covered benefits including bariatric surgery. What that means is simply this: even if a senior wants to pay cash in order to undergo minimally invasive weight-loss surgery, surgeons, being Medicare providers, can't accept it. In the last 10 years, my office has been inundated by frustrated seniors who would clearly benefit from weight-loss procedures and have offered sizeable sums of cash to have a surgeon perform the operations. But since all of the surgeons in the region are Medicare providers, we are legally prevented from providing this service.

I wish I knew what's going to happen in the future as our population ages and the number of overweight individuals age 65 and older grows. I suspect one of three things will occur that will allow minimally invasive weight-loss procedures to become more available for more seniors:

1. Medicare will raise its rates to a level that allows surgeons to provide the service without paying money out of their own pockets (not the most likely option).

2. Many more general surgeons offering weight-loss surgery will accept Medicare patients as they are growing their practices and refining their skills.

3. An increasing number of surgeons will drop their status as Medicare providers in order to accept patients outside the Medicare program. But while this will open the door for some seniors, it isn't the solution for the greater number of seniors who still won't be able to pay for the procedures independently.

Insurance and Finances

One of the reasons outpatient weight-loss surgery is growing quickly in popularity is that outpatient procedures are much less expensive than the inpatient procedures performed in the early days. And many patients are paying out-of-pocket.[97]

As weight-loss surgery has become increasingly recognized as safe and effective and no longer a mysterious, time-consuming and expensive open procedure, the demand has grown. Many more insurance carriers now cover weight-loss surgical procedures than did 10 years ago, but there are some insurance carriers that either don't cover the procedures or make it very difficult to get coverage. Some carriers place onerous obstacles and high hurdles in front of patients who want to undergo weight-loss procedures. Many try to make it so difficult that patients will give up their quests. Cynically, and despite the data showing how profoundly bariatric procedures extend life, some insurers require three or even six-month "weight-loss programs," with lots of documentation requirements, before they will approve the procedure.

Rather than giving up, many patients are opting to pay out-of-pocket. The decision has advantages and disadvantages, putting the patient in charge of many of his or her own health care decisions. But one definite effect paying out-of-pocket has is this: patients become highly cost-conscious consumers. And outpatient surgery centers are an economical option for safe and effective weight-loss surgery.

In my market, the Northern Nevada and Lake Tahoe region, in 2001, approximately 2 percent of the patients undergoing weight-loss operations paid cash. In 2007, approximately 8 percent of the patients were cash-paying patients. After the economic decline and The Great Recession, that percentage has remained about the same in 2012. In many other markets, the percentage of patients paying out-of-pocket rose and then fell with the economy.

For example, cost-conscious patients in the Northern Nevada region would find the outpatient surgery center price substantially lower than having a weight-loss procedure in an area hospital. An LAGB procedure at one of our hospitals, including all personnel and services (such as surgeons, hospital facility fee, anesthesiologists, assistants and equipment) would typically run $25,000 to $28,000. At an outpatient surgery center, the costs drop dramatically to approximately $12,000, including all of the costs listed above, plus extensive classes, nutritional counseling and preoperative education.

With more than 300,000 bariatric surgical procedures expected to be performed annually by 2020, and an increasing percentage of these being paid for exclusively by patients, there will inevitably be a greater demand for outpatient weight-loss surgery. If the cost differences between hospital and outpatient surgery centers remain as they do today, then most patients will continue to choose outpatient surgery centers for their procedures.

INSURANCE FRUSTRATION

With weight-loss surgery now proven to be so effective in extending life and improving health, the fairest system would be for it to be a covered benefit at a fair rate, just like every other proven medical treatment. That way as providers we could focus on doing the job we love to do: helping people live healthier and longer lives. Instead, some insurers won't cover weight-loss operations at all (making them available to only those who can afford to pay), some cover them fairly and Medicare and Medicaid "cover" them but pay the surgeons less than it costs to provide the services. I know this is frustrating for seniors and low income people, and it is frustrating for providers, too.

Certainly this problem is just a microcosm of the whole health care system. I recently learned that almost none of the primary care physicians in my community will accept new Medicare patients, because they cannot afford to accept the low rates. It's even a shock to my parents who need a regular doctor today, and what about the baby boomers that will all need primary care doctors tomorrow? The Affordable Care Act may bring many more people into the system, but only time will tell the long term effects it may have on access to life-prolonging metabolic and bariatric surgery.

Paying Cash for Weight-Loss Procedures: Concerns and Considerations

With a significant number of people paying for their own weight-loss operations when their insurance carriers won't, important questions and concerns are being raised. For example, what happens if complications arise and more surgery is required? What happens if after surgery the patient needs to be admitted to the hospital for ongoing care? And what happens if there is a complication down the road? Will an insurance company eventually cover these contingencies, or will the patient be exposed to future costs not initially budgeted for?

Partial solutions for these problems have been found at experienced centers like mine, but these questions have yet to be widely addressed within the current insurance environment. At this writing, many centers are embarking on programs to create insurance products or warranty products that will allow partial coverage for many, if not most, complications. Keep in mind that complications in weight-loss surgery are rare in the hands of an experienced bariatric surgeon. So, the discussion pertains to a small percentage of the overall population undergoing weight-loss procedures. Nevertheless, even if we are talking about 1 percent of a group of 300,000 people we are still discussing 3,000 people a year who may experience significant financial concerns if complications arise. Ultimately today there is no mechanism to completely avoid financial exposure for these potential complications.

Many centers are developing mechanisms by which additional surgical and hospital services may be at least partially covered with the initial costs of the weight-loss procedures. In some cases, these added coverages or benefits do add significantly to the costs of the procedure – anywhere from a few hundred dollars to upward of $2,500 per case. However, by paying the additional coverage, serious financial risks can be mitigated.[98]

When making your decisions on a weight-loss procedure, ask your surgeon and your outpatient surgery center staff if they offer such plans or even a less formal means of providing care and coverage should a complication occur. At many centers where there is yet no formal insurance or warranty-type coverage policy in place, agreements are in place to allow for a return to surgery in order to correct complications. Procedures in that event are provided for by the center and the surgeon at little additional cost to the patient. In some cases complications are taken care of at a cost to the patient that covers the expenses and equipment usage for such complications. (But even these "minimum" charges can run in the thousands or tens of thousands if major complications occur.)

This was the type of agreement my practice had reached in Reno with the inpatient and outpatient surgery centers prior to ever undertaking surgical weight-loss procedures. Now we provide a separate and formalized insurance or warranty policy for each and every patient paying cash for his or her weight-loss operation. It does not cover everything, and financial risks are still present with cash procedures of any kind, including bariatric procedures.

If you are considering a surgical outpatient weight-loss procedure and a formal coverage policy is offered, take it. I can't emphasize enough how valuable it will be to have coverage in place should a complication occur. The extra costs will be well-spent. My practice now offers a coverage policy for most major complications for most patients undergoing weight-loss surgery and paying without help from insurance. A premium is added to the overall fees, which partially covers the cost of additional procedures and hospitalization if such become necessary due to complications arising after surgery.

So, like all forms of insurance, in which we pay a small premium in exchange for coverage of a major potential expense (think of a car insurance policy), this concept involves pooling of risks across a large group of people. The funds from every premium go to pay for that rare case that involves an expensive complication.

Some centers require the extra coverage or policy, and the costs are automatically rolled into the fee charged. This is probably the best way to go. If it's the policy at the center you choose, it's there for your protection. The journey to successful weight loss and long-term health has plenty of challenges without adding the stress of potential financial hardship.

Patient Story: Francisca Q.

Procedure: **LRYGB**

Francisca chose the LRYGB procedure and was out of the operating room in 50 minutes. She stayed overnight in the hospital, going home in a little more than 24 hours. Since her procedure she reports that she has regained her energy and excitement about life.

What to Tell (or Not to Tell) Your Boss and Friends

What you choose to tell those around you is your business. Whether you wish to tell everyone that you are undergoing a surgical weight-loss procedure and enlist their help and support during your journey or whether you wish to maintain absolute privacy about this decision is up to you.

Years ago the logistics of weight-loss surgery required a substantial operation followed by a significant seven- to 10-day hospital stay and lengthy recovery that could last months after the patient returned home. Obviously if the person were missing from work or school for such a long period people were bound to notice and inquire. So, while not impossible, it was certainly improbable to expect a person would be able to maintain complete privacy about the operation.

In addition, before the modern, minimally invasive techniques, candidates for weight-loss surgery tended to be more seriously overweight. Because weight-loss surgery is a risk/benefit decision and in earlier years the risks were greater, it made sense to apply treatment selectively to those candidates who stood to gain greater benefits because their health problems were more severe. Since the results were more dramatic in those cases, results were much more likely to be noticed, as well.

Today things are different. Weight-loss procedures may only result in as little as a one-day absence from work or school. With such a short time away, there's a much better chance of keeping the decision to oneself.

Is secrecy the best course of action for you? That's a discussion to have with your surgeon and your spouse or best support person. And every answer will be individual. I will tell you that it is an important decision you need to make while planning your weight-loss operation, and you need to make it early in the process and share it with your surgeon and surgery center personnel so those involved can take steps to protect your privacy. There is no way to absolutely guarantee privacy, but there are numerous steps that can be taken by the surgeon, surgical staff and surgery center personnel that will markedly reduce the odds of third parties learning of your decision to undergo a weight-loss procedure.

Benefits of Remaining Open About Your Choice

There are benefits to not keeping your decision a secret. For one thing, you can avoid the necessity of lying and any awkward moments secrecy can cause. Keeping the weight-loss operation a secret is bound to lead to some of those awkward moments. The most common and nicest of these is when your friends, neighbors and co-workers begin to ask you what you're doing to lose so much weight. If you are planning to maintain secrecy about the operation, you will need to have an answer ready that you're comfortable using and can use consistently.

If you choose to keep your secret, try out your answer before you're ever put in the position of needing to use it. You may want to indicate you're in a medically supervised weight-loss program and exercising more while eating better. This answer has the advantage of being largely true while somewhat vague. But be prepared for people asking for many more concrete details at that point.

After trying this for a while, even in private, you may decide you are simply more comfortable telling people you had a weight-loss operation and are working very hard at medically supervised weight loss and exercise. Many people will respond positively to this. Those who have struggled with being overweight themselves will respect you for having the courage to do what they couldn't. Some will be jealous. And most will be happy for you. Almost all of them will have many more questions about your surgery, your surgeon and your decision to have the procedure, and usually these questions will reflect admiration for your decisions.

Occasionally you will encounter very ignorant attitudes and people who feel you took the "easy way out." It's up to you whether to try and dissuade them of this misapprehension or leave them to their own beliefs. If you choose to try and explain to them, you might want to mention:

♦ It takes hard work, commitment to a program of learning, changing behavior, exercising and adhering to the medically prescribed nutrition and exercise regimen.

♦ While the surgery only takes an hour, the process of getting from the decision to have weight-loss surgery to the procedure itself takes a lot of time and effort and classes and evaluations.

♦ It made no sense NOT to have the operation, given the health statistics with surgery vs. without surgery.

But mostly you will encounter a community of people who admire you for doing it, who support you and recognize your journey is a difficult one and one that required a great deal of courage and perseverance. This leads to another reason you might want to consider telling people about your choice: positive effects of having an open support group.

There are numerous studies that describe the benefits of successful long-term weight loss, and most of them point to personal group support as being key. Having a support person or a support group is helpful for long-term challenging behavior modifications of many types, such as stopping smoking or quitting drinking. The National Weight-Loss Registry data points out the importance of support groups for their database of long-term successful weight loss, and weight-loss programs such as iMetabolic® and WeightWatchers® have long relied on the positive support of group dynamics to further the goals of health and weight loss.

Don't underestimate the value of a support group, especially an organic group comprised of people you see in your everyday life. In addition, your surgeon may recommend or require you to attend a support group either before or after your procedure, or possibly both. These groups provide a forum for people who have had the same types of operations with the same surgical group to support and encourage each other on the weight-loss journey. If your focus is on privacy, it may not be possible for you to take advantage of this component of long-term weight loss.

One more consideration: If you choose to be open about your decision, you may be able to help other people. It is estimated that only around 1 percent of those people who could most benefit from weight-loss operations and enjoy longer, healthier lives ever actually undergo much-needed weight-loss procedures. Many fail to seek effective treatment for their health because they are stymied by concerns about how the procedure is perceived, lack of knowledge about the minimally invasive approach, fear of complications and the judgment of others who don't understand modern weight-loss procedures.

Your openness can help these people learn more about modern weight-loss procedures and other state-of-the-art medical procedures that could help improve the quality and length of their lives. Many patients tell me they only sought weight-loss operations after close friends led the way and then shared the experience, dispelling misconceptions, banishing fears that had prevented them from moving forward with much needed medical intervention. You really can help make a difference, and it may turn out to be one of the most surprisingly rewarding aspects of your own weight-loss journey.

Advantages to Keeping your Decision Private

There may also be some advantages to keeping your decision entirely private. For one thing, people around you may not always approve of or understand your decision to undergo a weight-loss procedure. Most of the time people react quite favorably and quite supportively, but not always. Sharing your decision to undergo a weight-loss operation means exposing yourself to the judgments of others, and this can be uncomfortable if someone in your circle lacks the knowledge and sophistication to appreciate why your decision benefits your health and longevity. I have heard a few stories over the years of patients whose bosses, mothers or siblings forever blamed the weight-loss operation for any health or physical problem that arose. One of my patients, who in the course of a year had sniffles, a sinus infection and a broken leg, found his sister erroneously blaming each of these events on a weight-loss procedure that had occurred four years earlier!

Sharing openly your decision to have a weight-loss procedure may help battle the ignorance of people around you with regard to weight-loss operations, but it may not be a battle you want to fight.

Another fact to consider when weighing whether or not to share your decision openly is that you just don't have to. Just as you might keep close counsel with respect to any other health problems you have experienced, you may wish to maintain the same level of privacy with respect to this decision. In the end, no matter what your boss, friends or family think or don't think, it is really none of their business.

So, in summary, as I see it, you have three options:

- The first option is to keep your weight-loss procedure decision a secret. This may spare you from some of the ignorant opinions of others and limit the topic as a conversation item.
- Be fully open and share your decision with those around you. This may provide some advantages of extra support and encouragement and may help others learn that they too could benefit.
- Be discreet but honest. I have seen a few people choose this middle ground. I have performed surgery on a number of famous people who

ultimately chose this approach. They wished to minimize the publicity surrounding their decision to undergo weight-loss surgery, and yet they wanted to be open with their immediate family and closest friends. They did attend limited support groups and, if asked, shared that they had indeed undergone weight-loss surgery. But they chose not to mention it unless asked directly about it. And in some cases they took measures to increase the discretion of the practice and the surgery center to decrease the sphere of people who learned of their decision.

Privacy

Your surgeon and his or her practice can help you maintain your privacy. Here are some of the ways:

HIPAA.

The privacy compliance law known commonly as HIPAA – Health Insurance Portability and Accountability Act of 1996 – works to some degree in your favor if you choose to maintain your privacy about a weight-loss procedure. Your surgeon and your surgeon's staff are required to adhere to HIPAA. Among the many provisions of this law is the strict requirement

I must admit that I personally measure success in terms of the contributions an individual makes to her or his fellow human beings.

~ MARGARET MEAD

that practice or center staff not reveal any of your private information, or even that you were a patient, with anyone that you have not authorized.

I should mention that HIPAA does nothing to protect your information from the people who can actually do you some harm, namely the insurance industry, the government and law enforcement entities at all levels who request access to your private information. But should a co-worker, a stranger, a friend, a curious neighbor, relative or a journalist call the office to inquire about your status, no information would be given without your prior authorization. I can't resist adding that such privacy concerns have long been a principle of medical care, and HIPAA codified the already widely pervasive privacy practices into a cumbersome law that involves an awful lot of trees felled to comply with the paperwork. Hopefully now the noble ethics of the medical field combined with the law work together to prevent abuses of disclosure of information. Some day real privacy advocates will protect your information from the people who might actually harm you with it by misusing it: the insurance industry, government, and law enforcement.

MAKE AFTER-HOURS ARRANGEMENTS.

Some practices will accommodate requests for high levels of privacy and discretion by making after-hours appointments. I have done this on a few rare occasions for very well-known politicians and personalities who wanted their decisions kept from the public. There is no guarantee your surgeon will accommodate your desires, but if you think there's a chance you'll be recognized, and the media will be interested in publicizing your personal decisions, it is certainly reasonable to ask for this type of accommodation. I have seen patients after 5:30 or 6:00 in the evening when nearly all my staff has gone home and there are no patients in the waiting room. While it's not an absolutely foolproof system, it does cut down on the number of people apt to see you coming or going from the weight-loss surgery clinic.

USE A PSEUDONYM.

Some practices, hospitals and surgery centers allow you to register under a pseudonym to avoid prying eyes becoming aware of your health or your status as a patient of a practice or facility.

In one case, a prominent physician in my community wanted to keep his weight-loss operation private. I allowed him to use a pseudonym because he was so well-known to all the doctors and nurses, hospital and health care employees in the community that the simple appearance of his name as a patient would have spurred inevitable conversations. A pseudonym served him well, and he shared his decision and the details of his weight-loss journey with only those close to him. (I have noticed that over time he has become a bit more open about it and even shares his decision with patients who are overweight in an attempt to help them understand weight-loss procedures as options for themselves. But it has been totally his choice to disclose this.)

It is your right to decide how much or how little to share with other people. Let your surgeon and the surgery center staff know your preferences and make certain you are satisfied with their ability to honor your wishes. Understand it is nearly impossible to entirely protect privacy in this day and age, but that your

MARY

A couple of years ago, I had a patient I'll call "Mary." She came to see me as the last appointment of the day. She sneaked in the door just as the office was closing, and we sat down and talked about her weight-loss goals. Mary was a well-known public figure whose personal "figure" had grown with weight gain in middle age. In addition to some early health problems of sleep disturbance, rising blood pressure and rising cholesterol, she increasingly felt self-conscious in performing her public duties and making appearances. Mary was also extremely concerned about protecting her privacy. She didn't want to disclose publicly or even privately that she was considering a weight-loss operation.

As we have with some other public figures who sought privacy protections, our office scheduled all of Mary's appointments after hours and scheduled her operation under a pseudonym. Mary underwent a successful outpatient LAP-BAND® procedure at our surgical center and stayed there a grand total of three hours. She has dropped more than 60 pounds, resolved the cholesterol, blood pressure and sleeping difficulties, and approaches her public responsibilities with greater enthusiasm and nimbleness. Thus far she has not had to disclose her personal decision with anyone publicly. She has begun to do so privately, but on her own timetable.

surgeon and surgical practice will take every precaution.

Weight-Loss Surgery and Mexico

In recent years a number of people seeking weight-loss procedures have chosen to go outside the country for them. With the economic downturn, saving every dollar is important, and non-U.S. surgical groups can offer enticingly low prices. Numerous sites in Mexico and elsewhere now advertise bariatric surgery (usually LAGB, but increasingly LSG and LRYGB) online in an attempt to attract patients to their sunny shores for operations. The primary appeal is lower costs – or at least the possibility of lower costs. But traveling to Mexico for weight-loss surgery doesn't usually make sense for several reasons. It incurs added risks, both medical and financial, and offers little recourse should problems arise.

While the websites set up to attract patients to foreign clinics tend to play up lower costs, think for a moment about the importance of the procedure you're considering undergoing. Think about how important the decision and the operation itself are to your life and your well-being.

Keep in mind that most experienced U.S. bariatric surgeons and program directors are very uncomfortable taking on the routine long-term management and band fills of patients who have chosen to go to Mexico for LAGB surgery. The chances of problems are too high, and the liability exposure too great, to justify taking on all the problematic cases done in Mexico. If you have your procedure performed in Mexico and develop complications after your return to the U.S., you may find it very difficult to find a physician willing to treat you in this country.

Is "saving" a few hundred or even a few thousand dollars worth the risk? You are considering an operation for long-term results. Will a low-cost version of a procedure give you those results? And consider carefully your health and safety. In the United States, part of the cost of medical care is the cost of oversight placed on surgeons, hospitals and outpatient surgery centers. These people and places are carefully monitored for safety, hygiene and expertise.

There are excellent surgeons and centers outside the United States; there is no question about that. And if you carefully research all the details and know the surgeons and facilities, then it is certainly possible to have a successful LAGB procedure. However, by the same token, I have personally intervened in a number of cases where patients have undergone failed or inappropriately performed weight-loss surgical procedures outside the country. A recent case was a young woman who lived in Nevada and traveled to Mexico because she could save $4,000. The LAP-BAND® was placed improperly, and she developed a very serious gastric obstruction requiring an emergency operation to correct. And the kicker? Her American insurance company not only wouldn't pay for her Mexican adventure, but they would not pay for any of the hospitalization or surgery required to fix that problem. Now she is paying off bills totaling more than $50,000. Hardly a savings.

Another case presented at a conference involved a patient who paid money to have a LAP-BAND® procedure in Mexico only to return to the United States with nothing but a few incisions and no actual band placed. What recourse do you have if something like this occurs outside the U.S.?

Think carefully before you decide to leave the country to have LAGB or any other surgical procedure. Ask yourself:

♦ How much money will I really save?
♦ Will my insurance company cover me if I have any complications after the procedure?
♦ Can I find a qualified doctor and bariatric surgeon to take care of me after I return from my out-of-country surgical procedure?
♦ What is my plan should a complication arise? Will I go back to Mexico, or will I seek a local facility and throw myself on the mercy of the staff?
♦ Do I have any personal or professional references to recommend the weight-loss surgeon that I am considering seeing outside the United States?

Food for Thought

♦ Along with the freedom of choice – to choose your surgical weight-loss procedure, your surgeon and your outpatient surgery center – comes the responsibility for your own health, safety and welfare: do your research thoroughly on each and understand the pros and cons of each choice you make.

♦ Your top consideration when choosing an outpatient surgery center for your surgical weight-loss procedure is to find a safe, comfortable and professional environment.

♦ If you prefer the security of a full hospital, keep in mind that every outpatient surgical center has a contingency plan if complications with your procedure arise, and many are physically attached to major hospitals.

♦ While surgeons recognize that adolescents are still developing psychologically as well as physically, the devastating effects of obesity need to be considered with regard to minimally invasive surgical weight-loss procedures.

♦ Minimally invasive weight-loss surgical procedures can help older patients lose weight, improve health, increase activities and elevate quality of life. In addition, older patients seem to tolerate the discomfort and inconvenience of the procedures and the accompanying anesthesia better than younger patients. A case can be made that the LSG procedure will serve seniors very well.

♦ Patients over 65 will have a harder time finding a surgeon to perform the procedure for them: Most surgeons and surgical centers will not work with Medicare, and patients over 65 are automatically covered by Medicare.

♦ More insurance carriers cover weight-loss surgical procedures than ever before, but some still refuse coverage, and some place huge hurdles between the patient and the procedure.

♦ If you choose to pursue your weight-loss surgical procedure by paying out-of-pocket, you need to be aware additional charges may occur if there are complications with your procedure.

♦ Many surgical centers offer agreements that allow patients to pay a premium in addition to fees for the procedure in order to partially cover the costs if complications do arise. No system completely eliminates financial risk.

♦ Whether you choose to tell anyone about the procedure you've chosen to undertake or not is your business. Your surgeon and surgical center will do work to protect your privacy if you choose to keep it secret.

♦ If you choose not to keep your procedure private, you may be able to help others with their choices and can also interact more with others who have chosen to have the same procedure or have already done so. There are numerous studies describing the long-term benefits of successful weight loss and most of them point to personal group support as being very important.

◆ Some people are seeking weight-loss surgical procedures out of the country to minimize costs. While there are some excellent clinics outside the U.S., most surgeons in this country will not work on a patient who is having complications from a surgical procedure performed outside of the U.S. If complications arise after your return, you may find yourself unable to find a qualified surgeon to help you. And you're apt to pay far more correcting complications than you saved in the first place.

Arriving at one point is the starting point to another.

~ JOHN DEWEY

5

Getting Ready

Having weight-loss surgery is a lot more than just walking into the surgery center and going under the knife. It represents a commitment to achieving something important, something very valuable for the long term: improved health.

Take advantage of the time before your surgery to plan your steps for optimum success. A weight-loss surgical procedure can be a powerful tool in your effort to lose weight and keep it off. But the surgery doesn't work all by itself – it takes hard work and commitment to success to achieve the kind of amazing weight loss possible when you set your mind to it and prepare.

Preoperative Phase

Once you've made the decision to proceed with a weight-loss operation and made your choice whether to keep that decision a secret or share it, you're entering the preoperative phase of weight loss.

At this point you'll be working with a weight-loss program through the surgeon's practice. If you have insurance, the program you're working with will be in the process of obtaining pre-approval on the procedure. Meanwhile, you'll be working on additional steps required by the program. Most likely these steps are going to involve consultations with a psychologist, a nutritionist or dietitian, and often they will involve attending some support groups.

For some people this all feels intrusive. They've made the decision to proceed, and now that's exactly what they want to do – proceed. Others use this time for exactly what it is meant for – education and growth. With a couple months to go before the operation, this is a time for learning everything possible, a time for maximum education about the whole process, the entire weight-loss journey.

BOOKS

To begin with, I think it's a terrific idea to buy a book or two on the subject. That way you'll understand things that might not have made sense to you when they were explained in the sometimes intimidating clinical setting, and you can look up answers to sudden questions that occur to you at 4 a.m. when your surgeon is at home, asleep, not available to answer them.

There are several good texts out there on bariatric surgery, including Weight Loss Surgery for Dummies by Kurian, Thompson and Davidson and Bariatric Support: Crossing Over to a New You, by Williamson. And of course I highly recommend anyone trying to lose weight read Doctor's Orders: 101 Medically Proven Tips for Losing Weight because the surgery is not the complete answer– we still need more tools to succeed in cutting calorie

> Thought is the sculptor who can create the person you want to be.
>
> ~ HENRY DAVID THOREAU

intake and losing pounds (and yes, I wrote that one.) It won a Bronze Medal in the 2009 Book of the Year ForeWord Reviews Health category.

Audio CDs and Audio MP3 Programs

Feed your brain with some positive messages and valuable tips about weight-loss success, health and fitness. It is said that we are exposed to more than 20,000 messages about food, sweets and carbohydrates during the course of the year. Think of the billboards, TV commercials and radio ads your senses take in every day. How many of those are telling your brain you should eat more goodies and load up on calories? That's right – a lot of them.

You can change the messages your brain receives by going out and finding some high-quality audio programs that promote good scientific principles and techniques for eating healthier and becoming fitter. Listen in your car, while you exercise or just play them at home. I have prepared several audio programs that cover technical aspects of weight-loss surgery and the surgeon's role in detail, discuss recovery time and how to maximize recovery and minimize downtime. These programs also explore in more detail what you can do to maximize your weight-loss success during the first six months and beyond. Visit www.iMetabolic. com to check out some of these audio programs that could really help you maximize your weight-loss success and reinforce sound principles of weight-loss and health.

Support Groups

It's an excellent idea to start attending support group meetings at your bariatric surgical center on a regular basis. At my practice, we offer weekly groups, with many different groups in different parts of town, so in our area it's easy to find one that fits a patient's schedule and geographic location. Your surgeon's office will know what support groups are available in your area.

Support groups serve a number of purposes. In addition to fulfilling the important goal of learning about the weight-loss operation you're going to undergo, a group offers a place where you can meet people who are also about to embark on the same journey you're going to follow, and those people who have already started. You'll meet patients and their loved ones who are at the same point in the process that you are, as well as those in different places. And you can make friends with people who have had common problems and now have common goals.

Support groups present opportunities to ask questions about the experiences of people who have already had their operations. You can ask questions you were too embarrassed to ask your surgeon or nursing staff or that you just keep forgetting to ask. You can ask questions your surgeon might not be able to answer because the surgeon hasn't experienced the operation from the inside out – unlike the person standing in front of you at a support group.

You may also meet people at support groups whose recoveries didn't go so smoothly. While nine times out of 10 weight-loss surgery goes as planned with no complications or problems, if you meet someone whose operation was difficult you have a chance to ask some questions. What were the complications? How did they happen? Was the surgeon caring, conscientious and committed to making sure there was a successful outcome? This is valuable information from people whose journeys may have diverged from the path yours will most likely take in the hands of an experienced surgeon.

PREOPERATIVE CLASSES

Preoperative classes will vary from program to program. But on the whole, most weight-loss programs will include a series of classes aimed at providing additional tools for long-term weight-loss success.

One thing you have to remember: Weight-loss procedures don't work in a vacuum. The operation is not a miracle cure that works solely by itself. Weight-loss procedures work with you.

That's one of the first things I tell patients. No surgery works by itself. No surgery is foolproof. Every surgery can be undermined. There is no operation that can be performed that will guarantee success in the long term. The only thing that is absolutely definitive in predicting success is your total and complete commitment to success.

If you can commit to making your weight-loss operation a success, if you've done your homework, found the right surgeon, and you are willing to do the work before and after the operation, you've got a fantastic chance of success.

But a person can fail. Any patient can have a successful operation and a lousy weight-loss program due to eating the wrong foods, avoiding exercise, failing to work on better habits and not making the right food choices. And that would be sad after there's been so much time and energy and money devoted to the weight-loss procedure, and so much hope derailed. One way to avoid failing after going to all the time and effort of having a weight-loss procedure is to take advantage of the classes, support groups, audio programs and books available with expert advice, guidance and motivation along the way – your goals are too important not to utilize everything in your favor!

For most people considering a weight-loss operation, the effort to lose weight in the past has been an uphill battle. Many people have had transient successes followed by long periods of failure and gradual weight gain over the years. But after their operations those same people now find that, with their continuing efforts, the battle is easily won. The pounds come off as never before, and better still, they stay off.

So, while surgery is not a silver bullet that magically results in weight loss, it is a highly effective weapon in the battle against those unwanted pounds. I often tell my patients that the operation will be a very potent weapon in the battle to lose weight – but it won't fight the battle all by itself. If you want the procedure to change your life, you have to participate; you have to make healthy food choices, exercise and stay focused on the goals of becoming healthier, fitter and happier. Want to really be successful? Read on and follow my advice in Jump-start Your Weight Loss and Keeping It Off Forever in the chapters ahead.

Patient Story: Shane B.

Procedure: **LRYGB**

Shane chose the laparoscopic RYGB procedure and was in and out of surgery in less than an hour. Following his operation he reports a new lease on life and higher energy levels than he's experienced in many years.

What to Expect in Your Preoperative Months

In our program, the first preoperative classes emphasize the importance of personal responsibility in succeeding in the weight-loss journey and discuss your personal metabolism. The classes that follow offer dietary counseling, a good deal of education about nutrition and the kind of calorie count we're looking for, explanations of what an energy deficit is and discussion of what sort of energy content is present with protein and with carbohydrates and with fat and alcohol. One of the first steps is a test of your metabolism, your resting metabolic rate or RMR. It tells you how your genes and your muscle mass have contributed (or conspired!) to determine the calories your body will burn in a day. That way, you can personalize all the diet advice to make it specific to your own metabolism

The next step of our preoperative program covers fitness and exercise and the important parts both play in weight-loss success. Fitness trainers contribute to the classes and prepare instructional materials and demonstrations. Participants get log books, pedometers, educational handouts and other supplies to help them on their road to healthier lives. A chef sometimes comes in to talk about cooking and provides valuable insight, cooking and shopping demonstrations (shopping demonstrations might seem unnecessary, but how many times have you gone home with an unintended bag of chips or gallon of ice cream?)

All of these elements form the backbone of the comprehensive long-term weight-loss strategy. These classes take place during that interim period between the time you've made the decision to avail yourself of a life-changing weight-loss procedure and the time you actually have your operation.

Education is one of the keys to successful long-term weight loss, and it's available to you in quantity during this time. I highly recommend you take advantage of it.

PREOPERATIVE LIQUID DIET

Approximately four weeks before your operation the staff at many weight-loss programs, including ours, will ask you to change to a liquid protein diet. You'll be getting your daily calories from liquid meal-replacement protein shakes, which do facilitate weight loss. (See Appendix B)

You may be wondering why you need to do this if you're having a weight-loss operation. There are several reasons, including the jump-start it gives you on weight loss after your procedure and the fact that losing weight before your operation makes for a safer procedure.

One of the critical reasons is to shrink the liver. In the last few years, data has proven that the liver shrinks disproportionately to anything else in the abdomen when one follows a protein-based liquid meal-replacement system for two weeks. Studies using MRI scanners and laparoscopy evaluations demonstrated the extent to which the liver shrank.[36]

Fine, you think, I want to lose weight, not have smaller organs. Actually, in this instance you do want smaller organs. During surgery, we sometimes have difficulty with very large fatty-infiltrated livers. The liver, and specifically the left lobe of the liver, has to be moved out of the way to give us access to the upper part of the stomach. If the liver is very large it has a tendency to crack, which can cause bleeding and complications. Sometimes this leads to changing a laparoscopic surgery to open surgery with all the attendant risks and complications: infections, hernias and prolonged hospital stays, to name a few.

So, something as simple as going on a four-week preoperative liquid meal-replacement diet can make a dramatic difference in the whole weight-loss operation experience. We have worked to make this liquid diet program more fun and more palatable by preparing some great recipes for delicious protein shakes.

We started instituting a practice of the liquid meal-replacement phase in 2006 and found the results were striking. Patients whose cases might once have caused us to expect to contend with large livers or cracked livers and bleeding complications or cases in which we might even have had to abort surgery because of a liver that was just too large were now no problem.

Now I very rarely encounter any difficulties due to overly large livers, because everyone goes on the preoperative liquid meal-replacement program, and pretty much everybody has nicely shrunken livers. Not every patient complies with the program, and not every liver shrinks the way we'd like it to, but for the most part, by the time the operation takes place, most people's livers have shrunken. While it's nice for surgeons not to have to contend with oversized livers, it's nice for patients, too – it makes for a smoother operation with fewer chances of complications and easier recoveries because we didn't have to drag a large liver out of the way.

A smaller liver isn't the only reason surgical practices have instituted weeks-long preoperative liquid meal-replacement programs. Such programs are an excellent way to begin weight loss. Many induction or initiation diets used by nonsurgical medically supervised weight-loss programs kick off with liquid protein meal-replacement shakes and lead to very rapid weight loss. We're doing a miniature version of those programs.

What happens with these rapid weight-loss liquid-diet programs is that people tend to lose two to four pounds a week. In some cases, patients who are starting out with a great deal of weight to lose may lose as much as six to eight pounds a week on a very low calorie liquid meal-replacement diet. With weight loss like this, in a very short amount of time you can lose 15 or 18 pounds with the initial weight loss achieved with very small intervention and very profound results. This helps start off the weight loss both physically and mentally – there's nothing like losing 15 pounds in a very short time to make weight loss seem like a real-world possibility. And if you're losing the weight as a precursor to a surgical weight-loss procedure, those are pounds you're likely never going to see again. It feels good.

In addition to all the other benefits, losing even 10 or 15 pounds before an operation makes going under anesthesia safer. It makes postoperative recovery easier because you have less weight to carry around, less body mass restricting movements of the chest, so breathing is easier, and oxygenation of the blood is easier. Really, the weight loss favorably affects virtually every organ system.

But something even more amazing is that those pounds you lose before surgery stay off after surgery and beyond. I co-authored a study in which we found that even three years after surgery, those that did the preoperative liquid diet kept off significantly more pounds than those who did not![99]

Want even more good news? We have found that people taking medications for blood pressure and diabetes can lose enough weight on the preoperative meal-replacement program that their blood pressure and blood sugar normalize, again making the upcoming operation that much safer.

So, there are a number of reasons the preoperative liquid meal-replacement diet is important, and I urge you to talk to your surgeon about it and to comply rigorously with your surgeon's recommendations.

Most people find the diet isn't that hard to follow. During the first couple days using only liquid shakes people get pretty hungry, and if they're not committed it's easy to fall off the program and eat something not on the recommended menu. But by the third, fourth or fifth day, most people find their bodies and appetites have adjusted. An intrinsic kind of appetite suppression seems to kick in and most people feel perfectly satisfied with the shakes alone. So, stick with it through the first critical days, and you'll find it becomes much easier, and you'll reap the benefits with rapid weight loss and a healthier body for your weight-loss operation.

MARK

I saw Mark in follow-up recently after his surgery. Mark had done very well initially after an outpatient LAGB procedure, but he struggled in his ongoing battle to lose more weight. Starting at 295 pounds, Mark lost 24 pounds during the preoperative weight-loss phase. So, he had a good initial jumping off point. His surgery went very smoothly, and he initially lost an additional 10 pounds in the first month. Over the course of the next eight months, Mark lost an additional 25 pounds, so that he then weighed 235 pounds, 59 pounds down from his original weight.

Mark's goal, however, had been to reach a weight of 190 pounds, where he felt the most comfortable. He had the LAP-BAND® adjusted several times and complained that the band always seemed to be either too tight or too loose. After several of these trials of adding and subtracting minute amounts of saline from the band, I counseled Mark that the problem did not reside with the band. The LAP-BAND®, I told him, is merely a tool and an imperfect one at that. It does provide him some degree of improved satiety and better appetite control. It also "puts on the brakes" for Mark when he might otherwise overeat. But it is certainly not a foolproof or magically effective device that results in effortless, unlimited weight loss.

More recently Mark has had some success transitioning to a focus on more sustained and regular exercise, and on developing and maintaining long-term successful habits such as eating a low-calorie, low glycemic-index breakfast every morning consisting of a shake or bar that is based on protein and vitamins. Eating breakfast allows Mark's body to kick-start his metabolism and results in the burning of more consumed calories during the day. Mark has continued to lose weight slowly and is taking more responsibility for his long-term weight loss.

EXERCISE

If you thought you were just going to spend the time between deciding on a weight-loss procedure and actually having it undergoing a few medical tests and waiting for insurance forms, think again. Not only are you going to be dieting and learning and going to support groups, but this is a great time to start exercising. You're preparing for your new life, and if you really want to succeed in that life you're going to have to make exercise a part of it. Starting before your weight-loss procedure just gives you a head start.

As with losing weight and dieting and shrinking your liver and reducing some of your risks from health problems, exercise can reduce your risk levels for the operation.

First off, surgical procedures are stressful. They're hard on the body, like any physical endeavor, and just because the operation is done to you rather than you doing it doesn't make it less stressful. If you can improve your physical condition – get stronger, improve your cardiovascular system – you improve your chances of coming through without complications.

Before a weight-loss operation you want to start an exercise program that will help you improve your conditioning, your cardiovascular status, your stamina, your strength and your endurance, all of which will help you move through your operation much more easily. Studies have shown that some of the specific pulmonary mechanics, the numerical measures of the effectiveness of your lungs, are significantly improved by preoperative exercise programs – that's exactly what you're looking for. [100, 101]

If that's not enough, exercise can help you feel better emotionally about your upcoming operation and it can improve your sleep. Not to mention exercise can also help you attain weight loss before your operation by increasing the calories you burn, thus lowering your risks further.

What kind of exercise should you do? That depends on you and what you like, but in general you should pick something you're comfortable with, something you enjoy doing and something you can sustain long-term. In many cases people choose to start with taking brisk walks. For people who have trouble with walking because of joint or back pain, exercise bikes, elliptical trainers and exercising in pools doing water aerobics (or one of many other exercises available today) may be better choices. Your exercise program might involve something as simple as buying five- or 10-pound hand weights and vigorously exercising your arms while you're at rest even if you can't do much in the way of walking or standing. But whatever you pick, it's helpful to start now and to keep at it every day.

Don't know how to start? Your surgery center staff should have some ideas. I try to provide ideas about exercise for every patient who walks through our door, whether or not the person decides on a weight-loss operation or chooses to work with a nonsurgical alternative.

For starters, all patients get pedometers so they can monitor how many steps they're taking in an average day. With the exception of those patients who have joint problems or problems walking, most people can and should add more steps to their daily routines.

Walking not only burns calories, it improves physical conditioning and helps prepare the body for the operation. Start with a goal of taking 8,000 steps every day. When that becomes easy, increase the goal to 10,000 and then 12,000. Our patients find with time and commitment and motivation they will hit their goals and head into their operations in much better shape than when they started with the extra steps.

ATTITUDE

I'd also like to suggest positive imaging. I know that might sound a little too much like new-age thinking for some readers, the idea that you can think positively and prepare psychologically for physical outcomes, but there is a good body of data supporting the idea that thinking positively and indulging in some creative positive mental imagery may improve the outcomes of an operation. So, as you learn more and read more and talk to more people as you get closer to the date of your weight-loss procedure, take some time to sit down and think through the experience and imagine all of it going smoothly and very positively.

Imagine yourself coming in for the operation, meeting the people who are going to be taking care of you, having very positive experiences with them. Visualize the operation going smoothly and see yourself coming out of anesthesia without significant pain and without nausea or side effects, and see yourself recovering with very little pain or discomfort. Visualize yourself embarking on the hard work to come while feeling energized and confident. As you continue to work with these positive images I think you'll find that you're setting the stage for the kind of positive experience with weight loss that you want.

How Much Time Off Will I Need?

You're going to want to ask your surgeon that, of course. But while different surgeons hold differing opinions on time off, there are some general guidelines.

First, you're probably planning to undergo a laparoscopic weight-loss procedure. With rare exceptions there is really no good reason for having an open surgical procedure unless you've had a great number of previous abdominal operations, had a previous gastric bypass procedure or there is some other very unusual set of circumstances. (Multiple previous abdominal operations means a high chance of extensive intra-abdominal adhesions or scar tissue. This scar tissue can make laparoscopic surgery impossible.) But for 98 percent of us, weight-loss procedures mean laparoscopic or minimally invasive procedures with keyhole incisions.

Assuming you're having a minimally invasive operation, one to two weeks off is a good ballpark. This is too much for some people and not enough for others, but it gives you an average. If your job requires heavy lifting or a lot of activity, you might want to take three or four weeks off. And it doesn't hurt to have a cushion so if complications occur you can take longer for recovery. But the amount of time you can take depends on your situation and your job and also whether or not you've disclosed the nature of your absence or kept your weight-loss operation plans to yourself.

Over the years I've seen many patients go back to their jobs, especially office jobs, within a matter of days. One patient who was an employee at my practice had a laparoscopic RYGB operation on Monday and came back to work on Thursday. I tried to convince her not to, but she was absolutely fine, physically, and it was important to her psychologically.

One of my colleagues at the hospital had an LAGB procedure one day and returned to his full duties the next day. So, it depends a lot on your motivation, your comfort level and your attitude.

Some people find they tire quickly and are more fatigued at the end of the day even after the recovery period. It can take a good six to eight weeks to get back to normal energy levels, but this is true of all kinds of operations and minor procedures. Medical science doesn't know exactly why this is, but it may have something to do with the stress of surgical procedures, anesthesia and recovery. It's simply a good thing to know and plan around so that you're not following up your operation with 12- and 14-hour days. Try to take off for two weeks, for certain, with the option of working a lighter schedule or being able to get extra rest during the weeks that follow.

It's also important to make sure you have a safety net if you have children or parents to care for. During the weeks leading up to your operation try to line up other people who can pitch in and take over these responsibilities. If you're the one who usually does the shopping and cleaning, you may want to even hire somebody to come in and help. You really need to give yourself time to focus on just you and your recovery.

> The thing always happens that you really believe in; and the belief in a thing makes it happen.
>
> ~ FRANK LLOYD WRIGHT

The Countdown

One Month Prior to Your Procedure

Along with the physical changes you're making before your operation and everything you're learning, this is a good time to sit down and talk with your loved ones about the journey you are embarking upon. You may have decided not to tell many people that you're going to undergo a weight-loss operation, but you probably need to have a core group of people close to you who will be supportive and there to help you along your journey. Talk to these people about what you're doing and, if you're comfortable doing so, share your hopes and dreams and goals for the operation with your friends and loved ones.

This is a good time to help those people who are close to you understand how important a step this is for you. Explain that this is something you have decided to undertake in order to live a healthier, better quality and longer life and that you're looking forward to spending time with them, maybe enjoying outdoor activities with family and friends or working on alleviating health problems you've begun to experience. Or tell them that you are working to make certain you don't succumb to the type of health problems that nagged your relatives or stopped your parents from living the lives they wanted to live.

Define Your Goals

You may have other goals that family and friends don't suspect. Maybe there's a hidden athlete inside you. Maybe you want to go rafting with the family next summer or climb a mountain. Maybe you have goals about your physical appearance. If you're not comfortable sharing your goals with others, review them when you have some time alone. Make a list of the things you want to do after your operation. Remind yourself of all the reasons you've sought a weight-loss procedure – for your health, for your longevity, for a chance to spend more time doing more of the activities you enjoy with your loved ones.

Write down your goals. Put them on your mirror or other places where you'll see them often and remember that what you're doing is embarking on a very important journey. It's very important for your long-term health and your long-term quality of life. And your long-term life.

The last month before your operation is a good time to attend preoperative classes and support groups. It's also time to review the things that need to be done before your operation. Double-check with your program that insurance authorization is underway. Make sure you have childcare or eldercare set up for the first week or two after your surgery when you're going to need a little extra time and assistance yourself.

Also, if you haven't done so, this is the time for two important steps that are required by all the national Centers of Excellence from the American Society of Metabolic and Bariatric Surgery and increasingly by insurance companies: the meetings with the dietitian or nutritionist, and a meeting with a psychologist (at least one meeting is required; others are optional).

Take advantage of these opportunities. I know some patients view them as simply more boxes to be checked off while getting ready for the operation and find them a bit of an annoyance, but many people find these visits very, very valuable.

PSYCHOLOGICAL EVALUATION

Many practices work with a panel of psychologists who have become very experienced at offering preoperative assessments and counseling for people undergoing weight-loss procedures. They are experts in behavior modification and in all aspects of the psychology of the weight-loss journey.

Sitting down with a psychologist before your weight-loss operation can be very valuable. The psychologist is there to offer some insight to you about what will work for you to succeed and what things you might think about to help you on your journey. The psychologist is also there, in part, to assess your suitability and candidacy for a weight-loss procedure. Insurance companies are in the habit of requiring a psychologist's approval before authorizing surgery, so this visit is usually one on the checklist of things to do before surgery is officially scheduled. This isn't a cause for concern – very few candidates are turned away on the basis of psychological evaluations, though some candidates are found to have deeper emotional issues that require some counseling or treatment prior to and after surgery. Identifying these concerns ahead of time will only improve the surgical outcome.

This doesn't mean you have gone into therapy or that anyone will know that you have seen a psychologist. But, if you do have ongoing concerns as you make the transitions in your life that a weight-loss procedure brings about, many of these professionals are willing to work with weight-loss patients on an ongoing basis.

Most of the changes from weight-loss procedures are positive, but some can be stressful. Changes in body image and how other people react to you and treat you can be a new stress in your life. Or weight loss may result in new attention from others, which can be stressful if it's unexpected. A psychologist can help you through your transitions or, if you're only working with the psychologist before the operation, help you prepare. So, the psychological evaluation is a valuable opportunity to learn more and interact with an experienced professional in the field of surgical weight loss.

EVALUATION

The same is true for the dietary or the nutritional consultation. Our dietitians are invested in seeing patients succeed. They're advocates of the surgical weight-loss process and have seen a great number of people come through and dramatically change their lives for the better.

But it's natural to feel a bit apprehensive before visiting with a dietitian.

By the time people are contemplating weight-loss procedures, they've already dealt with a good many people in their lives telling them what's what in weight loss, what to do, eat and think. Going to a dietitian when you're already overweight might feel threatening. It's natural to anticipate being told "no, wrong, bad." But it's not going to happen. Our dietitians are interested in your long-term health and well-being, and they're also interested in making sure you have realistic goals and a good understanding of the responsibility that you need to take for long-term success. Dietitians can offer some tremendous insights and ongoing counseling in terms of what foods are good choices for the long term.

PREOP LIQUID DIET

The dietitians often play a role in the all-important preoperative liquid meal-replacement diet that you should begin at this point. Your program staff will most likely have already given you details about it, and their version of this preop diet may be somewhat different from what I have outlined in Appendix B. The key is to markedly reduce calories, emphasize protein drinks, plenty of water, exercise and fiber.

Our dietitians meet with patients, perform evaluations, offer insights and suggestions, and they also teach some of the preoperative classes, giving you even more chances to interact and ask questions about nutrition and good food choices – tools necessary for long-term success.

We use the protein-based liquid meal-replacement program because we've found people succeed when we take all other choices away. You don't have to worry about what you're going to eat or drink during these last four weeks before your weight-loss surgery because it's all based on liquid shakes and liquid meal replacements. There isn't anything else.

I'll admit my outstanding dietitian and I fight about whether or not to let people have a bit of steamed broccoli every now and then, and I know she tells them to go ahead and do that if they're just dying for something to eat. It adds a little crunchiness and some additional nutrients without adding too many calories. But typically, I tell people to just stick with the liquid shakes and to not add even the vegetables.

Liquid Meal Replacements

The fact that you've been following a liquid meal-replacement diet during your preop month doesn't mean you're going to stay on it forever. The liquid meal-replacements work very well. They help you focus on your intake of protein, vitamins and fluid, and help you avoid everything else that could be detrimental to losing weight. They can play a helpful role in long-term weight loss, and can easily be prepared for breakfast or lunch, taking the place of a meal, especially one that might be high in carbohydrates. They're also a great snack, taking away hunger and replacing possible extra carbs with proteins and helping you keep your weight down.

But they're not a complete or permanent solution, and you're not expected to continue the liquid meal replacement diet forever. The months before surgery are the time to reshape how you think about food and to learn how to make healthier food choices. This is one place the nutritionist involved with your weight-loss program can definitely help out. Over the long term, you can use the shakes or bars for snacks or breakfast or when you need to refocus your weight loss and avoid a relapse of weight gain.

ONLINE EDUCATION

In addition to in-person preoperative classes, there are online classes available from many programs. Like many centers, we have made a decision to offer a great deal of material free to anyone online.

You'll need to set aside time for all your necessary appointments, and it might seem like there's a lot going on prior to your weight-loss operation – because there is. Take advantage of all the resources available. The more you learn, the better you'll succeed.

TWO WEEKS PRIOR TO YOUR PROCEDURE

Two weeks before your operation it doesn't seem like there's much left to do. By now you've had time to talk with your loved ones and support people, hopefully you've attended some preoperative classes, and your insurance authorization is underway. The date of your operation should already be set by now and circled on the calendar. What's left to do?

For one thing, if you haven't already started the preoperative protein-based liquid meal-replacement program, start immediately. If the center you've chosen doesn't offer this kind of program, take a look around at some other centers and see if you can make sense of the programs they're offering.

You can also order protein meal-replacement products online that will allow you to put together your own two-week program. That way you've still got time to achieve the results that patients do at the centers that employ this kind of program.

If your program does prescribe a meal replacement program, then stick to it religiously. You want to begin making some changes in your diet and in your way of thinking about food and drink that you will want to sustain for the long term, and these can start with the liquid meal-replacement program.

During this time you're also going to pay strict attention to what you drink. Some programs rule out all carbonated beverages, but I don't think a little carbonation prior to your operation is going to hurt. Just make sure whatever you choose is a zero-calorie drink.

There are a wide variety of zero-calorie beverages on the market today, from Diet Snapple to Diet 7UP. I do advise against drinking caffeinated beverages, simply because of the diuretic effect, which can cause some dehydration. After an operation, many people feel you shouldn't drink carbonated beverages anymore, but I have several personal friends who have had LRYGB and LAGB procedures, and they are able to drink carbonated beverages without too much trouble.

HERBAL REMEDIES

This is also the time to discontinue herbal medications, supplements or remedies you may be taking. Many people don't regard herbal products as medicines and forget to tell their doctors about them. In recent years research has uncovered dangerous side effects of common herbal products in people who are undergoing surgical procedures.[102-103]

It is very important to tell your doctor about herbal medicines you're taking. Many people are unaware that quite a few herbal or so-called "natural" remedies have serious side effects including bleeding. (The American Society of Anesthesiology recommends every patient stop all herbal remedies two to three weeks prior to an operation because of side effects.)

Garlic, ginseng and ginkgo biloba have all been shown to increase bleeding. Kava can increase the sedative effect of anesthetics. Ma huang (ephedra) increases blood pressure and heart rate. Saint-John's wort alters an important enzyme of the liver that metabolizes many drugs. So, reduce the risks for your operation. Tell the doctor about any of these herbal products and discontinue them for the next two weeks.

At two weeks out from your operation you should be up to 8,000 or even 10,000 steps a day on your pedometer, and be attending preoperative classes. You've probably picked up a couple books on bariatric surgery and want to finish them before the date of your operation. You've talked to loved ones and tried some positive visualization. What else?

For one thing, you need to make sure you've set aside enough time for your recovery. Make certain all arrangements are in place for your time off work. You don't need last-minute panics cropping up or people asking if they can e-mail you or call you, especially if you haven't revealed that you're going to be gone for a weight-loss operation rather than a trip. Childcare arrangements should be double- and triple-checked, and if you're taking care of a parent or older loved one, make sure you've got arrangements for someone to take over that caretaking responsibility as well. You don't want to spend the time just before your operation stressed out, making arrangements, and if you have to cancel or postpone your operation, your surgeon may not be able to accommodate you in your preferred time frame. You've worked hard to get here – now you need to make sure that hard work all pays off.

ONE WEEK PRIOR TO YOUR PROCEDURE

Most practices recommend you stop any medications that cause blood thinning prior to an operation. If you're taking prescribed blood thinners like Coumadin, it's important to discuss that with your surgeon long before your operation (see Chapter 3). Typically your surgeon will recommend you go off Coumadin for a period of five to seven days before your operation. In some cases, the surgeon may make additional arrangements for you to be on another kind of blood thinner, though most of the time the decision is to simply stop the blood thinner prior to surgery.

For milder prescribed blood thinners, including aspirin, ibuprofen or naproxen, this is something to cover with your surgeon individually. I generally have a standard recommendation to stop these medications five to seven days prior to an operation, but there are times when people need to stay on them. In such cases, it's really up to each individual surgeon to make the call. In my practice, if people have a strong reason to stay on their aspirin, I let them stay on because I think the risk of bleeding is quite small. But there may be other surgeons who would recommend stopping them altogether. It's a matter for you to discuss with your surgeon. For anyone undergoing LRYGB or LSG, I strongly recommend stopping ibuprofen and all other NSAID drugs because of the risk of ulcers.

One week or more prior to surgery, clarify with your doctor's office the list of the other medicines you take and which of them you should keep taking right through to surgery. Generally you will be instructed to keep taking your usual medicines. Beta blockers, in particular, are proven to protect against perioperative heart trouble, so keep taking those if you are on them.

Usually your surgeon will ask that you visit the hospital or surgery center around a week before your operation to register and go over paperwork, and to have some preoperative tests. (More tests? Yes, I'm afraid so.) These last-minute tests usually include an EKG, a chest X-ray and some blood work. Even if you've had all these done before, they're usually required again close to the operation date so that the results are up-to-date and reflect your health status as you undergo anesthesia and the operation.

Two Days Prior to Your Procedure

Okay, this might sound crazy, but the most important thing to do two days out from your operation date is triple-confirm the date and time and location of the operation.

It sounds silly. But imagine the huge stress it would cause if it turned out you were planning on going to the wrong place at the wrong time on the wrong day – or any of the above. Figuring it out at the last minute might save the surgery, but it will cause you to be stressed and rushed, which is not the experience you want to have.

So, two days before the operation, confirm exactly where you're supposed to be and when, and take the time to double-check with the people who are going to help you the day of your operation.

Support Team

For some people, as many as two or three support people might be necessary, but one intelligent, supportive person is often the right number. This is the person who is going with you to the hospital or outpatient center and who will accompany you through your journey.

I think it's very helpful to have your support person or team with you to hear everything the doctors and nurses tell you before and after your operation. Someone who is not undergoing the procedure is probably going to be a little more relaxed and might ask better questions and retain more of the information. Then that person can help you through those first days after your operation when you're apt to be sore and need the most assistance.

Typically, it's going to be a spouse or best friend who will support you through the weight-loss operation, driving you to the facility, remaining through the procedure, listening to the information from doctors and nurses and seeing you home again. A few days prior to your operation is a good time to discuss with your support person or team exactly what's going to take place and what you should all prepare for.

In the case of LAGB procedures, more than 90 percent of procedures can be done in outpatient facilities. So, your support person is going to bring you to the facility early in the morning, most likely, and help you prepare for your operation. Your support person can stay while you have your IV placed, move with you to the preoperative area and meet with the surgeon and wait during the operation. After your operation your support person will meet with the surgeon again, and, after your recovery period, take you back home.

If your support person can spend the night with you after you return home, so much the better, and it wouldn't hurt to have support for the next couple days. Most people don't need someone to wait on them hand and foot, but it's nice to have someone who can do the cooking, bring you things to drink or read or extra pillows and walk with you when you're not walking at your usual brisk pace and need someone with a little extra patience. While most people are physically capable of going it alone after most outpatient surgeries, I don't think there's anything more valuable than having a best friend or partner who can be around for a few days. After the first couple days you'll probably feel more like yourself, but in the beginning it's nice to have the support.

If you're having an LRYGB procedure, the advice is a little different.

You should expect an overnight hospital stay, or even two nights (at our center most patients now spend one night, but a minority do stay two nights). With rare occurrences, the stay can be longer, three or four nights, or in rare cases of complications, longer than that.

THE DAY PRIOR TO YOUR PROCEDURE

Some people want to go out for one last big meal, a celebratory blowout, and, in Nevada, where I practice, the casinos have big, beautiful buffets that can be really tempting. But your blowout could blow it, ruining the two-week or longer meal-replacement diet you've been carefully following and probably making you feel worse than you might expect. I strongly advise against this.

The day before your procedure is a good day to review what you're going to be doing the following day, review where you're going to be and when you need to be there, make sure your support person is up to date with your plans and double-check that your rides are arranged.

The day before your operation is a good day to have quiet time at home. It's a good day to reflect on your goals, to look at the progress you've made so far, to visualize a successful outcome to the operation coming up and daydream about the new life your future holds.

Some programs have preoperative medications or preoperative bowel preparation or cleansing, so you might end up taking the entire day off work. Your surgeon will give you specific instructions, as different programs use different procedures. At our center, we recommend a bowel cleanse for all patients undergoing LRYGB surgery or complex revision procedures but not for LAGB or LSG. While not critical to the success of the operation, the bowel preparation does empty out the intestinal system and can help reduce postoperative constipation, bloating and potentially even infection. In the early days of gastric bypass, there was a chance of bowel perforation and contamination, and the risk of infection was lowered by cleansing out the bowels ahead of time. Today, experienced laparoscopic surgeons almost never encounter that type of problem, and, as a result, most centers have dropped the requirement of the bowel preparation except sometimes for LRYGB.

The day prior to your operation is a good day for long, brisk walks, for continuing your exercise program and for taking care of any last minute arrangements you need to make. Set aside time for a good night's sleep.

Generally speaking, if you're taking medications for ongoing health conditions, such as heart conditions, high blood pressure or any other significant medical conditions that require ongoing medication, you should continue to take your medicines the day before your operation. In most cases, we actually recommend patients take them the morning of an operation, but only with the smallest sip of water. We want the stomach as empty as possible for the procedure.

DIABETES

People with diabetes – a fairly common medical condition in patients considering weight-loss procedures – are the exception to the medications rule, as the need for medications to control the condition has likely dropped over the previous several weeks. On the day before your operation, if you've been following the preoperative meal-replacement diet, your blood sugars should have fallen (your medication requirements, should you have any, have probably fallen also in the last four weeks). So, if you have diabetes, the day before your operation, when you're having your meal-replacement shake again and nothing else, you may not need much in terms of insulin or oral medication due to the cumulative impact of your meal-replacement plan.

Keep a watch on your blood sugar. Try to target a range of 120 to 150. It's okay if it creeps a little higher, you just don't want it to fall too far below 100, because you don't want it to really bottom out and be in the dangerous 50 to 60 range the night or morning of your operation. Remember, you won't be eating anything the next morning, so let it drift up a little.

If you do take insulin regularly for diabetes, most practices and most endocrinologists recommend you take only half the normal dose the evening before your surgery. You're not going to even have a protein shake or a cup of coffee the morning of your operation. The most you're going to have is a sip of water to wash down any regular important medications.

THE DAY OF YOUR PROCEDURE

Welcome to the day of your operation. You've worked long and hard to get here. There are only a few more steps.

First thing: Don't eat. The number-one reason operations get canceled at the last minute is that the patient had something to eat or too much to drink. In that case the anesthesiologist is faced with a person who is significantly overweight and also has what is referred to in anesthesia as a "full stomach." Full-stomach anesthesia is only performed in emergencies when there's no choice – and weight-loss surgery is not a trauma situation, nor should it be. A full stomach causes too high a risk of aspiration, where stomach contents can come upward and be breathed into the lungs.

You've worked so hard and taken all the trouble to arrange time off and put together a support team and arranged childcare and everything else you've done in the last two months, it would be a shame to waste it. So put nothing in your stomach the morning of your operation but your prescribed medications with a sip of water.

You'll probably want to bring your CD player or your iPod with you and a book or magazine, because inevitably we ask you to arrive early in case of last-minute issues that need to be resolved, problems or questions with your laboratory studies or any other minor complications. Some waiting or downtime is an inevitable part of the process, and it is far better to expect it, be patient and have something with which to pass the time. Plan to wait a little to register or check in as a patient, to have your IV started, to talk to the nurses, to talk to the doctors and to be wheeled into surgery.

Typically your lab studies will have been drawn several days or a week before your operation. Now the anesthesiologist, surgeon and operating room team will have one last look at your health and documentation, the history and physical provided by the surgeon's office, and the preoperative X-ray, EKG and blood work.

If anything was profoundly abnormal in the lab work it likely will have been picked up before the day of your surgery, and your surgeon will have discussed it with you. Occasionally, however, something is missed until the day of surgery, so you have to plan for contingencies.

Every once in a while the anesthesiologist or surgeon or hospital staff realizes that for some reason the surgery has to be postponed. It doesn't happen often, but it does happen. Don't be shocked. Just roll with the punches and do whatever additional testing is required, and hopefully the situation will be resolved, and the operation can either go ahead or be rescheduled. But most of the time, even last-minute issues can be resolved. In such cases, the patient has simply spent a little more time enjoying music or a book and talking with loved ones.

This is the morning you'll meet the nursing staff. You'll change out of whatever comfortable clothes you wore to the facility and into the hospital gown countless television shows have made fun of (for good reason; you may want to ask for two gowns – one that closes in back and one that closes in front, so you don't have embarrassing exposure). Hospital or center staff will place your IV so you can receive fluids. If you do have diabetes, the nurses will check your blood sugar to make sure you're in a safe range for your operation.

At this point you'll meet the surgical team members. If I'm your surgeon, I'll come and visit with you and your support person. Our anesthesiologist will also come and spend a few minutes describing the anesthesia planned. This is the time to ask any last-minute questions or talk over any last-minute concerns and make sure I know where to find your loved ones so that I can go and talk with them as soon as the surgery is over.

And, now, it's time. You've done good, hard work preparing for your operation. You've done a great job with your exercise program, followed your liquid meal-replacement program, learned everything you can about weight-loss surgery, attended support groups and preoperative classes, worked on understanding the range of tools you'll need for success, and, most importantly, you've decided to take 100 percent responsibility for your weight loss. You're taking a very important step for your long-term health, your longevity and your quality of life, and so you're going into the operation with the most positive outlook and the most positive thoughts you can possibly have!

And now, the journey begins!

.The first problem for all of us, men and women, is not to learn, but to unlearn.

~ GLORIA STEINEM

Food for Thought

♦ Before a weight-loss operation, you will likely have consultations with not only the surgeon but, most likely, a psychologist, nutritionist or dietitian and possibly a physical trainer. You'll have the opportunity to attend support groups. Each step is an opportunity to learn and prepare for weight-loss success. Learn all you can.

♦ Books are a great way to get answers to questions you didn't think of when talking to your surgeon, or those questions that occur to you only in the middle of the night. See the reading guide in the Resources section at the end of this book.

♦ Audio programs are another great way to learn about successful weight loss while driving to work or working out. Visit www.iMetabolic.com.

♦ Support groups offer a way to meet other people who have already experienced the procedure you're about to undergo and ask questions from those who have experienced the operation from the inside out.

♦ Preoperative classes can give you the long-term tools to make your surgical weight-loss procedure a success. Some classes may be available online so patients can check out teaching modules based on the specific operations they've chosen.

◆ In the last several weeks before your procedure you will probably be on a liquid (meal-replacement shake) diet in order to lose weight before the operation. Losing weight before the operation has a number of benefits, including shrinking the liver (which makes the procedures safer).

◆ The last several weeks before your procedure will also involve an exercise program. The healthier you are going into the operation, the faster the recovery time.

◆ The weeks before your procedure are also time to double-check all arrangements the surgical center is making with your insurance carrier and your own arrangements for childcare and/or eldercare during your recovery. It's also a good idea to double-check on your own support team.

◆ One week before your procedure you'll be doing the last of the blood work and medical testing. Confirm what medicines you will continue taking and which, in any, you will stop.

◆ Two days before your procedure, double-check all arrangements – where you're supposed to be and when. The day of the surgery is a bad time to be rushed and panicky or to wind up at the wrong facility.

◆ The day of your procedure you do not eat. Your surgeon will advise you which prescription medicines to take. There will probably be last minute medical tests run before your procedure starts, so come prepared for short waits.

◆ While you may have butterflies about the operation, remember everything you've learned and how far you've come and start looking forward to your new life!

6

Success After Weight–Loss Surgery

To succeed in creating a new you, you need the right tools. The surgery itself is one powerful tool, but there are many more that you need in your tool chest to succeed.

Not everyone who undergoes a surgical weight-loss procedure fully internalizes the important methods necessary to keep the weight off. Some programs don't spend enough time on the educational components of successful weight loss and, to be honest, many patients have told me they were so excited about having surgery and their chances for a new future they failed to recognize the importance of the information they were receiving. They didn't understand it was important to learn every facet of medically proven weight-loss science.

I've been fortunate enough to have helped thousands of people lose weight successfully through surgical and nonsurgical weight-loss methods. So if you've already had a surgical weight-loss procedure, or if you're just about to have your operation, or if you had your operation a year ago, it's time to marshal all your enthusiasm, resources and dedication to the singular goal of losing weight. You can lose weight and keep it off; you can do it with the right tools, the right information and the right program.

I will show you how.

Take a minute and think back over what you've done in the last few months. You've found a bariatric surgeon to work with and scheduled appointments, gone through the lab testing and required medical procedures in order to be accepted as a candidate for surgery. You've probably attended educational classes as part of your program and learned better eating habits. Hopefully you've had a chance to take advantage of support groups offered through your weight-loss program and met with other people who are going to have or have already had the procedure you're about to undergo. Maybe you've met with a nutritionist or dietitian, and taken a good hard look at how you have been eating and how you need to start eating.

It's likely that for the last four to eight weeks you've been following a liquid protein diet of meal-replacement shakes so you've probably already lost quite a bit of weight while preparing for your operation. Good for you! This is a promise of good things to come.

Here's what to expect now that your new life is about to begin.

Keep Doing What You've Been Doing

In the last few months you've created all kinds of new habits, followed a liquid meal-replacement program to lose weight preoperatively. Hopefully you've utilized tools available to you through your surgical program to make preoperative weight loss easier and get more information on everything to do for long-term weight loss. Don't stop! If you continue to take advantage of educational materials and support groups like you did before your operation, you give yourself more tools for success.

Having gone through preoperative classes and met with experts, you will probably have heard the answer to every question about your procedure three times over. But when you come out of your operation, you may still find you have questions, and once you go home from the surgical facility, you're going to either have to call someone or wait for an appointment with your surgeon's office to ask those questions not related to critical medical care. Some questions you'll either have to answer for yourself or wait for follow-up appointment with your doctor, questions such as: "Can I move all my furniture on the second day out of surgery?" (No!) or "Has anyone else ever felt this particular sensation?" (probably Yes). If you've taken advantage of the support groups in your area, chances are there's someone else in your group who has had the same procedure you have and can answer your questions or provide support when you're feeling doubtful or worried.

Many weight-loss programs build in support mechanisms, so there are plenty of resources for questions that might arise. Take advantage of all the resources available to you and keep in touch with your support network; don't go it alone.

If you've been educating yourself with audio programs, don't stop once your procedure is over. The more knowledge you have, the more tools for success you have. In our country today we're exposed to approximately 20,000 messages about food in the course of a year, and most of those messages are about the unhealthy kinds of food. Advertisers bombard us with images and messages, most of which are garbage we could do without. So why not replace them with healthy messages?

Recovery

With today's laparoscopic procedures, when you wake in recovery it's likely you'll only have been under the effects of an anesthetic for 30 minutes to an hour. For the rest of the world, not much time has passed and not much has happened. For you, the entire world has just changed for the better.

When you first wake, you'll be in the first stage recovery room. This is where you'll emerge from anesthesia, and it's unlikely you'll even remember being there. If you've never had a surgical procedure or awakened in recovery, the room is nothing more than another hospital area, much like the area you were moved to for preoperative work. It's a calm place, with nurses and staff present to take care of you.

Recovery isn't a private area, though, only sectioned off with curtains, and there will be other patients recovering there as well so there's usually no way for your family to join you there (because there's no way to protect the privacy of the other patients). You'll still have an IV and will still be wearing your stylish hospital gown. If I'm your surgeon, I'll probably come in to make sure recovery is progressing well, though it's unlikely you're going to remember seeing me there.

Don't worry – you won't be in recovery for long. As soon as you're awake and declared stable, you'll be moved to a second stage recovery area, often a private room, where your loved ones can visit.

Physically, every person feels a bit different, but many people can expect to feel some pain or discomfort from the operation. This will most likely be felt at the abdominal incision areas and in the upper back, chest and shoulder blades. These upper chest and back pains are caused by what is called referred pain, meaning nerves that are irritated by the laparoscopy gas at the diaphragm or upper abdomen create the sensation that the chest, back and shoulder areas are actually hurting. Just let your nurses know what you're feeling and they can work to keep the discomfort down to a tolerable level.

Nausea is one of the most frequent side effects of anesthesia, so don't be alarmed if you feel nauseated or if you vomit while you're in recovery. The sensation will pass as the medicines wear off and time passes.

Some people feel groggy after undergoing surgery and anesthesia, while others feel bright and alert. Just be prepared to go with the flow after you wake up, and remember that the sensations are temporary and will take some time, sometimes many hours, to wear off.

YOUR FIRST DAY

Your first day home you're probably going to be moving pretty slowly. You'll be sore at the site of the incisions and probably feel tired more than anything else. If your procedure was a LAP-BAND®, you may feel the site of the access port placement is the most uncomfortable in the first days.

It's a good idea to have someone with you for the first 24 to 48 hours. You may want someone to offer support when you're walking around, or bring you liquids, or simply talk to you when the nerves kick in. Even though weight-loss operations are minimally invasive and very safe, every operation holds trepidation for the person experiencing it. Simply stated, if you have a support person or people to spend those first few nights with, it can be both helpful and comforting.

You're probably not going to experience complications from your procedure. While there's no way to state for certain that your surgical procedure will be 100 percent risk-free, today's minimally invasive outpatient operations are extremely safe. If you experience symptoms that are different than what you expected or you have severe, unexpected and worsening pain, go to the emergency room. But I don't expect you're going to run into anything that will send you to the ER. You can resolve most normal symptoms (if they don't resolve themselves in a short space of time) by calling the nurse or the doctor's practice during normal working hours.

One of the best ways to retain some peace of mind is to do your homework before surgery. Read, review and talk to as many other people as possible so you know ahead of time the kinds of symptoms, pains and feelings you might experience after surgery. Then when you experience them for yourself, they won't seem scary. Ask about wound drainage, fevers, cough, food sticking, nausea, pain, diarrhea and sore throat.

Sometimes symptoms develop in the stomach or gastrointestinal system that warrant tests to diagnose a potential problem. These tests may be ordered by a primary care physician or bariatric surgeon and are generally routine studies. The most common are abdominal ultrasound, upper GI series and upper endoscopy, which are routinely covered by most insurance plans. Every plan is different, though, with different co-pays and deductibles, so it pays you in the long run to be well informed about what's covered on your plan and what isn't. If you don't have insurance and paid for your procedure yourself, the fees for these tests can add up quickly and become quite expensive, so it's best to be prepared and know what could, potentially, be coming.

I want to be very clear that the best way you can take your procedure into your own hands and reduce your risk of complications is to be very choosey about who you select to perform your operation.

Your First Week

Some people go back to work during the first week after a laparoscopic gastric banding procedure. I usually recommend taking a full week off to rest and recuperate, but not everyone needs that much time. One colleague of mine went back to work on Tuesday after having the procedure on Monday and managed quite easily with routine office work; it was important to him psychologically to get right back in his game. For those people who have undergone a gastric bypass or laparoscopic sleeve procedure, I suggest taking two weeks off.

You should do what works for you. If you've chosen to keep your procedure a secret, which is totally up to you and which is a choice your surgeon's practice will honor and support, you'll want to have scheduled a little extra time in case there are complications or you just don't feel as up to snuff as you'd expected. While it's not a bad idea to follow the guidelines above for the amount of time you take off, the biggest side effect most patients experience is fatigue by the end of the day.

And if you're feeling great on day two and you want to head right back into real life? Good for you! When returning to normal activities use common sense and listen to your body. Every doctor will give you different advice about what you can do and when, but you'll probably be cleared – or even recommended – to start taking walks your first day out of the surgical facility. Beyond that, if something hurts, don't do it. Listen to your body. Start working out gently. Use five pound hand weights. Walk on a treadmill or use an elliptical machine. Be active. But if you're hell-bent on moving the refrigerator, you want to wait about six weeks.

WHEN YOU'RE GOING TO BE YOURSELF AGAIN – ONLY BETTER

Feeling better doesn't follow an exact timeline. It's different for everyone, but usually it's a gradual, week-by-week process. The exact date you look in the mirror and say, "I feel better than ever!" may be different from someone else's and probably doesn't happen just like that for anyone. What I've found with patients is that somewhere around week six or week eight, the person suddenly looks back at how life was and then looks at how life is now and sees just how great things are.

That's worth working for.

Weight Loss after Surgery

One of the things you'll be doing in the first couple weeks after your procedure is losing weight. People lose the most weight by far right after surgery. Weight-loss programs have become increasingly successful in helping people lose substantial weight before surgery too, so you've probably already gotten a healthy start on losing your excess body weight. Typically if you've been following a liquid protein meal-replacement program you've already lost somewhere around 12 to 20 pounds, or substantially more. But in addition to the weight you've already lost, you'll probably experience a significant amount of weight loss directly after surgery. This is partly because you'll likely be eating less substantial food and not have much of an appetite, so you may have a jump-start on that weight loss of something like five to 10 pounds in two weeks. Everyone is different, and the amount of weight lost in the first two weeks depends in part on how much extra weight you have to lose. A less overweight person may not lose as many pounds right away as someone with significantly more to lose, but the percentage of overall weight may be the same. In addition, sometimes people retain water and actually gain a few pounds right after surgery, so don't get discouraged.

After the first two weeks, as you continue to follow the nutritional plan for your new life, weight loss will continue, but at a slower rate. Set a goal for losing all of your targeted excess body weight over the next 12 to 18 months or so. By then you may have lost all of your excess weight and will need to eat in a way that respects your procedure and maintains your healthy body weight. Or you will be substantially closer to your goal weight and be ready to – you guessed it – set a new goal for losing more pounds in the months to come.

Rate of Weight Loss

Everyone loses weight at a different rate. There's no magic number of pounds you'll lose every week and no number that marks you as having won the race or failed utterly. The rate of weight loss depends on you, on how you minimize calories, maximize movement and follow all the guidelines for your postoperative new life.

After laparoscopic Roux-en-Y gastric bypass (LRYGB) or laparoscopic sleeve gastrectomy (LSG) surgery, most studies have shown a rapid loss of weight over the first 12 to 18 months, after which the weight typically stabilizes. Many surgeons recognize this time period as a kind of "golden window" during which a person should try to lose as much weight as possible. After this, the focus shifts to maintaining all the weight that has been lost, maintaining good habits and enjoying life at this healthier new weight.

With the laparoscopic adjustable gastric banding (LAGB) procedure, many studies show a target weight loss of a pound per week as being a good goal. Over the course of a year, that adds up to 52 pounds – pretty respectable weight loss.

But not everyone has the same starting weight or the same metabolism, or even the same level of motivation. Some people will probably focus harder and diligently lose more weight than this over the first year, while others may lose weight more slowly. After years of helping people get started losing weight after surgery, my own philosophy is to recommend you try to set an ambitious goal and really focus on losing the maximum weight you feel you can in the first year, while adhering to the healthy diet recommendations in this book.

Keep in mind that the more you weighed at the time of your procedure, the more quickly you can lose weight after your procedure. If you lost a substantial amount of weight before your procedure, your post-procedure weight loss may be slower than average (but then, you have less to lose). You'll probably lose the most weight in the first six months, and continue losing for the first 18 months after an LRYGB or LSG operation or for as many months or years as it takes to reach your goal weight after LAGB.

Your metabolic rate influences your rate of weight loss, so comparing yourself to someone else who's had the same procedure can be frustrating. Men often lose weight faster than women because they have more lean body mass (muscle mass) and therefore a higher metabolism. The slower your metabolic rate, the slower your weight loss.

Also keep in mind that regaining some weight 18 or 24 months after LRYGB is fairly common. Often the weight regained is roughly 5 to 10 percent of your weight loss. So if you've lost 100 pounds, it's not uncommon to gain back five or 10 pounds. Don't get discouraged. Your weight goals are more than just numbers on a scale. It's also important to look at the medical problems you've cured by losing weight, the energy you've gained and your newfound quality of life.

Postoperative Diet Progression

After your procedure I recommend a four-stage diet before you start your regular postoperative lifelong eating plan. Following my recommended guidelines in a four-stage plan can prevent many postoperative problems with eating, including food sticking, belching, nausea, vomiting, dumping syndrome and the failure to achieve your weight-loss goals. If it seems onerous to have gone through all the preoperative weight-loss food plans and the operation itself only to come out the other side and find more diet recommendations, remember that following the recommended instructions will lead to greater weight loss.

STAGE 1 – CLEAR LIQUID DIET

You'll be on stage 1 of the diet plan while you're in the hospital after your procedure, and some programs recommend it for a week or so after you go home. Unless your doctor has suggested different parameters, it's a good idea to stay on clear liquids for at least the first three days after your procedure. Anything you can see through is considered a clear liquid. While in the hospital, make certain you are consuming only clear, sugar-free, non-carbonated liquids, regardless of whether or not there are other options on the tray. It is possible for the hospital to make a mistake in this regard, and in your best interests to catch and correct it.

Foods allowed in Stage 1 include:

- ◆ Decaffeinated tea, hot or cold
- ◆ Sugar-free gelatin or popsicles
- ◆ Sugar-free, non-carbonated beverages such as Crystal Light or Propel
- ◆ Broth, such as beef, chicken or vegetable

After your procedure you may find your tastes have changed and foods that used to taste good are now too salty or too sweet. If this happens to you, and some of the foods you're allowed in Stage 1 are unpleasant to you, try diluting your liquids with water. Remember to sip your beverages, taking sips throughout the day to stay hydrated..

STAGE 2 – FULL LIQUID DIET FOR DAYS THREE THROUGH SEVEN POSTOPERATIVE

After you're released from the hospital or surgical facility, you need to be following a liquid diet for the rest of the first week after your procedure. This is to give your stomach time to heal. During this time you need to make certain you follow these guidelines:

♦ Servings should be no more than about three tablespoons per meal. Use standardized measuring spoons to measure portions.

♦ Drink water or zero-calorie beverages throughout the day. You need to take in 45 ounces of fluid or more daily.

♦ Make sure what you're drinking is sugar free.

♦ Eat your meals slowly, taking 20 to 30 minutes per meal.

♦ A liquid or chewable multivitamin should be part of your daily routine at this point if you can tolerate it.

Following is a list of foods that are liquid or semi-liquid at room temperature and may stimulate your appetite if you're having trouble convincing yourself to get all your nutrients.

♦ Sugar-free popsicles

♦ Nonfat or 1 percent milk

♦ Creamed soups made with nonfat or 1 percent milk

♦ Thinned mashed potatoes

♦ Thinned sugar-free yogurt, plain nonfat yogurt

♦ Thinned hot cereal such as Cream of Wheat or Rice, blended oatmeal

In order to take in enough fluids, you'll be sipping beverages throughout the day. Other than water, you can have beverages that are low-calorie or have less than 10 calories per eight fluid ounces, including Fruit2O, Propel sports drink, Crystal Light, sugar-free Kool-Aid, broth, decaffeinated coffee and tea (no sugar or creamer, though you can use a sugar substitute), flat diet sodas (you don't want carbonated drinks at all) and sugar-free gelatin.

STAGE 3 – SMOOTH FOODS DIET FOR DAYS EIGHT THROUGH 13 AFTER YOUR PROCEDURE

As you start your transition back to solid foods you'll want to eat foods that have been pureed in a blender or food processor. You want to consume foods that have the consistency of applesauce. Continue eating by consuming your protein before your other food groups; you may get full before you finish the protein alone. Continue to avoid high-calorie, high-sugar foods.

Servings are now two to four tablespoons per meal. Remember:

♦ Eat your protein first.

♦ Drink only low-calorie beverages between meals.

♦ Eat five or six small meals a day, about every three hours. If you have very little appetite, still at least make an attempt to eat every three to four hours.

♦ Avoid the habit of eating and drinking at the same time because it will flush the food through your stomach and you will not get the full benefit of feeling satiated.

♦ Sip your beverages through the day to stay hydrated.

♦ This is a great time to enjoy a liquid protein meal-replacement shake – try one of the awesome recipes at the end of the book.

♦ Don't forget your vitamins. Chewable, liquid and sublingual work best.

STAGE 4 – SOFT FOODS DIET FOR DAYS 14 THROUGH 28 POSTOPERATIVE

At this point you can add soft, whole foods to your diet – those foods that are easy to chew or mash with a fork – and you can have servings of ¼ to ½ a cup per meal. Use standardized measuring cups to determine portion size and cut food up into very small pieces, chewing each thoroughly.

Remember:

♦ Eat protein first.

♦ Experiment with solid foods one food at a time (so you can pinpoint any that cause trouble).

♦ Eat three small meals and two to three small snacks every day.

♦ Do not eat and drink at the same time. Drink beverages 30 minutes after you eat.

♦ Aim for 64 fluid ounces a day – water or zero-calorie beverages – and sip.

♦ Take your vitamin and mineral supplements as directed.

ENHANCING WEIGHT LOSS

Once you're back to eating regular food, a month after your surgical weight-loss procedure, your plan should include a balanced diet of high-quality protein, vegetables, fruit, whole grains and healthy fats. The good news as you look to changing the way you've always eaten is that it's very likely your tastes have changed since your procedure – it may be easier to stay away from those high-fat, high-sugar foods you used to enjoy because they just don't appeal to you anymore. This is helpful, because you need to commit to your changes of eating habits not just until you lose the excess weight, but forever.

The diet principles for life aren't that hard to follow. You still need to eat your protein first, in the form of legumes, lean fish, cottage cheese and whatever other healthy proteins are allowed on your nutritional program.

When trying to enhance your weight loss, look at some of your daily eating behaviors and habits. Make certain your portion sizes are small and in keeping with your nutritional program, but continue to take in calories. Eating too little (fewer than 600 calories per day over several weeks) can stall weight loss just like eating too much can. If you don't take in enough nutrients, your body goes into starvation mode – your metabolism slows and your body hangs on to every calorie, which prevents you from losing weight.

Other points to keep in mind when trying to enhance weight loss: Eat your protein first, vegetables second and carbs last if you still have room for them. Avoid high-calorie foods and eat set meals at set times rather than grazing. Grazing, or eating little bits throughout the day, can slow weight loss considerably. While you've been advised to eat set meals every three hours, this is not the same as grazing. Grazing is a behavior that involves nibbling handfuls or small amounts of whatever is available throughout the day.

Enhancing your weight loss involves more than just attention to food and nutritional habits. Is intentional physical activity part of your daily life? Exercise is essential for both weight loss and weight maintenance, so get moving.

As for charting your progress and seeing how far you've gone on your journey, weigh yourself at least twice a week when you're actively losing weight and maintaining weight loss – this means forever. Studies show that weighing-in on a daily basis is associated with the most successful long-term weight loss.

These are just a few of the tips I've found over the years. If you're interested in more, please check out my book, Doctor's Orders: 101 Medically-Proven Tips for Losing Weight. This book offers scads of scientifically-validated weight-loss tips that anyone can follow. (Available now; order at www.iMetabolic.com or on Amazon.)

Your First 100 Days After Surgery

Three months after your surgery is one of your milestones. You've already lost a great deal of weight and met some of your goals. Good for you. This is a great time to set some more ambitious goals for your weight-loss success. Your plan should be to read and accumulate as much information as you can on successful weight-loss strategies, network with as many other people who have successfully lost weight as you can, and to set target goal weights for yourself for the coming months. Then, and here's the fun part, I want you to plan and arrange celebrations of those milestones with some special events with friends and family.

For example, let's say you had set a goal of losing at least 10 percent of your excess body weight before your operation. That means if you were 100 pounds overweight, you had promised to lose at least 10 pounds. If you followed my guidelines for preoperative weight loss, you probably lost well over 10 pounds and probably more like 20 before you ever had your surgery. So at the time of your procedure, you had 90 percent of the overall total to lose.

So let's set a goal of losing at least 20 percent more in the next 100 days. And on the one hundredth day, having achieved your goal, you should celebrate. I'd say buy the tickets now and invite your best friends to a concert or some other special event that takes place around that time. Let everyone going with you know what the celebration is for and hold yourself to your goals.

For most people, losing one to two pounds per week in these first 100 days is very achievable. For people with more weight to lose, or people with more discipline to exercise more and who stick strictly to meal-replacement shakes and bars, two to four pounds per week is often possible. You know your body. You know how determined you are and how hard you've worked; now set your goal.

If you're an LSG patient, by the end of your first three months you have already experienced:

♦ Weight loss (hooray!)

♦ Healing and resolution of the soreness from surgery (though you may still feel discomfort at times and with certain activities)

♦ Regained energy

♦ Familiarity with the vitamin regimen you must adhere to (a specially formulated bariatric multivitamin)

♦ Improved exercise tolerance – walking farther and more frequently

If you're an LRYGB patient, by the end of your first three months you have already experienced:

♦ Weight loss (hooray!)

♦ Healing and resolution of the soreness from surgery (though you may still feel discomfort at times and with certain activities)

♦ Regained energy

♦ Familiarity with the vitamin regimen you must adhere to (a specially formulated bariatric multivitamin, a separate calcium-vitamin D supplement, and a separate vitamin B12 supplement

♦ Improved exercise tolerance – walking farther and more frequently

If you're an LAGB patient, you are likely to have:

♦ Weight loss (hooray!)

♦ Experienced one to two adjustments or fills of the LAP-BAND®

♦ Learned to tell when you're full or have eaten enough and when you have eaten too much.

♦ Celebrated some important milestones in your weight-loss journey (30 pounds lost or finally less than a certain body weight)

By the end of the 100 days, you should be returning to life with a vengeance. Many of my patients are more active than ever before, and more energized by the weight they've already lost. Most or all potential complications related to surgery and healing should have already have been solved.

But every person is different and every person who has undergone a weight-loss procedure is battling a different set of physical and psychological obstacles. The key is to set goals, commit to them, remain forward-thinking and work hard to achieve those goals.

Why Your Friends May Be Your Saboteurs

So, one day, not so long after your procedure, your friends invite you out for drinks, dinner and conversation, just the sort of thing you did all the time before you started your weight-loss journey. And you used to be the life of the party, right? At least you contributed heartily to everyone's fun, and having a few drinks probably added to the atmosphere.

But what about now? You don't want to just turn them down and abandon your social life entirely, but can you still enjoy something like drinks and dinner with friends? I know a lot of you are probably thinking, If I start with a couple drinks with friends, it will lead to a lot of calories in the drinks and I'll probably give in and start eating some of that delicious bar food, and knowing the calories in foods like hot wings and deep fried hors d'oeuvres, you're right to be concerned. But what do you do?

Let me just say that successfully managing to continue a social life with your friends and enjoy their company, even going out to restaurants and bars – this is a very advanced level of difficulty! It's actually one of the most difficult situations you're going to face after your procedure. If you consider that every situation or encounter is associated with a level of challenge, then this part of your adventure can be considered about a level nine out of 10.

Getting around such temptations involves preparation. It begins with planning and preparing yourself for the situations you know you're going to encounter. It begins with identifying the things that normally lead you to drink too much and eat too much, taking matters into your own hands and planning how you're going to respond.

I don't recommend tackling this project too soon after your surgery. When you do make the decision to join your friends for an evening out, do some pre-event planning, visualizing and strategizing beforehand. Imagine exactly where you're going with your friends, what people typically order, how many drinks most of your friends are likely to have, how long you're going to be in the bar or restaurant and what kinds of restaurant or bar food you're going to be exposed to. If you're on a liquid protein meal-replacement plan, take your protein bar or shake with you and stick to your plan. Know ahead of time what you intend to eat at the restaurant or bar so you're not tempted to dive into the goodies with or without encouragement. You can bring your own drink or order club soda, which, while it doesn't taste that good, can be slowly sipped, takes time to consume and has no calories. Or order a diet soda.

You'll also want to concentrate on what's going to happen when it's time to decide whether or not to order dessert. You might even go as far as imagining your friends encouraging you to live it up and eat and drink "just this once."

I want to be clear that I don't think your friends are intentionally trying to sabotage your weight-loss efforts. What they are doing, however, is indulging in behaviors you've educated yourself to avoid. And they may be trying to get you to "relax and live a little" for this one night without understanding the ramifications that has for your overall plans. If your friends are thin or normal weight, most likely they don't understand the amount of effort it's taking you to pursue your weight-loss goals or how much damage could be done by letting go "just this once." Protect yourself and plan for your friends' good intentions before you're confronted with them.

Your friends aren't weight-loss experts. They haven't spent years researching the negative effects of weight gain and obesity. They probably haven't read a mountain of academic papers describing the skyrocketing risk of diabetes that starts with even modest weight gain. They may not be aware that overweight people are 10 times more likely than normal weight people to lose a limb to amputation, go blind, suffer renal failure, or have a stroke due to diabetes.

The fact that your friends don't understand the changes you're making isn't terribly surprising, is it? But now you've educated yourself and taken steps on the weight-loss path to improve your health. You've identified your problems and your goals, and made a commitment to yourself to achieve a specific goal of a specific number of pounds lost, and to achieve a major improvement in your health and longevity. You've taken 100 percent responsibility for your own success. Now's the time to apply that self-discipline when you're thinking about going into familiar situations with old friends. And if you're comfortable talking with your friends about your goals and concerns, ask them to help you stay on your healthy new path even when you're going out. Sometimes friends who would encourage bad behavior will encourage good behavior if asked to play watchdog.

Don't let the evening get out of hand. Plan ahead of time for a reasonable escape clause, a reason to leave early if you need to.

Enjoy yourself. Have a good time with your friends, being out, at a movie, dancing or just talking in a restaurant. Food doesn't have to be the center of the entertainment. Your goals are highly valuable and you've learned so many healthy behaviors. You can succeed at this. Just remember you're on a mission, one that's extremely important for your long-term welfare and happiness, and these social occasions are a kind of test of your commitment. Don't be deterred from your mission. You are too important.

Plateaus

By the end of your first year after your operation, weight loss might be slowing, but many people go on losing weight. After LRYGB and LSG surgery, it's commonly reported that the average person loses weight for around 18 months, and then generally plateaus. It's also commonly reported that after LAGB surgery, the average person loses weight more slowly but continues to lose weight over the course of several years (and beyond, according to many studies). But every individual is different, so you shouldn't expect that you're going to necessarily conform to an average.

If you've hit your goal weight and are where you want to be, good for you! Keep up the good work. If you're still on your way there, don't panic. You're still losing weight, just at a slower rate.

But if the weight loss has stopped, and week after week is going by without a drop on the scale, you may have hit a plateau.

After all the work leading up to your operation, after the initial jump-start of weight loss and probably close to a year of losing weight steadily, nothing can be more maddening than having the weight loss slow. Or even stop.

This is a plateau, and it's frustrating and aggravating when the weight stops sliding off because it can happen with no change in your actions. You haven't been cheating. You haven't been overeating. You haven't stopped exercising. In short, you haven't done anything wrong, you're short of your ultimate goal weight and you feel like you could have gotten this far without undergoing a surgical procedure.

Don't get discouraged. I know that's easy to say and hard to hear. But plateaus are a normal part of weight loss. There's no set time for a plateau to occur and no set time for how long it will last. You haven't failed, and the operation hasn't failed you. You'll be losing weight again as soon as the plateau breaks. The bad news? As soon as you get comfortable with the weight loss again, you may hit another plateau. Weight loss is kind of like a balky car engine – it happens in fits and starts rather than a smooth, continuous burn. Plateaus are why so many people get frustrated and give up. Don't do that! You're still winning.

On the other hand, plateaus can be because of some subtle change you've made in your day-to-day behaviors and eating. Have you started snacking on nuts or changed where you go or what you do for lunch? This is a good time to make a careful review of what you're doing, what you're eating and how your exercise regimen may have changed. If you don't have it in hand, this is definitely the time to buy a pocket calorie guide and begin carefully tracking your daily calorie intake.

While you're waiting for the weight loss to start again, there are things you can do to keep your mind off the plateau and on the overall journey to health. Try reviewing your overall long-term goals to remind yourself where you're headed and how far you've come. Keep a food journal and check to see if your eating or drinking habits have changed recently. Maybe you're eating more carbohydrates or drinking sugared soda or just consuming more calories – any of these could have caused the plateau.

TIPS FOR GETTING OFF A PLATEAU

There are steps you can take to help break a plateau. See your bariatric surgery doctor and discuss a battle plan. To start with, make sure you're eating enough calories. It's been mentioned before but bears repeating: If you consistently eat too little (fewer than 600 calories a day), your body goes into starvation mode and protects itself by hanging onto every calorie and every pound. Also, make sure you're still eating your protein first when you sit down for meals, because protein is absorbed more slowly than other foods and gives you more energy to burn. Follow the protein with your vegetables and, if you still have room, a portion of complex carbohydrates. Do not finish everything on your plate!

Make sure you eat breakfast every day (small, protein-based); breakfast helps your metabolism wake up in the morning and stimulates healthy weight loss. If you don't break your fast in the morning, your body gets worried you're not going to feed it and hangs on to every calorie. My protein shake every morning has 172 calories, makes me feel full, and tastes amazing. Find something like that for yourself and stick with it.

If the plateau lasts for months rather than weeks, you can check in with your physician. Some procedures allow for fine tuning, like the LAP-BAND® or REALIZE™ Band, which can be tightened during an office visit so that weight loss starts up again. Your doctor may recommend you re-test your metabolic rate with a breathing test, and keep a food journal. You can also check in with the nurse practitioner or nutritionist for your surgical program, who may be able to help you tweak your eating plan. Prescription weight-loss medications can play a role, and I utilize them in our clinic for just this circumstance. You don't have to do this alone.

You can also add back in some of the techniques you may have been using earlier in your weight loss journey. Keep a food journal and make sure you're mindful of how much you're eating every day. You can make notes in your journal when you find you're hungry between meals about whether it seems to be head hunger or stomach hunger, meaning are you eating for emotional reasons, recreational reasons or because you're actually hungry?

Keep track of how often you're eating. Grazing, which means eating little bits throughout the day rather than sitting down for scheduled meals (or in addition to those meals), can slow weight loss considerably and even cause you to gain weight instead. Know what you're going to eat, how much and when.

Continue to weigh yourself at least twice a week, but remember the scale doesn't tell the whole story. Look at the other successes you've already achieved such as reduced joint pain, a decrease in the numbers or amounts of medications you're taking, you're not as short of breath, tying your shoes is easier – make your own list of successes. You can also attend a support group to get an idea of how other people have dealt with plateaus. Again, you don't have to do this alone.

Follow-up Appointments

You're not, actually, going to be out there all alone on your weight-loss journey after your procedure. Most surgeons and surgical practices recommend follow-up appointments after surgery for at least the first year, and many suggest at least annual visits after that for the rest of your life. Follow-up appointments can help you keep on track losing weight, answer your questions and concerns about your health after your procedure and keep you up to date on the latest information on weight loss.

Top 10 Roadblocks to Success after Weight-Loss Surgery... and Ways Around Them

1. THE "FIX ME" ATTITUDE.

This is usually seen in someone who is looking for an outside force to do the work of creating weight loss or someone who's going to say, "The surgery didn't work" as soon as the results aren't there. The downfall behind the idea is that the operation (or pills or shots or hypnosis or any other outside solution or force or magic) is going to do all the work. Of course not. You are. You've done all the work to get here. You're going to go on doing it because you're committed to success.

Don't get caught in this syndrome. Take ownership of your life and your health and your weight. Only you have the power to change and succeed. You've got the tools – go for the success.

2. CATCHING UP ON SLEEP IN CLASS.

This is the person who readily admits to not paying attention during the preoperative classes and instructions. Sometimes patients tell me they were just too excited about having the surgery to realize the information they were receiving was all that important. They didn't focus on the principles, didn't take advantage of the education and ultimately failed to do much of the homework.

Don't do this! Invest in the entire program and pay attention to every nugget of information that comes your way and every possible tip to help you achieve long-term weight loss. Details are important. Use every bit of education you can.

Make use of down time by listening to the AudioDiet series, "Success with Weight-Loss Surgery," in your car, your home, on planes, wherever you're going.

3. REVERTING TO BAD HABITS.

This is the person who walks right back into their old lives with their new body. Wednesday night pizza with the gang. Weekend ice cream outings with the kids. These are traditions, aren't they? And there are business lunches and all those networking events – won't it look strange if you don't have a roll or eat dessert? What about drinks after work where so many deals and connections are made? In short, people like this have made half of the commitment – they've made the changes to this point, but now they want to take the new body back to the old habits, consuming tons of useless calories in social situations because that's part of the routine.

You have to change the routine. And if that change sounds threatening and the routine sounds familiar and comforting, realize that the routine wasn't working. If it had been, you wouldn't have just had a weight-loss surgical procedure. Change your routines. Get better, healthier ones. Your buddies will live. You might even encourage them to make some healthy changes in their lives too – wouldn't that be something to be proud of?

4. TESTING THE LIMITS OF THE PROCEDURE.

This person expects that if the procedure was performed properly it should function well to completely limit excess calories, excess quantity or the wrong sort of food. So the patient tests the limits, as if the restriction of the procedure will physically stop the person from eating past the point where he or she should have already stopped. As if, in fact, the procedure was a physical presence, a policeman, maybe, standing in the room and preventing that person from going overboard. "If I can eat it," this thinking seems to also suggest, "then it must be all right. Otherwise the restriction wouldn't allow me to. Right?"

Wrong. It's still up to you. Minimally invasive outpatient weight-loss operations don't change the need for self-determination and responsibility for your own actions. Just follow the recommended advice and eat the smallest quantity you can eat and still feel satisfied after you leave the table. The surgery is a tool to help you lose weight and keep it off. Tools need us to actually wield them.

5. MALADAPTIVE EATING, OR "BUT THESE FOODS GO DOWN SO SMOOTHLY."

I've had patients tell me certain foods go down smoothly, so they gravitate toward them. Even with gastric bypass surgery and the hoped-for dumping syndrome (an intolerance to sweets that results in unpleasant physical symptoms and should be a deterrent) some people find certain sweets or milkshakes go down easily. Milkshakes, cheeses and chocolates are classic examples. This behavior just begs to defeat the weight-loss objective. Another example is high-calorie cashews or any other high-calorie snack you're tempted to nibble on all day long.

During your preoperative educational work, you probably met with a registered nutritionist or dietitian at least once. Hopefully you have utilized the information from those meetings and can still put it to work after your operation. Now that you've had your procedure, make it a point to continue learning everything you can about what you can and can't eat and what you can do to keep yourself from snacking. Success is often best achieved by planning for that success for all you're worth and leaving nothing to chance.

6. TRADING NEW PROBLEMS FOR OLD.

Alcohol with its seven calories per gram can sometimes go down quite smoothly and a person with an addictive psychological eating pattern might find solace in alcohol. Although it's not as common as some media reports might lead you to believe, there are some patients who turn to alcohol after weight-loss surgery. Whether this is truly a transfer of addiction or simply the fact that a certain percentage of us drink too much alcohol whether we've had a weight-loss surgical procedure or not, the fact is alcohol contains a lot of calories and leads to weight gain. It's also very damaging to the stomach lining when drunk excessively and can cause serious, life-threatening stomach ulcers.

Don't trade one solved problem for a new one, and get help if you think you are heading down this path.

7. NOT EXERCISING.

Whether due to injury, disability, pain, dislike or just a lack of commitment to regular exercise, lack of exercise can be one of the reasons for poor results following a weight-loss procedure. Remember, there's always some method available for getting physical every day, even for people with severe degenerative diseases or amputees or people with disabilities. Use small hand weights, try swimming and exercising in water.

Many creative methods exist for you to find ways to use your muscles and build lean body mass. It doesn't have to be hours every day. It does have to be consistent. Shoot for at least 30 minutes a day.

8. LETTING LOW SELF-ESTEEM SABOTAGE SUCCESS.

I've seen a number of people over the years fall into this category because they never internally accepted they were worthy of such profound change in their lives. The feeling some patients have of not being worthy may spring from depression or low self-esteem or in some cases the idea their spouse loves them because they're fat and they might even lose this spouse if they lose the weight.

A good therapist can help dispel these self-destructive thoughts and help you get back on track to weight loss and a healthier life. A key early step in successful weight loss is recognition of your own self-worth and a commitment to succeed.

9. *LETTING OTHERS SABOTAGE SUCCESS.*

Sometimes a spouse, friend or relative can actually work against your best interests when you're trying to lose weight. It might be because you used to be the eating buddy or because this person hates seeing you go off to exercise because you're not there spending time together or because it makes his or her own feelings of guilt flare up. It may be because you've always liked the little treats this person offers – high-calorie snacks, baked goods and other treats that derail weight loss. Most of us need only a little encouragement to do what's easiest: skip the workout, enjoy a movie on the couch, skip the protein shake and have a milkshake or dessert.

Saboteurs need to be identified and confronted immediately. If they really love you, they'll help you on your journey to a healthier life, not derail your efforts. If the behavior continues, you'll need to find some fortifications against it or limit your exposure to the saboteur. You've come too far to be derailed!

10. *MAGICAL THINKING.*

"If I lose the weight, something bad will happen." This is the person who, deep down, clings to the belief there must be something wrong with being skinny, which leads to an irrational belief that losing the weight will lead to negative consequences. This may be fear of a health problem, fear of problems with relationships because of a change in appearance or maybe a fear of change because nothing bad has happened yet, so why tempt fate? I've actually had morbidly obese individuals tell me they were afraid to lose the weight because they'd have excess skin, not realizing they already have the excess skin, and the excess weight, and the excess threats to health.

Listening to internal voices that make excess skin or any of these other perceived negatives sound important will lead to weight gain. Arm yourself with information and quiet those nay-saying voices. Excess skin, for example, is a great problem to have. Think of it: You've lost so much weight that instead of diabetes and blindness to worry about, your main focus is on excess skin rolls. Those can be removed if they really bother you. You will look and feel so much better at that lower weight that any excess skin will be an afterthought. And by the way, it's not excess skin. It's the same skin but without the fat.

Rewards

You've made a huge change in your life by undergoing an outpatient weight-loss procedure. You've made a lot of positive changes in your life just to get to the procedure itself, and afterward you've continued losing weight, eating healthy and working out. It's entirely possible you feel you deserve a reward for persevering, but if your rewards so far have been big meals with family and friends or special treats, you're suddenly faced with what to do to celebrate.

Some of the rewards of surgical weight-loss procedures are inherent in the procedure itself. Just think about what you have to look forward to now:

1. *PREVENTION AND FUTURE BETTER HEALTH.*

Even if you weren't experiencing complications from your health yet, there were health consequences in your future if you didn't take steps to lose weight and maintain that weight loss. That's why an entire surgical team agreed with your choice and went forward with you. The biggest reward you could have given yourself is a renewed future and a promise of greater longevity and health to go with it. Weight loss may not remedy or stave off every disease, but it does lessen risks of diabetes, high blood pressure, heart disease, sleep apnea, complications from high cholesterol, asthma and some forms of cancer. That in itself is a great reward.

2. NEW AND IMPROVED HEALTH.

If you were already suffering from a weight-related health condition, chances are preoperative weight loss has already had a beneficial effect on your health. Postoperatively, most conditions that weren't cured with preoperative weight loss will continue to improve, or even resolve completely. Asthma and sleep apnea are improved or resolved entirely with weight loss. Cardiac function and hypertension (high blood pressure) improve drastically following weight loss, as does fertility. Gastrointestinal reflux disease and diabetes can both be lessened or cured by laparoscopic weight-loss procedures and hepatic steatosis, a form of severe fatty deposits on the liver that can lead to problems with liver function and the immune system and is a leading cause of non-viral, non-alcohol-related cirrhosis, improves markedly after surgical bariatric procedures.

3. FREEDOM.

One airline advertises low fares by promising, "You are now free to move about the country." Well, you're now free to move around without the restrictions being overweight imposes on movement and without embarrassment when seats are too small or seatbelts not long enough. You'll feel better and be less fatigued at the end of the day without having to carry around the excess weight.

4. EXPECTATION OF LONGEVITY.

A 10-year study published in the New England Journal of Medicine that tracked men and women ages 50 to 71 concluded that excess body fat is a recognized harbinger of disease and early death, and that being above normal weight is associated with early death.[104] Congratulations! You've taken action to make sure you're not part of this statistic.

5. *POSITIVE FEEDBACK!*

Who doesn't like getting compliments? Take them! They're yours, and you've earned them.

REWARD YOURSELF

When you want to do something nice for yourself, and you're maintaining your weight and respecting your body and the changes you've made to it, and enjoying and the opportunities you've given yourself, try some of these rewards:

1. *BE NICE TO YOURSELF.*

A massage is a nice way to give your new body a healthy treat, and it feels wonderful, especially when you've been exercising.

2. *GET DRESSY.*

Once you find yourself in a new size, you're going to want new clothes that fit the new you. Enjoy dressing the new you – you've worked for the opportunity. If you're still losing and don't want to invest a lot of money in each size along the way but still want to celebrate each new, smaller size, check out shops in your area that carry stylish, pre-loved clothes at easy to swallow prices. Our center offers a clothing exchange for people moving down the size ladder. Your program may have similar options, or you can email for information at info@sassesurgical.com or communicate with us through the website or www.Facebook.com/Dr.Sasse.

3. *GET ACTIVE.*

If you've been missing hiking or skiing or fishing or playing golf or any of a myriad of activities that take you off the sofa and out of the house, what a wonderful way to reward yourself for your hard work – by doing something healthy as well as fun!

4. GET HAPPY.

Do you love to ice skate or read romance novels and never have the time? Is there a hobby you haven't given yourself time to pursue? Or is there something you collect? As you reach your weight-loss milestones, celebrate by giving yourself time to pursue activities that make you happy, or add to a collection. You're looking for healthy, zero-calorie ways to celebrate your successes.

5. GET OUT.

If travel's been too difficult because of your weight, you no longer have those restrictions. Start exploring those places you have always wanted to see.

Rebound Weight Gain And How To Avoid It

My hope for you is that after your weight-loss operation, you experience healthy weight loss and improved health. I hope you lose weight consistently, achieve your goal weight and live happily ever after. In many ways, your future weight and health are up to you. It's your responsibility to watch what you eat and include exercise in your life, but, that said, there is a phenomenon that can cause weight gain even after a successful operation. It also happens often when people go on diets, lose a significant or desired amount of weight and then go off the diet. I call it rebound weight gain.

Usually with rebound weight gain, once you start gaining weight again, more weight comes back than you lost in the first place. The undesirable phenomenon works something like this: If you've lost weight very quickly, you may have also lost nutrients and may have burned muscle mass as well as fat. The more lean muscle mass you have in your body, the better you can burn calories and create energy and lose or maintain your weight. But with a restrictive diet low in protein that includes rapid weight loss and little muscle use, instead of burning excess fat, you're burning too many nutrients, especially those easily utilized proteins that are supposed to build that lean body mass. That's the opposite of healthy, sustainable weight loss.

The more lean body mass you have, the easier it is to lose weight. So the more muscle mass you have, the better you're able to keep off fat, but in order to have muscle, you have to eat to maintain it, and that means going right back to eating nutritious foods and balancing your proteins, fats and complex carbohydrates. Even if you've had a successful weight-loss operation, balancing everything you eat to try and maintain muscle and continue to burn fat can feel like a tricky business.

If you don't maintain an adequate protein intake, the body begins to demand food to make up for the nutrients it was missing. Because your body was deprived of the powerful building blocks it needs, proteins and nutrients, it strives to make up the difference as fast as it can. As a result, you feel hungrier than ever before as the result of a biochemical process. Your muscles want to be fed. They're demanding it. And the more you feed them, the faster you regain the weight.

COMBAT REBOUND WEIGHT GAIN WITH A CALORIE-RESTRICTION PROGRAM AND PLENTY OF PROTEIN AND VITAMINS

One way to combat rebound weight gain is by using supervised calorie restriction, which is a different concept than dieting, and if used properly can lead you down the path to long-term weight-loss success. Our clinic has just such a plan and tests your metabolism before you start it. Sometimes we employ prescription medicines to help boost the weight loss.

The basic principles of calorie restriction are:

1. *THE RESTRICTION IS NOT PERMANENT.*

Calorie restriction isn't meant to be forever, which makes it a workable program for many people. There's something dreary about thinking you're going to eat from exactly the same program for the rest of your life. With calorie restriction, you're looking at a few weeks or a couple months. You set your timelines, state your goal weights and work to avoid rebound weight gain or short-circuit any rebound weight gain that has already started. The nice thing with this plan is that you can switch to it whenever you need a positive jolt of weight loss. You'll still be building muscle and burning fat, so at the end of your calorie-restriction period, you shouldn't experience rebound weight gain.

2. PROTECT LEAN BODY MASS.

Muscle mass helps you burn body fat. You can build lean muscle by exercising and eating protein. This doesn't mean you have to pump iron for hours every day, only that you need weight-bearing exercise every week and you need to make certain you're eating enough clean protein. Or you can drink your protein. Protein powder shakes can supply good, clean energy that, coupled with weight-bearing exercise, will help you build lean muscle and burn fat. Look for a good protein powder with a variety of amino acids and adequate vitamin content.

3. REDUCE CARBOHYDRATE CALORIES.

Carbs are fast, easy, satisfying and usually taste good. They also cause a spike in blood glucose and stimulate secretion of insulin and leptin into the bloodstream. That's what makes you feel good so fast. It's also what makes you hungry again so fast, because these nutrients are used so quickly. If you eat protein instead of carbs, you'll still raise blood sugar levels, but it will be a slower, less powerful rise, and fats don't stimulate a rise in blood sugar or insulin at all, which is why the majority of science-based weight-loss advice today includes some kind of carbohydrate restriction.

4. KNOW WHAT YOU WANT BEFORE YOU START.

Plan out how much weight you want to lose and understand that you're going to resume a healthy eating plan once you get there. The nice thing about calorie restriction is you can make these decisions for yourself rather than following a prescribed three-month program or swearing yourself to a lifestyle change and expecting you're going to make a lifelong change in your eating habits. Very likely you've already made several changes in your eating habits to accommodate weight loss and to adhere to dietary guidelines after your weight-loss procedure. Calorie restriction allows you to make a change for short duration in order to correct a problem, same as you'd eat soup when you're sick. You simply choose to follow a very simple eating plan (protein powder meal-replacement shakes) for as long as you need to in order to meet your current goals, then return to the new healthy eating patterns you adopted after your operation.

You probably followed a liquid protein meal-replacement diet before your procedure, but if you didn't, it's a great way to lose weight fast. By replacing every meal with a low-sugar, high-protein shake, you can easily drop your daily calorie intake to 800 or 1,000 calories a day. You can buy protein powder in bulk and mix your own shakes or buy them pre-mixed in single serving containers. By using only the protein powder meal-replacement bars and shakes you reduce your margin of error. There's no room to make bad food choices because there are no choices to make – you're going to be eating evenly spaced meals throughout the day that will consist of protein bars and shakes. It's fast, easy and effective.

Calorie-restriction programs are also used in the weeks before bariatric surgery. If using meal-replacement protein shakes and bars to lose weight sounds familiar, you might have followed a similar program before your procedure, and maybe it was called something else. Studies have shown that losing weight before a surgical weight-loss procedure makes for a safer operation, so chances are you've followed some plan like this before, and it wasn't all that bad last time, was it?

Calorie restriction works well in the short term to produce quick results in a defined timeframe. It's a good technique to use to jump-start weight loss if you've hit a plateau, and it works as both a transition to new, healthier eating habits and to induce rapid, healthy weight loss.

Jump-Start Your Weight Loss: Medically Supervised Rapid, Safe, Effective Weight Loss

Want to get the best results possible? Want to lose some significant pounds early on, and improve your energy level, health and positive attitude right away? Then you need to focus on specific and proven guides to healthy, immediate weight loss.

Jump-starting your weight loss after a minimally invasive weight-loss procedure actually begins before surgery. The preoperative diet puts you on a path to healthy weight loss through a calorie-restricted diet that is rich in proteins, vitamins and minerals. Over 90 percent of the people in my practice have lost significant pounds prior to ever arriving at the operating room. Accomplishing this feat isn't easy, but it is important and achievable with a structured plan. (For an example of the structured preop plan I use in my practice, see Appendix B).

Now, you've just had surgery, how do you jump-start your weight loss? The first task is to set a short-term goal. (Your long-term goal should be to reach a BMI of 25, or as close to it as possible, and stay there.)

Your short term goal may be, for example, something along the lines of lose 40 pounds in 90 days.

Losing 40 pounds in 90 days sounds too good to be true – it's nearly one pound every two days. It's fast, and it's an attractive idea, especially when losing those pounds will translate into improved glucose metabolism, decreased erosion of joints, improved breathing and cardiovascular function, and a better energy level. In fact, losing those 40 pounds may be just the ticket to enable you to feel good about exercising more and reaching that long-term goal of a BMI of 25.

Which doesn't mean you're not going to look skeptically at a claim like lose 40 pounds in 90 days. You might even be asking yourself Why would anyone want to do this? and Is this healthy?

Those are both good questions. And the answers to those questions are: *For improved health* and *Yes*. Using scientific-based and evidence-based medicine with respect to weight loss, you can lose 40 pounds in 90 days safely – and keep it off long-term.

ALL CARROTS, ALL THE TIME – NO THANKS

There is compelling medical data supporting the benefits of starting a serious multidisciplinary, comprehensive medical weight loss program to lose weight. That's all well and good – but now what?

The key behind this kind of rapid weight loss is to keep it healthy. And there are ways to do this. But are there ways to lose this kind of weight and do it in an unhealthy manner?

Of course there are. And we've probably all been guilty of some version of unhealthy rapid weight loss at one time or another. Many fad diets and get-thin-quick schemes focus on calorie restriction, which is at heart the way to lose weight. The only formula that actually works for weight loss is to take in fewer calories than you expend, which is probably going to mean restricting calories and increasing physical activity.

But when restricting calories for weight loss means eating only one food (all carrots, all the time, as many as you want, because realistically, how many carrots does anyone want?) or restricting an entire category of foods along with very low calorie intake, there may be temporary weight loss, but it's not the healthy way to get there. If you've ever tried one of these diets (and many, many of us have) you've probably found at the end of the diet that you experienced more hunger and a resulting rebound weight gain that can actually start the same day the diet stops. Surgery definitely changes the equation and markedly reduces hunger, but we don't want to invite extra hunger from the body by using an unsound diet technique.

So how do you lose 40 pounds in 90 days the healthy way? By losing the weight while preserving the lean body mass. This means burning the excess fat in your body, not the lean muscle. Starvation diets and diets that restrict calorie consumption severely (and possibly to one or two foods) tend to savage the lean muscle mass in the body rather than burning fat, a type of cannibalization of the body by the body. While it's possible to experience a sense of euphoria while losing weight this way, it is neither healthy nor likely to be as successful long term.

40 Pounds in 90 Days – The Healthy Way

In order to burn fat instead of lean body mass it's necessary to utilize a diet that is focused on adequate protein and nutrient uptake. What that means is you need to eat enough of the right kinds of food to feed your muscles. At the same time, you need to utilize those muscles during the weight loss period in order to signal to the body with your own hormonal and biochemical reactions that the muscle is to be utilized and sustained during this period of weight loss. This way instead of breaking down muscle, you'll break down fat and the result will be greater preservation of lean body mass.

It's a pretty simple formula, really. It just means we need to preserve the maximum amount of protein or lean body mass and burn the maximal amount of fat or adipose in our bodies.

One last note before we get to the How To – is everyone going to lose 40 pounds in 90 days? No. Different body types starting at different weights will lose different percentages at different rates. Some people will lose more than 40 pounds, especially after Sleeve and Bypass procedures. Other variables come into play as well – the more you cheat, the more you eat, the less you exercise – the less you'll lose. The more you follow the program, the more you're apt to lose. It's up to you.

How To

Remember that formula for weight loss? Take in fewer calories than you expend. That's the basis for losing 40 pounds in 90 days. The first step on this weight loss journey is to create a calorie deficit. What that means is you're going to eat fewer calories than you burn during the day.

So let's talk about calorie intake and calorie output. Calorie intake describes the net amount of calories (or nutrient energy) you receive from food and drink in a 24-hour period. Calorie output is the calories (or energy) you burn throughout the day, whether you're working on a computer or running a marathon. As long as your calorie output – the calories you burn – is greater than your calorie intake – the amount you eat – you will lose weight.

Basically we burn calories all the time. Sitting and doing nothing, watching television or working on a computer, you're still burning calories. Simply by being alive you're burning calories. You're just not burning enough calories.

And chances are many of us are consuming too many calories, not just more calories than we burn, but too many altogether. An average fast food lunch can run anywhere from 1,500 to 2,000 calories. When you figure the average person needs a ballpark number of 2,500 calories daily (this figure may be higher for men, lower for women, and depends on body mass) you can see that many of us get more calories than we can burn in a day.

So the answer to the How To question is to create an energy deficit. If your normal daily intake is around 2,500 calories, and that's what you function on, and you drop that to 2,000 calories – which isn't that difficult – you'll lose an average of one pound a week. Okay, maybe that doesn't sound earth shattering, but if you multiply one pound a week times 52 weeks in a year, you've just lost over 50 pounds, simply by reducing your calories by 500 a day.

To be maximally successful in this early postoperative period, I recommend two things: one, test your body's resting metabolic rate (RMR), and two, concentrate on meal replacement shakes.

In most medically supervised weight-loss programs you're going to sit down with your doctor and figure out how to create a calorie deficit by taking the amount of calories you normally take in (call it a ballpark figure of 2,500 daily) and figuring out how much weight you want to lose over what period of time, then restricting calories so that you burn enough calories every day to make that goals.

It's even better if you can eliminate the guesswork. The RMR test is one in which the patient breathes in and out through a mouthpiece attached to a hose and a machine that carefully records the exchange of oxygen for carbon dioxide. The result is a very accurate calculation of the daily calories the body burns at rest, the resting metabolic rate. It varies a good deal from person to person, based on their genetic makeup and their existing muscle mass. But after this test is done, a calorie target can be precisely calculated, and individualized, to map out the path to 40 pounds lost in 90 days.

If you're taking in 2,500 calories a day and restrict your diet by 500 calories a day, you'll lose approximately 12 pounds in 90 days. Which is a positive result, but not what we're looking for. In order to lose 40 pounds in 90 days, you'd need to take some 1,500 calories out of your diet so your daily intake is somewhere between 800 and 1,000 calories.

This is a significant restriction of calories, and it is made markedly easier by the surgery that reduces hunger and restricts the stomach. But it's important to remember that it takes focus and persistence to stay on the calorie target path, since it would be possible to easily blow it one day just at breakfast.

MEAL REPLACEMENT BARS AND SHAKES

To achieve safe, effective weight loss in a short time right after surgery, I recommend focusing principally on meal replacement shakes for such rapid weight loss. Protein-based shakes should run about 180 calories and contain a full complement of vitamins and minerals. The big advantage of centering your diet on these shakes is that you can have highly nutritious meals with little difficulty digesting them easily after surgery. The best of them will produce some good sense of satiety and taste good. Five of these per day results in 900 calories, a very good place to be for significant weight loss.

One reason for using the replacement meals is the amount of protein in them. When you're losing weight quickly, you definitely want to keep up your protein intake. Research supports the idea that more than 100 grams of protein a day is beneficial during rapid weight loss in order to maintain lean body mass while losing adipose (fat).

A second reason to focus on the shakes is that your stomach may need some time to heal and adjust after surgery. Many regular foods may disagree with your new stomach, causing unpleasant side effects like nausea, so it is best to make a slow transition from liquids to solids anyway. Just extending that transition for a longer time to stay focused on jump-starting your weight loss with protein shakes proves to be easy on the tummy and great for the weight loss.

And finally, another benefit is the simplicity of the replacement meals. Sure, you could try to lose the weight on 800 or 1000 calories a day of food, but we've found planning the meals to stay in that low calorie range is challenging at best, and very few of us are able to create a diet plan day by day, week by week, and stick to it for 90 days while creating the energy deficit we want and keeping the protein levels up. As much as we'd like to believe where there's a will there's a way, this is definitely the hard way and most people fail when they try it. Removing choices and making the whole thing simple by going with the replacement shakes is the successful route.

MEDICATIONS: SOME NEW ONES

I don't generally prescribe weight-loss medications after weight-loss surgery, but there are some instances in which I do. What is important is to know that there are effective medications that can help by modestly suppressing appetite and augmenting weight loss when a person is struggling. In my experience, at least

90 percent of patients after Sleeve Gastrectomy and Gastric Bypass experience profound appetite suppression and don't need any pharmaceutical help, especially in the first year. But a few people don't gain the benefit of such profound appetite suppression – modern science has yet to figure out why these outliers are wired differently – and they may benefit from a prescription drug if they are struggling with weight loss.

Two new medications were approved by the FDA in 2012, and each successfully led to significant, modest weight loss in prospective, randomized controlled trials lasting two years. Called Belviq and Qsymia, these drugs represent the best pharmaceutical treatments available, and some bariatric surgeons and physicians will employ them, as we do, in specific cases to augment weight loss. Phentermine, a cheaper, and also modestly effective appetite suppressant, can be a helpful adjunct for some people who are struggling with persistent hunger despite the surgery.

GET MOVING

Fitness and exercise are a part of any successful weight loss program. You might wonder how you're going to embark on a workout routine when you're only taking in 800 or 1,000 calories a day.

That's where the exercise coach comes in. Exercise is vital to maintaining that all-important lean body mass. "Use it or lose it" definitely applies to your muscles during weight loss. An exercise coach can help sharpen your focus and recommend specific exercises that work around injuries and emphasize your strengths. But even a simple workout plan that emphasizes daily walking will go a long way to helping you achieve your goals. In short, I tell each and every patient to make a commitment to walk 60 to 90 minutes a day, every day. In the National Weight Control Registry Database, this exact regimen was what distinguished those who kept their weight off for years, compared to those who regained.

I go one step further and ask for a commitment to a goal: running or walking in an organized event such as a local 5K, 10K or even a half marathon.

But Is It Safe?

There are some risks associated with a low calorie diet, but they're very few. We've been discussing all along that this would be a post-surgical, physician-supervised weight-loss program, and having a doctor or physician's assistant or nurse that you're scheduled to see periodically throughout the 90 days is a definite safeguard.

Past that, the risks are smaller than the reward. The biggest concern would be with people who have a health condition such as kidney damage or underlying renal insufficiency. Someone with kidney function issues may require adjustments to the protein in the diet. Protein is processed through the kidneys which might get overloaded and not be able to handle the load.

But for people with normal kidney function, an 800 to 1,000 calorie a day physician-supervised weight-loss program can lead to the successful loss of 40 pounds in 90 days and the health benefits far outweigh the risks. Studies have shown that as soon as people start losing weight, they start seeing health benefits. Losing as little as 10, 20 or 30 pounds can result in a drop in blood pressure and cholesterol levels and already there is a decreased risk for adverse health risks from heart attacks to other coronary events.

It may be challenging, but it's worth it.

Keep Your Eye on the Prize

Forty pounds in 90 days is fast weight loss. Many of my patients lose over 10 pounds before surgery, and then 40 more in the first 90 days. That's a whopping 50 pounds in three months, and it can be life-changing. That doesn't mean that some weeks can't start feeling like forever. When you find yourself tempted to cheat, or even quit, and you're looking for some inspiration, go back and look at everything you've accomplished so far and what you want to accomplish from here.

Go back and look at your goals, especially if you've written them down. These are the deeper reasons you chose to lose weight. Post a new sign on that bathroom mirror reminding yourself that you are on a mission to achieve something great.

Jump-starting your weight loss, losing 40 pounds in 90 days may sound miraculous or impossible but it's neither. After surgery, you are newly empowered with a stomach that is actually suppressing appetite and helping you to achieve this goal, rather than the other way around. With a physician-supervised weight-loss program, an eating program that allows no more than 800 to 1,000 calories a day, and the addition of physical exercise in your daily life, you can change your life, your health and your energy level in 90 days and keep it off long-term. It's a short-term investment that can make all the difference in the world.

Keeping It Off Forever

Now for the most exciting and most challenging part of your journey: Keeping the weight off for a lifetime. What's the secret?

You've gone through so much hard work in order to have the operation – qualifying for it, paying for it, getting time off for it – there are hundreds of things you've had to do and you've learned it wasn't as easy as requesting the procedure. Then you underwent the actual procedure and took time off to recover, possibly battled through complications and problems postoperatively, gained strength and energy, healed up, got over the soreness and regained your endurance – very likely that was challenging, too. And after that you set your sights on the next phases, the early period after surgery, the first month, the first three months and the first year, setting goals for each phase, marshaling your strength, maintaining your focus and determination, and achieving your goals. All of this took hard work and perseverance. So how could I possibly be saying that the last part of your journey is the most challenging yet?

I say it because now that you've made your way through those battles, I know you're ready for the final challenge, the most difficult and challenging battle of all: Keeping it off forever.

It's possible that keeping the weight off is considered so challenging because of the way it's perceived, but it's true that keeping it off is a phase of your weight loss that has no limits. There is no endpoint. It's not a finite task you can accomplish then breathe a sigh of relief and pump a fist in the air. It is an unending burden, when we phrase it that way, and who wants an unending burden?

NOT UNENDING HARDSHIP, BUT MANY SMALL GOALS YOU CAN ACCOMPLISH AND CELEBRATE

Before you get discouraged by the concept of forever or start thinking too much about lifelong deprivation and avoidance of anything that tastes good, take a minute to rethink the way you look at the future.

You've come so far and accomplished so much. What I'm talking about here is a chance to extend that great sense of accomplishment into the future.

Overall goals can be met with smaller, more easily achieved goals along the way, like weighing less than 200 pounds by a certain date, then less than 175 and so on as you move closer to your goal weight. In each case, there is a definable milestone ahead and the process of meeting goals becomes a matter of keeping your eye on the prize, working toward that goal and achieving it. So before you get fuzzy-eyed looking off into the blue, uncertain future, look at what lies just in front of you. What's the next goal for you? Where's the next milestone?

FORGET THE LONG-TERM FUTURE – LET'S FOCUS ON THE NEXT GOAL

I know – this isn't the advice you're used to hearing. A lot of attention is placed on long-term goals in life, those goals pertaining to careers and homes, how much money you want to make, where you want to live, who you want to be. Without setting these goals, you might never achieve them. But without breaking them down to manageable short-term goals, you might become overwhelmed by them.

Probably you did the same thing with your preoperative weight-loss, breaking down the overall weight-loss goal into manageable weight-loss chunks, losing a percentage of weight by each goal date. Now I want you to focus on short-term weight and health goals again, because just like other long-term goals, without short-term, manageable milestones and health goals it's much more difficult to maintain the approaches and behaviors that have gotten you this far.

So let's break down this long-term future into some short-term goals. I recommend a six-month goal. At this stage of the game, a six-month goal might be for you to weigh in six months from now at exactly the same weight or below by two to five pounds. If the next six months involves the winter holiday season, then such a goal is truly a challenge. Simply maintaining your weight through the holidays is a daunting challenge that's worth the energy and effort – and it's cause for considerable celebration when you achieve it. On the other hand, if your weight has not dropped to where you would like it to be, then your six-month goal needs to be more aggressive. If you want to lose 20 pounds over the next six months, you need to do a mental calculation and figure out how many pounds you need to lose every week or every month to achieve your goal.

And once you've reached your six-month goal, you're allowed a celebration, a reward (not food!). But then, guess what? Part of the celebration of achieving your goal is – that's right – setting a new goal. It's time to set another six-month goal.

In addition to these six-month goals you're setting for midyear and end-of-year, it can be helpful to take a look at the calendar and set some additional goals for your weight and your health. This is the time to make use of your own personal vanity for your advantage. By this I mean that while it's unhealthy to live your life focusing on what anyone else thinks about you, in this one instance it's a helpful, motivating tool for you to use public occasions and family events as a motivating tool to keep you on your weight-loss path.

Let me give you an example. Aunt Marge is getting married in September. Let's say it's now February and you are looking for reasons to maintain your weight-loss mission and keep up your motivation. Why not make use of Marge's wedding and the plans for seeing a lot of family members who remember you as being very overweight as a tool to keep yourself motivated?

Then look ahead at the calendar to other occasions. Think of other times, places or events where you'll be meeting new people, seeing old friends, visiting family members, making a speech, or any other appearance that involves interaction with others. Think back to how you felt at such events when you were more overweight. Think back to how self-conscious you felt, how much time you spent wondering what people were thinking about as they looked at you. Think about what it felt like both emotionally and physically to go to these events and interact with all these people. Now stop and think about attending these same events now that you have accomplished so much. Think about what it will feel like to visit with these same folks who probably never accomplished anything as difficult as losing the weight you have. Imagine how good it will feel to look these people in the eyes and enjoy their company rather than worrying about what they're thinking. Imagine how good it will feel to tell them about your journey and what you've accomplished (if you choose to do so).

There may be people who want to ask you how you managed to lose the weight and keep it off, and you may take pride in telling them about the hard work that you've done. And whether or not you tell anyone about your challenges and goals, you'll feel better about the experience of attending the event at a healthier weight and with a sense of achievement. So spend a few minutes and visualize that date. Visualize Aunt Marge's wedding and all the people you will meet, run into, talk to and visit with. Then use those images to motivate yourself for this next short-term goal.

There's no limit to short-term goals. Each time you reach one, look ahead to the next. Take time to celebrate your accomplishments but always be looking at what you can accomplish next.

Short-Term Goals Become Long-Term Accomplishments

Focusing on short- and mid-term goals is one very important strategy for maintaining your focus and discipline in your weight-loss journey. As you can tell by now, the journey doesn't end, but rather changes along the road. You never reach a place where you can forget about your weight, start eating anything you want, stop exercising and expect you'll maintain a healthy weight.

You've learned what it takes to succeed at losing weight. By doing so, you've joined the elite company of people who have accomplished something very difficult and very worthwhile in their lives. Now it's time to be certain that you're maintaining conditions in your life that will allow you to continue this success. What can you do to maintain this success for the long term?

You Don't Have to Go It Alone

If the future looks a little intimidating as you start your new life, remember, while you may be ultimately responsible for your own weight-loss success, you can still enlist the aid of others as you go.

For starters, you'll probably have routine visits with your bariatric surgeon's practice. Most of the best practices recommend you stay in touch with the surgeon for the long term. I strongly suggest you continue follow-up appointments every few months for the first year, then at least semi-annually thereafter, forever.

There are a number of good reasons for return visits to your surgeon or surgeon's practice, all aimed at benefiting you as a patient in achieving your long-term goals. As new findings are released in the field of bariatric medicine and weight loss, your surgeon's office can keep you up to date with information that can make your weight loss or weight maintenance easier or give you suggestions when you're facing challenges. And if there are medical complications or concerns along the way, your bariatric surgeon's practice is well versed in solving what may seem mysterious to your primary care physician.

From the medical standpoint, collecting data on how patients are doing after surgery for the next several years helps us have an accurate weight record. It also allows us to gain accurate information on that patient's health, information that helps us become better as a practice and deliver better care to others in the future.

BELIEVE IN YOURSELF

You've already accomplished so much. You already know this, but it bears repeating: No one has done this but you. You are the sole person who has achieved all of this success and no one can continue the success except you. No program or friend or advisor will do it for you. Many people and resources can help, but you are the one who is going to make it happen.

To do this, you must believe in yourself. You must believe you're worth it. You must continue to believe that you're deserving of the good health and compliments, rewards, jobs, money, romantic opportunities and good feelings that come along with living at a healthier weight. You deserve all this and more.

QUIET THE VOICES OF NEGATIVISM

In believing in yourself, you must also silence the voices of negativism. You must set aside all those objections that tell you things like, "My skin looks too wrinkly when I lose weight," or "Some of my friends won't like me as much if I am no longer the fat person," or "My spouse may get angry with me if I start getting more attention from the opposite sex." These are all voices of negativism in one form or another. They're each possible reasons to abandon the cause, excuses to give up on the program of losing weight and becoming healthier. They emanate from your conscious and from your subconscious mind and they all have one thing in common: They must be ignored.

Your goals of losing weight are far too important to be derailed by any of these objections. Placed within the context of your entire life, almost nothing you can do will have as positive an impact on your life, on your health, on your quality of life and your longevity, than losing this weight as you have set out to do. What possible objections could justify abandoning such an important goal? Take stock of those voices of negativism and learn to ignore them. Your future depends on it.

Tell me about your success on Facebook.
*Connect at **www.facebook.com/drsasse**.*

Appendix A

Weight–Loss Surgery Graphs and Statistics

The following graph illustrates some early results of outpatient weight-loss surgery.

Sleeve Gastrectomy: percent excess body weight lost

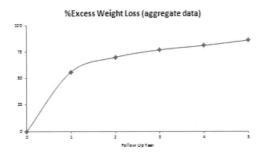

%Excess Weight Loss (aggregate data)

Appendix B

Recipes for Success

I developed and designed a step-by-step meal plan to help patients ease into their liquid diets and achieve the recommended weight loss prior to surgery. Many people ask why preoperative weight loss is necessary: the simple answer is that it makes the surgical procedure safer. A 10 percent loss of excess body weight is a healthier choice for surgery.

The meal plan below includes the liquid diet. The purpose of the liquid diet is to reduce the size of the liver, reduce abdominal fat and make the surgery safer. If the patient's body mass index (BMI) is greater than 50, the patient may need to follow the liquid diet phase of this plan for more than four weeks, as directed by a surgeon.

I recommend a preoperative meal plan that begins as soon as you know you are going to have a weight-loss procedure. You have decided to change your life for the better, so seize the day! Use that motivation to start losing pounds and cutting carbohydrate calories now. This diet will result in weight loss (and how nice to know you will never see these pounds again), and also liver shrinkage – both lead to improved patient safety during surgery.

PREOPERATIVE MEAL PLAN

This preoperative diet plan has been specifically designed to help you lose weight more easily and achieve your required weight loss before surgery. By achieving the requested weight loss before your operation, your surgical procedure should be safer and your body healthier for the surgery.

Note: If you are diabetic, have renal insufficiency or cardiac health issues, please call your primary care provider for suggestions on medication adjustments and clearance to begin the preoperative diet. If you have questions, you should talk with your surgeon or the dietitian in your program.

PHASE 1 GUIDELINES

Phase 1 can be started at any point but you should start at least four weeks before surgery or at least six weeks before surgery if your BMI is greater than 50.

Phase 1 can be followed for several weeks, but allow yourself enough time to stay in Phase 1 for at least a week.

Breakfast	2 scoops of protein powder with 8 ounces of water and ice
Snack	Choose from the list provided below
Lunch	Frozen/microwaveable entrée with 300 calories or fewer, 1 to 2 cups veggies
Snack	Choose from the list provided below
Dinner	Frozen/microwaveable entrée with 300 calories or fewer, 1 to 2 cups veggies
Snack	1 scoop protein powder with 4 ounces water and ice

PHASE 2 GUIDELINES

Phase 2 should be started at least three weeks prior to surgery, or at least five weeks prior to surgery if your BMI is greater than 50.

Phase 2 should be followed for at least one week.

Breakfast	2 scoops protein powder with 8 ounces water and ice
Snack	Choose from the list provided below
Lunch	2 scoops protein powder with 8 ounces water and ice, 1 to 2 cups veggies
Snack	Choose from the list provided below
Dinner	Frozen/microwaveable entrée with 300 calories or fewer, 1 to 2 cups veggies
Snack	2 scoops protein powder with 8 ounces water and ice

PHASE 1 AND 2 SNACK LIST

This list provides allowed snacks for Phases 1 and 2 of your preoperative diet. These items should be eaten at the specified time on the meal plan. No substitutions can be made to this list.

1 medium apple
1 small banana
1 cup any berries
1/2 small cantaloupe
2 cups honeydew melon cubes
2 cups watermelon cubes
1 medium nectarine, peach or orange
1 medium pear
1 hard-boiled egg
1 stick of string cheese
1/2 cup 1 percent cottage cheese
6 oz plain yogurt (add Stevia, Splenda)
10 almonds or 7 walnut halves
1 stick of jerky

GENERAL GUIDELINES FOR THE PREOP DIET

Begin this preop diet at least four weeks before surgery. If your BMI is greater than 50, you will need to begin at least six weeks prior to surgery.

Please follow the meal plans as written. The meal plans have been designed to provide you with an eating pattern to help you start a habit of regular eating after surgery, eliminate grazing and make surgery safer. No substitutions are allowed.

Most microwave meals are higher in sodium. Because the other food choices on the plan are low sodium foods, this meal plan averages sodium intake below the recommended 2300 mg sodium per day.

Take a multi vitamin/mineral supplement daily to get in the habit (for after surgery).

Eat at scheduled meal and snack times. After surgery, you will be eating 5 to 6 times per day.

A few tips:

Eat slowly. Aim for 20 to 30 minutes per meal.

Practice chewing each bite 20 to 30 times.

Practice separating drinking and eating.

Mix your powdered shake mix with water only (ice and blender ok!). DO NOT add fruit to your shakes. It is okay to add sugar-free flavorings such as cooking extracts, sugar-free flavored syrups and cold coffee.

Drink 64 oz of zero or low calorie liquids daily in addition to your shakes. Examples include:

Water
Crystal Light
Propel
Vitamin Zero Water
Sobe Lean

Sugar-free Kool-Aid
Tea with sugar substitute
Coffee with sugar substitute, 1 TBSP or less of creamer/milk
Broth (helps take away hunger)

PHASE 3 GUIDELINES

Phase 3 should be started at least two weeks prior to surgery or at least four weeks before surgery if your BMI is greater than 50. This is the mainly liquids phase of the meal plan. You may continue to eat the vegetables with lunch and dinner. You do not need to take a multivitamin on this phase.

Breakfast	2 scoops protein powder with 8 oz water and ice
Snack	1 scoop protein powder with 4 oz water and ice
Lunch	2 scoops protein powder with 8 oz water and ice and 1 to 2 cups of veggies
Snack	1 scoop protein powder with 4 oz water and ice
Dinner	2 scoops protein powder with 8 oz water and ice and 1 to 2 cups of veggies
Snack	2 scoops protein powder with 8 oz water and ice

VEGETABLE LIST, LUNCH AND DINNER

For all phases, add one to two cups of vegetables from the list below to your lunches and dinners. Vegetables may be eaten raw, as a salad, as a vegetable soup, or cooked in many ways. Do not add any oils, sauces, butter, salad dressings or condiments such as cheese or bacon bits or ketchup.

You can use freely anything from this list: flavored vinegars, lemon juice, salt, herbs, spices, hot sauce, garlic, jalapenos, soy sauce and mustard. You may use Pam-type spray to cook with.

A word of caution! If you are unaccustomed to eating raw vegetables, you may want to limit your intake to one cup daily to prevent problems with gas.

Vegetables allowed on this meal plan include:

Crookneck or Zucchini Squash
Green Beans
Green, Red, Yellow, Orange Sweet Peppers
Lettuce (up to 4 cups per day)
Mushrooms
Onion
Radishes
Spinach (if raw, up to 4 cups per day)
Other leafy greens
Tomatoes
Brussels sprouts
Bean sprouts
Bok Choy
Asparagus
Broccoli
Cabbage
Carrots
Cauliflower
Cucumber
Celery

Additional Snack Options, every phase (limit to 2 servings per day)

1 cup sugar-free JELL-O®, sugar-free popsicle, 6 oz V8 or tomato juice

AMAZING SHAKE RECIPES

For everyone who is utilizing medically recommended shakes as liquid meal-replacement, these recipes can provide a wonderful resource. For who among us can truly enjoy the same "Chocolate" flavored shake over and over again? Variety is the spice of life.

Medical literature shows clear evidence that meal-replacement shakes serve an important and highly effective role in weight-loss programs. A proper shake contains the protein and nutrients necessary in order to control the appetite while allowing the user to lose weight in a healthy way. By following some of the recipes listed below, you'll find you don't have to sacrifice flavor and variety to stick with the meal-replacement shakes and go the distance with your diet.

What these recipes accomplish is a magnificent service – adding flavor and variety to the hard work of achieving a weight-loss goal. Enjoy every one of these recipes, and may they bring you even greater success on your weight-loss journey.

The iMetabolic Perfect Meal high protein meal-replacement powder consists of whey protein isolate together with vitamins and minerals. It has no lactose, gluten or artificial sweeteners. Of course, there are a variety of protein powders and pre-mixed liquid protein meal-replacement shakes on the market. Look for those that offer low calorie counts, low carbohydrates and high protein content.

Following are just a few of the wonderful recipes available for everyone drinking protein shakes. Each recipe creates one serving. For each of the following recipes, place cold water and ice into blender, followed by protein powder and other ingredients. Blend for 45 to 60 seconds. Serve chilled.

Creamy Iced Mocha

2	scoops chocolate flavored protein powder
1	cup ice
4	ounces cold water
1	teaspoon sugar-free chocolate syrup
¼	teaspoon decaffeinated instant coffee

Banana Orange Dream

Banana and orange, blended to dreamy perfection.

2	scoops banana flavored protein powder
1	cup ice
4	ounces cold water
¼	teaspoon sugar-free orange gelatin powder
¼	teaspoon vanilla extract

Chocolate Decadence

2	scoops chocolate flavored protein powder
1	cup ice
4	ounces cold water
1	teaspoon sugar-free chocolate syrup
¼	teaspoon butter extract

Cinnamon Meow Roll

2	scoops vanilla protein powder
1	cup ice
4	ounces cold water
1	teaspoon butter extract

cinnamon to taste

Chocolate Covered Cherries

2	scoops chocolate protein powder
1	cup ice
4	ounces cold water
¼	teaspoon sugar-free cherry gelatin powder

Strawberry Cheesecake

2	scoops strawberry protein powder
1	cup ice
4	ounces cold water
¼	teaspoon almond extract
¼	teaspoon butter extract

Caribbean Smoothie

2	scoops orange protein powder
1	cup ice
4	ounces cold water
¼	teaspoon banana extract
¼	teaspoon coconut extract
¼	teaspoon sugar-free strawberry-kiwi gelatin powder

Banana Nut Bread

2	scoops banana protein powder
1	cup ice
4	ounces cold water
¼	teaspoon almond extract
¼	teaspoon vanilla extract

cinnamon to taste

You can also create your own amazing shake recipes. Start with a base of two scoops of protein powder from the base group, add one (or more) flavors from the second group, and spice it up with your favorite flavors from the third group.

Base protein powders – start here with two scoops of one of the following:
Chocolate protein powder
Vanilla protein powder
Strawberry protein powder
Orange protein powder
Banana protein powder

Flavors (add one – or more!)
Sugar-free flavored gelatin powder
Cooking extracts
Sugar-free Italian syrup
Decaffeinated instant coffee
Crystal Light

Spice it up! – add to taste:
Cinnamon
Nutmeg
Apple Pie spice
Pumpkin Pie spice
Ginger
Anise
Allspice

Appendix C

Which Band is Right for You?

With two medical device companies now each offering a laparoscopic adjustable gastric band in the U.S., which band should you choose?

Initially only one laparoscopic adjustable gastric band was available in the United States, the LAP-BAND®. The LAP-BAND®, now sold by Allergan, Inc., was developed by the Inamed Corporation, an American company based in Southern California. After many years of testing, and large clinical trials outside the U.S., the LAP-BAND® came to America in 2000, where its popularity has grown immensely as an effective, minimally invasive outpatient weight-loss surgical option. Significantly, in 2011, the FDA expanded the approved indication for the LAP-BAND® by allowing it to be used for patients with a BMI as low as 30 who have an obesity-related health condition.

For many years, a rival band known as the "Swedish adjustable gastric band" had been in use in other parts of the world, especially Europe. The Swedish band was acquired by Johnson & Johnson Services, Inc., and its surgical instrument division, Ethicon, Inc. In 2007, the Ethicon band was granted approval for sale in the United States, so now you have a choice.

The Ethicon band has since been renamed the REALIZE™ Band. The REALIZE™ Band is now competing head-to-head with the LAP-BAND® after a six-year head start in the United States by Allergan's product. This new competition has lead to many questions among our patients:

♦ Is there a difference between the two bands?

♦ Is one better than the other?

♦ Will surgeons offer both bands or just one?

Like other experienced U.S. bariatric surgeons, I have a significant multiyear experience with both the LAP-BAND® and the REALIZE™ Band. I am well-versed on the published literature of the two medical products.

What are the differences between these bands, and are they significant? To begin with, both bands share a great many features in common:

♦ Both are meant to be wrapped around the upper part of the stomach in what is essentially the identical position.

♦ Both have an interior balloon that lies in direct contact with the stomach, and it can be filled with saline.

♦ Both have tubing that connects to an access port that is placed in the deep subcutaneous abdominal wall tissue at the level of the muscles or fascia.

♦ Both bands act as "restrictive" procedures that lead to weight loss by restricting the stomach pouch and creating fullness and satiety.

♦ Both bands have more than 15 years of high-quality data supporting them and demonstrating effectiveness in weight loss and resulting health improvement.

And so both bands are remarkably similar in their design and in the way they work.

However, the REALIZE™ Band uses a slightly different design in the internal balloon. The REALIZE™ has one size and one size only. It has had very little change in its basic design for 15 years. The balloon is considered a low pressure balloon and one that accommodates a volume of up to 10 cc of saline.

The LAP-BAND® by Allergan has undergone several design changes and currently is offered in two different sizes: the "AP Standard" size and the "AP Large" size. Some surgeons find that with very large patients, and especially large men with more fatty tissue around the upper stomach, the AP Large band is easier to place and more effective. Over the years, the Allergan LAP-BAND® has gradually evolved to a low-pressure, larger balloon size that accommodates more volume, in the range of 10 to 14 cc of saline. Both AP bands involve an internal balloon system that is in contact all around the stomach, where it is placed. With prior designs of the LAP-BAND®, the balloon did not reach all the way around, and this appeared to be related to a somewhat higher rate of erosion.

Another feature that distinguishes the REALIZE™ Band is an access port that involves a mechanism to secure the port to the abdominal fascia and muscle tissue with some self-applying titanium hooks instead of hand-sewn stitches. Ethicon believes that this system will allow an easier placement of the port and will be favored by surgeons because of its convenience. Some surgeons believe this system leads to slightly less discomfort at the port site, some surgeons believe it leads to slightly more discomfort for the patient, but either way, port site discomfort is an uncommon complaint in either band.

In my opinion, the currently available designs of both the REALIZE™ and the LAP-BAND® offer many very similar features, namely the circumferential 360-degree balloon and a very low risk of serious complications, of erosion or slippage. It is available to many millions more patients because of the expanded FDA approval of the LAP-BAND® to lower BMI individuals. Time will tell whether there are any important differences in outcomes, weight-loss results or the risk of complications over time. I believe that both of these bands share much in common, but our practice, like the majority of others in the U.S., has gravitated toward the newer AP design LAP-BAND® primarily because of the appeal of the circumferential balloon design and the perception that patients are losing weight more successfully with it.

What is clear is that each company will continue to market its band with great energy and effectiveness. It is very likely that direct consumer marketing will lead to patients requesting a specific band by name. It is also likely that individual surgeons will prefer one band over another because of differences in pricing or ease of placement or historical familiarity. It is also the case, as with any instrument or device in the medical industry, that hospitals and surgery centers will face intense pressure to utilize only one brand of band. This pressure occurs because the manufacturers exert enormous pressures on hospitals and hospital systems to remain loyal to an entire line of products, devices and surgical instruments, or face steep price increases.

What is the Future of the Bands?

What will the future hold? With many years of high-quality studies demonstrating effective long-term weight loss and health improvements with both of these bands, it is highly likely that both of these bands will remain in the marketplace for many years to come. While the LSG procedure has gained popularity and the band procedures have declined in the U.S. in recent years, we are reminded that the band procedures are best considered in a different category: truly outpatient, reversible, adjustable procedures that involve no cutting or stapling. And now that around 80 million Americans qualify for the LAP-BAND® under the new FDA approval, and with these weight-loss medical devices are in the hands of two major medical instrument suppliers, it is also very likely that we will see increased marketing and competition.

Increased marketing will undoubtedly spread the message about the safety and efficacy of gastric banding to more overweight people who could benefit from it. For this reason alone, tens of thousands of lives will likely be saved or prolonged in this country every year. Greater competition may also bring reduced costs for these devices down the road but may also bring more pressure on hospitals and surgery centers to align themselves with one supplier or another.

The FDA approval Allergan's Lap-Band in 2011 for use in patients with a lower BMI – now down to a BMI of 30 for individuals with obesity-related health conditions – is perhaps the most important piece of news in recent years involving obesity treatment. The approval brings tens of millions more Americans into range for the procedure, and it sets the stage for a large increase in the number of bands being placed in the future. Additionally, modifications of surgical techniques, such as the addition of the Imbrication procedure to the LAGB, appear to boost the initial weight loss success of the LAGB procedure. Furthermore, the outpatient nature of the LAP-BAND® procedure and its reduced invasiveness when compared to stapling surgical procedures makes it possible to fill what some doctors call the "treatment gap" between diet and exercise (which usually doesn't work) and stapled surgical procedures (which some view as too invasive). Time will tell if band placements go up or decline as procedures like the LSG become more accepted.

Should You Choose One Band Over the Other?

Ultimately, you should make informed choices about every aspect of your health and medical care. If you are considering the laparoscopic adjustable gastric band, then odds are that you have researched the most effective, and least invasive, ways to lose weight for the long term. While most U.S. surgeons moved to the AP Lap-Band system when it was released, a case can be made that either the REALIZE™ or the LAP-BAND® is a smart choice to improve long-term health, quality of life and longevity. Both appear very durable and effective for the long term, and both are placed comfortably in an outpatient setting, thus minimizing time off from work or activities. Only the LAP-BAND® device is approved by the FDA for the BMI 30-35 range currently. In time, other factors may emerge which distinguish the bands to a greater degree, but I would recommend you talk over the topic with your surgeon and move forward when you feel comfortable with the choice you are making.

Appendix D

The Top Misadventures
with Outpatient Weight-Loss Surgery
and How to Avoid Them

1. A LEAK

An anastomotic leak is a leak or disruption of the connection that is made in laparoscopic Roux-en-Y gastric bypass surgery, or another stapling/cutting procedure (LSG,MGB,BPD) between the tissues of the stomach and the small intestine. Leaks are a serious problem because they lead to a dangerous intra-abdominal infection known as peritonitis. This usually mandates a return to surgery, usually within hours of detection of the problem, to repair the leak. Sometimes this urgent complication requires an open procedure with a long midline abdominal incision. If unrecognized or not treated early, a leak can lead to serious illness, difficulty breathing and the need for prolonged intensive care unit support and care, as well as more surgery. But in the vast majority of cases, a leak will be corrected and the patient will recover with no long-term problems.

A leak, like any other complication, is best avoided entirely. If it occurs (and there is always a small percentage chance of a complication occurring), then it is best recognized very early and treated aggressively. While there is no 100 percent foolproof method of averting leaks, studies have shown that the incidence of this serious problem drops dramatically as the surgeon becomes more experienced. You can maximize your odds of avoiding this serious complication by choosing an experienced surgeon with an excellent track record. Surgeons who have managed to reduce the incidence of leaks down to the 1- or 2-percent range have done so through careful technique, avoidance of tension on the tissues and application of a regular and routine test for minor leaks either during or directly after surgery.

The signs that a leak may have occurred are high fevers, racing heart rate, increase of pain, shortness of breath, nausea and vomiting. Often all these things occur at once.

The best thing you can do to prevent leaks or mitigate their effects is to put yourself in the hands of an excellent, experienced surgeon.

I have heard it suggested that overly vigorous exercise, coughing or a major fall could cause enough trauma to disrupt the suture line and create a leak, but this data is doubtful. The overwhelming majority of leaks that occur in this and any other intestinal surgery occur without any such particular trauma.

If a leak does occur you can help the surgical staff. If your nurses and surgeons are concerned about a leak, do everything you can to cooperate with investigations or studies that they want to order so that an answer can be arrived at immediately. Often the fastest and best way to both diagnose and treat a leak is to go back to surgery and operate either laparoscopically or sometimes with an open procedure. In LSG, a delayed leak may be best treated with an endoscopic stent.

2. VOMITING AND DEHYDRATION

Inevitably, after a person has undergone a gastrointestinal operation of any kind, the stomach and intestines will have some recovering to do before they begin working normally again. One of the most common side effects after an abdominal or gastrointestinal operation is nausea and vomiting. Anesthetic gases and pain medicines also have the side effect of causing nausea and vomiting. In most cases these symptoms appearing after a weight-loss operation do not present a very serious problem. The symptoms can be treated with anti-nausea medicines. Sometimes over the course of a few hours the symptoms can resolve and a person may still be discharged home in a timely manner without a prolonged hospital stay.

However, in a few cases, the symptoms do not subside and a person may experience persistent nausea and vomiting that requires intravenous fluids and hospitalization. The worst problem arises when these symptoms have occurred after the patient is discharged home.

What can you do about this problem? The first thing is to make sure that you are able to tolerate liquids fairly reliably before you go home. It is true that sometimes in the hustle and bustle of modern hospitals and surgery centers both patients and hospital staff are anxious to move along in the process and get the patient home in an expeditious fashion. Sometimes patients are exhibiting more optimism than realism and think "I'll be fine" even though they haven't been able to hold down even two sips of sugar-free apple juice.

So, take stock of your situation and make sure that you are in fact able to drink at least a small amount over the course of a couple of hours before you make the journey home. This will give you peace of mind and avoid anxiety that stems from finding that you're not able to tolerate any oral intake.

There are a couple of other things that you can do to pre-empt this problem. One of them is to make sure you are very well hydrated the day and evening prior to your operation. I advise my patients to drink a good deal of extra liquids the night before an operation. This helps avoid the dehydration that can occur after an operation.

Finally, I would say that if you are at home and the nausea and vomiting occur despite your best efforts, try to intervene early with the use of anti-nausea medications. Your doctor can prescribe them (I prescribe them preoperatively so that the patient can have them on hand, just in case), and if you use them early they may help reduce the nausea and allow you to tolerate some liquids. Newer anti-nausea drugs can be taken as a dissolving sublingual pill or even as a suppository. If the problem is persistent and doesn't look like it's going to resolve, then it is usually best to call your doctor's office. You may need to return to your doctor's office or surgical center for IV fluids. Usually after going home it is safe to wait overnight before moving to the step of returning to the hospital, but you and your doctor or the doctor's nursing staff can help advise you in that matter.

3. HEART, LUNG, KIDNEY AND OTHER ORGAN PROBLEMS

Every kind of health problem that could occur in the outside world walking down the street can occur in the hospital or in the time frame immediately following surgery. Surgery and anesthesia can both put some stress on the heart, lungs and other organ systems and can lead to some underlying problems with these organs manifesting in a serious way. Such problems are not common, but a small chance always exists of these types of issues arising. For example, people with underlying heart disease may experience heart attacks or abnormal cardiac rhythms after operations. Likewise someone with intrinsic lung disease (for example, a long-time smoker) could experience problems breathing or develop a lung infection. There are unlimited numbers of problems that can occur, although complications are rare in a high-quality, high-volume bariatric surgical practice.

What can you do to protect yourself? Again, the answer is prevention. It is critically important that you notify your doctor and your doctor's team of the underlying health problems that you have experienced in the past. It is important not to minimize these problems, and it is important to follow through with any recommended tests or evaluations so that these issues can be thoroughly looked into prior to surgery and anesthesia. For example, if you have had some heart trouble that you were told was not terribly severe in the past, it is still important to mention it to your doctor. The doctor may want to have you undergo a cardiac stress test just to be sure. Comply with these important investigations. They could save you from serious postoperative complications.

4. You Think Something is Wrong, but You Can't Get Any Answers

This is an extremely frustrating problem that stems from a lack of communication from the hospital nursing staff or the surgeon and the surgeon's staff to you and your family. Sometimes there actually is no serious problem or complication but only a worry or anxiety about one. Sometimes there is a complication that is unfolding and studies are in progress to help reveal the problem, but no answers have been received. Worse, there is a serious problem and the doctor is aware of it but she and her staff are too busy to communicate with you or your family.

How can you avoid this problem? The best answer lies in prevention or avoidance of the problem. As you interview surgeons and examine surgical practices, ask the questions from the beginning about communication. Ask: How will I be able to reach you or your associates, and how will you communicate with me? If I feel something is going wrong and call your office, will a nurse relay information to someone and get back to me in a timely fashion? These are all reasonable questions to ask your surgeon and the surgical staff. Nowadays, many surgeons work closely with Physician Assistants and nurses who may be in charge of communicating information; in most cases you will be best served accepting that they work as a team. Likewise, you can expect the outpatient surgery center staff to be in communication with you and your family if any problems or questions arise. Ninety-nine times out of 100, the surgeon, surgical staff and the outpatient surgery center staff are working hard to make your experience a positive one and are appropriately investigating potential problems or questions that arise. If a problem is ongoing, such as a reaction to medication or a potential surgical complication, generally you need to take a deep breath and give the professionals a bit of time to gain an understanding of the potential problem. So, don't expect constant and immediate communication on every issue that crosses your mind but do expect forthright communication if it appears there is a problem.

If you find yourself in the worst possible scenario, in which a serious problem is developing and no one will tell you anything about it, you need to have your allies and advocates get on the phone and call the physician's office as well as the outpatient surgery center or hospital nursing staff. Sometimes just getting an answer such as "we are getting an X-ray to check on that potential problem" is all it takes to allay anxiety. Keep in mind that if you are at home already and facing such worries, it is usually necessary to go back to the hospital to get definitive answers by undergoing investigative studies.

5. BLOOD CLOTS

Blood clots in the large veins of the leg (deep vein thrombosis) used to be a fairly frequent and severe complication of weight-loss operations many years ago. This problem can cause painful leg swelling but also a potentially very serious breathing problem if a blood clot travels up the venous system to the lungs. Blood clots are more apt to occur if a person is seriously overweight, and they are more likely to occur if a person is undergoing a long operation during which time the person remains immobilized on an operating table. The blood in the venous system pools, stagnates and becomes still, like a river that stops flowing. At that point a person can develop a clot. The good news is that with modern laparoscopic weight-loss surgery, the incidence of blood clots has plummeted. In our series of approximately 3,000 cases there has been no documented blood clot occurrence.

The reason for this is probably the high level of vigilance that experienced bariatric surgeons bring to this particular problem. Most centers employ sequential compression stockings that use a pneumatic squeezing mechanism to keep the venous blood circulating in the legs. In addition, many surgeons and their staffs will also use injections of low-dose blood thinners to keep the blood from clotting abnormally.

What can you do to prevent a clot? First, ask the surgeon and the nurses about their protocol for prevention of blood clots. It would be very unusual for an experienced, high-volume weight-loss surgical center to fail to employ a vigorous blood clot prevention program.

You can also ask the surgeon how long procedures generally take. Since minimally invasive weight-loss surgery in the hands of experienced surgeons generally takes around an hour or sometimes substantially less, there is little time for blood clots to form in the legs. If your surgeon answers that routine weight-loss surgical procedures take six or seven hours, it's time to look for a different surgeon.

If after your operation you suspect that you have developed a blood clot (symptoms are a hot, red, tender, swollen calf), you need to tell your nurses and doctor immediately. A blood clot can be diagnosed with a simple ultrasound test and treated with blood thinners.

There are steps you can take to prevent blood clots from forming after surgery when you are at home resting. Be active. Move your legs. Pump your feet. Stand up and walk. Get outside. All of these recommendations are meant to keep the blood circulating and keep problems from developing.

6. BLEEDING

Surgical bleeding is not as common as many people imagine, yet it is still possible for serious bleeding to occur and for a person to require blood transfusions. This kind of problem would be exceedingly rare in an LAGB procedure in an experienced surgeon's hands (probably on the order of one in 1,000 cases) and quite uncommon also in a laparoscopic RYGB or LSG procedure (in the 1 percent range). Bleeding can occur because there are blood vessels that need to be divided. There are also structures, such as the liver and spleen that can bleed just from mild trauma to them. This can occur even with routine surgery. Bleeding is best dealt with by early recognition and treatment with either blood transfusions or a return trip to the operating room to identify and stop the source of the bleeding.

There are actually a few things you can do before your operation to reduce your risk of complications from bleeding. Your surgeon will generally advise you prior to surgery to stop taking any medicines that thin the blood and increase your chances of bleeding. These include aspirin, ibuprofen and all of the nonsteroidal anti-inflammatory type medicines. Usually it is recommended to stop these medicines five to seven days prior to an operation. In addition, if a patient is taking a more potent blood thinner called Coumadin, then the surgeon will generally advise stopping this medicine also. Special arrangements can be made for people who must have their blood thinned due to a mechanical heart valve or other special situations. Talk with your surgeon about these conditions and how to manage them.

The second thing you can do pertains to bleeding that occurs from a specific site: the liver. The liver is the largest organ in the abdomen and a place where a great deal of fat storage occurs when people gain weight. Virtually everybody who is considering a weight-loss operation has an excessive amount of fat stored in the liver, a condition which is aptly named "fatty liver" or hepatic steatosis. I describe this condition because it leads to a greater chance of fracture or bleeding from the liver during an operation, and it can be dramatically improved over the course of a mere few weeks time preoperatively.

How can you improve such a condition? By decreasing the fat storage. To accomplish this, many surgical programs ask patients to embark upon a vigorous weight-reduction and fat-reduction program lasting anywhere from two to 12 weeks before operations. This strict program consists of a liquid diet that normally runs about 800 calories per day. Several studies have shown that the liver shrinks dramatically with this preop liquid diet program, and the risk of bleeding (as well as other problems such as conversion to an open incision) are lessened with this preoperative liquid weight-loss program. So, ask your surgeon about a preoperative liquid diet. Follow the guidelines religiously. Don't cheat, and you will significantly reduce your odds of several serious problems and complications, including bleeding.

7. CONVERSION TO AN OPEN OPERATION

For many years, all weight-loss surgery was done with an open technique. This meant that a long incision was made, usually from the lower breastbone area down well below the navel. There are even a few surgeons who still argue today that this is a preferred technique even though a great deal of data and experience exists that such open surgery brings with it much longer recovery times and higher rate of complications related to the incision and wound itself. Open surgery also compromises the mechanics of the lungs and leads to greater respiratory insufficiency and respiratory complications after surgery when compared to laparoscopic surgery. With all due respect to surgeons who would still defend the open technique, it is, in my view, an antiquated technique that has been replaced by a procedure that is safer, faster and more effective: laparoscopic or minimally invasive surgery.

So what happens if your experienced laparoscopic surgeon runs into trouble and the problem can't be solved laparoscopically? The surgeon will have to convert to an open operation. This occurs in up to 2 percent of cases, even in the experienced hands of a laparoscopic surgeon performing gastric bypass surgery. It is far from the end of the world, but it would be nice to avoid this particular event since it inevitably leads to a hospital stay of at least several days, and often a week, and it brings with it the issues related to wounds and breathing and other risks I describe above.

Like any surgical risk, the risk of conversion to open surgery cannot be entirely avoided. However, your odds can be improved substantially by two major preoperative efforts. One is selecting the finest laparoscopic bariatric surgeon you possibly can, and the second is making yourself the best possible surgical candidate you can. The former involves careful research and interviews. The latter involves working hard night and day to improve your physical health and reduce your weight.

So, if your surgeon requires a four-week preoperative weight-loss program, you should consider that the bare minimum. Make a target for your own personal plan of success maximization to lose a minimum of 30, 40, 50 or even 100 pounds prior to your operation. This means starting a daily exercise program, wearing a pedometer, fighting against carbohydrates, hunger and junk food night and day, and then transitioning to a very strict all-liquid low-calorie weight-loss program. Nearly anyone reading this book has lost many pounds before and can do it again; and this is perhaps the most important time in your life for you to lose weight: prior to bariatric surgery.

It may seem a strange irony that you are seeking help to lose weight through surgical intervention only to now be told that in order to safely undergo surgical intervention, you must first lose weight. And yet the facts are that your risks during an operation will be significantly reduced if you lose weight beforehand. You have the power to lose pounds before your operation. For this one short-term, finite and highly important time period, you must dig deep to find the motivation and resources to lose these pounds prior to your operation. You will dramatically improve your chance of success and reduce your risk of complications, including the complication of converting to open surgery.

8. STOMACH ULCER FORMATION

It is increasingly recognized that stomach ulcers can form in the early weeks and months following LRYGB. This has not been found to be a significant issue with LAGB. For patients undergoing gastric bypass, however, ulcers can be a serious problem. They can lead to pain, nausea and vomiting and can become difficult to treat, sometimes causing swelling or scarring that narrows the stomach outlet, or they can result in a perforation that requires surgery. This problem has been increasingly recognized and may occur in up to 5 percent of cases after gastric bypass.

In order to avoid this, avoid agents that cause damage or irritation to the stomach lining and promote ulcers. These include, chiefly, alcohol, tobacco, nonsteroidal anti-inflammatory drugs, or NSAIDs (ibuprofen, naprosyn, etc.) and corticosteroids such as prednisone.

There may be more that you can do. It is increasingly recognized that a common bacterium known as helicobacter pylori plays a role in the formation of stomach ulcers in LRYGB or LSG as well as in the general population. So, more and more practices are now testing for the presence of this bacterium even before surgery and treating it with the antibiotics that kill it in order to lessen the chances of later stomach ulcer formation. Ask your doctor if this is a test the surgical practice performs. These measures may not completely eliminate your risk of ulcers, but the studies would suggest they would probably reduce the risks by as much as 90 percent.

9. STOMAL STENOSIS

There are a few different ways in which the stomach or intestines can become blocked or obstructed after LRYGB or MGB. These blockages tend to occur after someone has gone home from the hospital. The first way is that the anastomotic site of the stomach to the intestine (the connection where the stomach and intestinal limb are sewn together) scars down tightly over a few weeks. This blockage results in a gradual intolerance of foods as the person is attempting to progress to a more solid diet in the weeks following surgery. It is best treated with an endoscopy, where a lighted flexible camera is inserted down the esophagus, and the opening is gently stretched. The treatment is usually highly successful, especially if done quickly after the onset of the problem.

There is probably fairly little you can do about this preoperatively, other than (once again) seeking a skilled and experienced laparoscopic surgeon and optimizing your preoperative weight loss, both of which make the procedure technically easier. There is evidence that the factors that lead to stenosis often involve tension from the tissues, and this may be improved in part by a very successful preoperative weight-loss program. Following an operation, it is important to monitor your symptoms and assess how well you are doing as you progress from liquids onward through pureed foods and on to solids. If over the course of several weeks you find that your ability to swallow and eat is worsening rather than improving, then you need to let your doctor know right away. A stenosis could be forming, and the best diagnostic test is an upper endoscopy. Long delay in recognition of the problem usually makes it much more difficult to treat and fix.

10. CONSTIPATION

Okay, constipation may not seem like a really serious problem, but it can be. One of the main reasons people become constipated after an operation is that the narcotic painkillers prescribed all cause some degree of constipation through a slowing of the bowels. Add to this the fact that you are not eating much, and it can become a bit confusing when one should expect a bowel movement. In rare cases, people may become very seriously bloated and experience pain due to constipation, which can be avoided.

Simple advice for avoiding this complication is to drink plenty of fluids in the days preceding your operation. If you have a tendency to become constipated anyway, you need to anticipate that this will likely become worse after an operation, especially if you're taking narcotic pain medication. (The most common narcotics used after bariatric operations are oxycodone, hydrocodone, codeine, morphine and hydromorphone, with trade names like Lortab, Vicodin, Norco, Percocet, Roxicet and Dilaudid.) Ask your surgeon or your nurse about this preoperatively. Take stool softeners and fiber regularly prior to the operation.

After your operation, you should expect your bowels to begin working again within three or four days. Any longer than this usually warrants treatment with a laxative.

Looking Toward the Future

What is the future of weight-loss surgery? None of us has a crystal ball, but it's clear that procedures for weight loss have, in the past 15 years, become much less invasive and also much more effective at achieving weight loss.

The bar has been set very high. Future innovations will have to show that they can achieve excellent weight results to compete with the LAGB, the LRYGB, MGB and the LSG – and that won't be easy. Future innovations will also have to prove that they are less invasive or at least no more invasive and no riskier than what is available now. This will also be challenging.

It's difficult to tell at this point if the NOTES procedures will one day play a major role, but at least some of the new technology available appears offer potential benefit to patients. On the other hand, it's hard understand to how some of the new NOTES procedures (removal of the gallbladder, for instance, via an internal incision in the stomach or vagina) are any safer or better than the current standard of minimally invasive, or laparoscopic, surgery. The full scope of risks has yet to be determined, and some of the procedures that involve internal incisions will incur risks of leak or infection that may be very serious, even if rare. Robotic surgery technology at this point offers a technologically interesting but massively expensive set of tools to complete a procedure that most surgeons can do well in under 60 minutes with standard tools and tiny incisions. Whether insurers will continue to pay for all the extra technology remains to be seen.

I do believe incision-free endoscopic technology will one day play a role as a weight-loss procedure, at least in revising stretched pouches and possibly as a primary weight-loss procedure. Today and in the near future, however, surgeons will continue to perfect and refine laparoscopic minimally invasive procedures to make them safer and more effective for long term weight loss and better health.

Recovery and Beyond

Making a decision to undergo weight-loss surgery is a big step toward better health and a better life. The day you undergo the operations is the day you start a new journey. You're bound to have questions:

- What is important?
- What do I eat?
- How do I cope with the cravings from my old life?
- How do I deal with people who knew me as the "fat person" I no longer am?
- And most importantly: What are the proven keys to weight-loss success for the long term for someone who has undergone a weight-loss operation?

Over the years, so many people have asked me these questions that I began writing down the answers. The result is a guidebook for people who have undergone weight-loss operations and now want to maximize their success and live the fullest life possible. After Weight-Loss Surgery: Losing weight, avoiding rebound weight gain, overcoming plateaus and maintaining a healthy weight for a lifetime is available through Smashwords as an e-book.

The bottom line is that you can succeed in losing the weight and keeping it off forever after a weight-loss operation. All you need are the right tools. And it turns out that researchers have helped us all identify some strategies that truly work, including some pretty simple ones that make a big difference over the course of a year. I spent a year compiling those scientifically-proven techniques and tips and put them together in a book called Doctor's Orders: 101 Medically Proven Tips for Losing Weight. Visit our website www.iMetabolic.com for this book and others in The Sasse Guide Series that will assist those on this journey.

Glossary

Anastamosis: tissue connection of the stomach pouch to the intestine.

Anastamotic stricture: narrowing of the tissue connecting the stomach pouch to the intestine.

ASC: Ambulatory surgery center or outpatient surgery center.

Band with Imbrication: laparoscopic adjustable gastric band with imbrication (folding) of the stomach with sutures.

Bariatric: the branch of medicine dealing with weight loss.

Biliopancreatic diversion: a bariatric procedure involving reduced absorption of nutrients. In BPD, a portion of the stomach is removed and the ileum is connected to the proximal stomach. The duodenum and jejunum are bypassed and their secretions flow into the distal ileum through a new anastomosis.

BMI: Body Mass Index, a measure of the height and weight. Normal BMI is 18-25.

Bowel obstruction: a blockage of the intestines.

Cardiac arrhythmia: irregular heartbeat .

CAT scan: an imaging study used for diagnostic purposes, using X-ray technology to create a 3-D image.

Center of Excellence: a designation from the American Society of Metabolic and Bariatric. Surgery or the American College of Surgeons denoting an experienced program that has passed certain criteria including a site inspection and satisfactory outcomes reporting.

Cholecystectomy: gall bladder removal.

Coumadin: an oral prescription blood-thinning medication.

Comorbid: a coexisting illness or condition (for example, hypertension is a comorbid condition related to obesity).

CT scan: same as CAT scan.

Deep vein thrombosis: blood clots in the large veins of the leg.

Degenerative joint disease: wear and tear on the joints, causing arthritis and damage to cartilage and bone, often caused by and exacerbated by weight gain.

DS: Duodenal switch procedure: a bariatric surgical procedure that involves removal of 70 percent of the greater curvature of the stomach, and a malabsorbtive component that takes the ingested food to a common intestinal channel, bypassing the duodenum and proximal small intestine.

Dumping syndrome: a syndrome noted by symptoms of flushing palpitation, sweating and nausea that comes from rapid intake of sugar or high osmolality nutrients (like sugars) following gastric bypass.

Dysphagia: difficulty swallowing, often described as food "sticking."

Eating disorders: maladaptive eating behaviors. In obesity and bariatric surgery, the most common types are: binge eating, defined by over-consumption of food and a loss of sense of control; nocturnal eating disorder, characterized by eating after eight p.m. or waking in the middle of the night to eat; grazing: eating small amounts very frequently throughout waking hours.

Endoscopy: a nonsurgical procedure to examine an organ using a flexible fiber optic tube passed down the esophagus.

Enoxeparin: an injectable blood thinner medication also known as low-molecular weight heparin.

FDA: Food and Drug Administration.

Gastric bypass: laparoscopic Roux-en-Y gastric bypass, the most popular weight-loss operation in the United States.

Gastric pouch: term used to describe the small stomach pouch created in gastric bypass surgery.

Gastroesophageal reflux disease: a common condition, worse with weight gain and obesity, in which stomach acid travels upward to the esophagus, usually giving an unpleasant sensation of heartburn.

Gastrointestinal: pertaining to the stomach or intestinal system, digestive system.

Gastrojejunal anastamosis: the area of connection from the stomach pouch to the intestine.

Ghrelin: a hormone produced in the stomach and pancreas that increases hunger.

GLP-1: glucagon-like peptide-1, a hormone secreted by the intestinal cells involved in metabolism and hunger; GLP-1 stimulates insulin release from the pancreas and causes a feeling of satiety in the brain.

Glycemic index: a numerical system that measures the rise in circulating blood sugar a carbohydrate triggers.

Glycemic load: a ranking system for the carbohydrate content of foods based on their glycemic index and size of portions.

Heart arrhythmias: irregular beating of the heart; some arrhythmias can be persistent and dangerous or require medical treatment.

Heparin: an injectable blood thinner.

Hepatic steatosis: a form of severe fatty deposits on the liver that can result from obesity and lead to liver dysfunction and cirrhosis.

Hernia: a weakness in the abdominal wall fascial tissues, creating a bulge, commonly occurring in the groin region, the umbilical region, or in the area of old surgical scars.

Hormones: chemicals secreted by tissues of the body's organs that travel through the bloodstream to exert an effect on another part of the body.

Hypoxia: low levels of oxygen in the blood.

Inferior vena cava: the large veins that bring the returning blood from the legs back to the heart.

Imbrication: a procedure in which a part of the stomach is folded and sutured in order to shrink it rather than removing a portion or bypassing the stomach.

Intragastric balloon: a procedure in which an endoscope is passed through the mouth and esophagus into the stomach to deploy a balloon there, leading to a feeling of satiety.

Jejunal limb: the portion of the intestine used to connect to the stomach pouch in laparoscopic Roux-en-Y gastric bypass surgery (also called Roux limb).

Keyhole incision: a small incision made on the skin of the abdominal wall in laparoscopic surgery, usually measuring 5 mm to 12 mm in length (less than half an inch).

LAGB: laparoscopic adjustable gastric band.

Laparoscopic: surgery performed using a camera system and small, thin, specially designed instruments inserted through the abdominal wall, a type of minimally-invasive abdominal surgery; from laparos (abdominal) and oscopy (meaning using a camera to view what's inside the abdomen).

Laparoscopic sleeve gastrectomy: a newer weight-loss procedure in which a large portion of the stomach is removed and the remaining stomach is made into a smaller, thinner, tubular structure.

LAP-BAND®: the brand name of the Allergan laparoscopic adjustable gastric band.

Leak: a complication of weight-loss surgery in which stomach or intestinal juice may pass outside of the stomach or intestine, causing infection or peritonitis.

Lean body mass: the portion of the body mass that is not body fat; consisting of muscle, skeleton and organs, the lean body mass plays a key role in determining a person's metabolism rate.

Leptin: an important hormone produced primarily by fat cells in the body; leptin causes a long-lasting feeling of satiety. Leptin resistance may be linked to obesity.

LRYGB: laparoscopic Roux-en-Y gastric bypass, a bariatric surgical procedure in which a small proximal stomach pouch is created and connected directly to the intestine, thus bypassing the lower stomach and the duodenum.

LSG: laparoscopic Sleeve Gastrectomy (LSG), a bariatric surgical procedure in which around 75 percent of the greater curvature portion of the stomach is removed. In mid-term studies of less than 10 years, LSG produced weight loss results only slightly below those of LRYGB.

Marginal ulcer: formation of an ulcer or sore on the inside lining of the stomach pouch.

Medically supervised weight-loss program: nonsurgical physician-supervised program to lose weight, often involving diet, counseling, behavior modification and, sometimes, specially designed meals and prescription drugs.

Medicare-certified: approved by Medicare, the federal national health insurance plan for the elderly and disabled.

Metabolic rate: the rate at which the body burns energy, as measured in kilocalories per day.

MGB: Mini-Gastric Bypass, or Loop Gastric Bypass, a bariatric surgical procedure in which a small proximal stomach pouch is created and connected directly into a loop of small intestine, thus bypassing the lower stomach and duodenum.

Multidisciplinary weight-loss programs: medically supervised programs which utilize contact with experts from related disciplines including psychotherapists, nutritionists and exercise coaches.

Natural orifice transluminal endoscopic surgery (NOTES): an emerging type of surgical procedure in which a natural orifice, such as the mouth, can be used to insert the surgical instruments and camera, minimizing any external incisions.

Open surgical procedure: a surgical procedure that involves cutting through the abdominal wall and opening the abdomen.

Open Vertical Banded Gastroplasty: an open abdominal procedure popular in the 1970s involving placement of a nonadjustable, firm silicon band in the upper stomach.

Outpatient surgery: surgery in which the patient is expected to go home the same day. Often, in the eyes of insurance plans or regulators, this means within 24 hours.

Outpatient surgery center (also known as ambulatory surgery center, or ASC): a center or facility devoted to ambulatory or "day" surgery, in which patients go home after surgery, usually within 23 hours.

Outpatient weight-loss operation: any of the weight-loss surgical procedures performed on an outpatient basis, in which the patient undergoes the operation and goes home within 23 hours.

PCOS: polycystic ovarian syndrome, a condition involving hormonal abnormalities, weight gain and ovarian cysts.

Peritoneal cavity: the space inside the abdomen where the intestines are.

Pneumatic sequential compression stockings: worn by patients during surgical procedures, these squeeze the legs, ankles and feet to propel blood up the veins and back to the heart in a manner similar to normal muscle contractions; use of pneumatic sequential compression stockings reduces the risk of blood clots during and after surgical procedures.

Pre-diabetes: early stage disorder of glucose control, a less severe impairment of the body's metabolic system which leads to elevated glucose levels; defined as a fasting plasma glucose of 110-125mg/dl or a glycated hemoglobin level between 5.7 and 6.4 percent.

Preoperative liquid diet: use of liquid meal-replacement protein shakes in place of meals to promote reduction of liver volume and weight loss before a weight-loss surgical procedure.

Pseudotumor cerebri: a brain condition that causes severe headaches.

Pulmonary: having to do with the lungs.

Pulmonary embolus: blood clot in the lungs.

Pulmonary hypertension: an advanced state of high blood pressure in which the heart and lungs have become damaged over time.

Radiology: the field of medical imaging using X-rays, ultrasound, CT scans and other imaging techniques.

REALIZE™ Personal Banding Solution: the name for the Ethicon laparoscopic adjustable gastric band.

Rebound weight gain: the phenomenon of re-gaining some or all of the weight lost after dieting.

Referred pain: when nerves stimulated by injury, trauma or a surgical procedure create a sensation of pain in another part of the body.

Roux limb: the part of the intestine used to connect to the stomach pouch in gastric bypass surgery (also called the jejunal limb).

Satiety: the sense of feeling full or satisfied.

Set point: the concept of a body weight that is defended by hormonal and metabolic mechanisms; for example, when a person weighing 200 pounds loses 20 pounds through dieting, hormonal changes occur that serve to promote weight re-gain by slowing metabolism and increasing hunger.

Sleep apnea: a condition in which proper sleeping is impaired because of the floppy tissues in the throat and neck obstructing the air flow. It can range from minor snoring to severe life-threatening cessation of breathing during sleep.

Stent: a long hollow tube that can be placed inside the esophagus, stomach or intestine; extend across a narrowing or a disruption in a site of tissue connection.

Stomach pouch: the upper portion of the stomach that is formed into a small-volume reservoir after gastric bypass surgery.

Stomal stenosis: a narrowing of the connection point of the tissues; in bariatric surgery this is most commonly at the site of the connection or anastomosis of the stomach pouch to the intestine.

StomaphyX™: no longer available, an endoscopic device for revising stretched gastric pouches; it consists of a soft flexible scope passed down the esophagus with surgical instruments attached to approximate tissue and shrink the pouch; other similar procedures show promise for revising stomach pouches.

Swedish Band: now called the REALIZE™ Band, an FDA-approved medical device for weight loss that consists of an adjustable band placed around the upper stomach connected via tubing to a subcutaneous reservoir port for adding saline.

Thromboembolism: blood clots that form within blood vessels and break off and travel within the blood stream.

Transfer of addiction: the concept of changing from one addictive behavior, such as binge eating, to another addictive behavior, such as substance abuse.

Urinary incontinence: loss of control of the urinary bladder, resulting in involuntary passage of urine, often with coughing or sneezing.

Venous stasis disease: slow transit of the blood returning from the legs upward toward the heart, resulting in swelling of the veins and soft tissues of the legs, related to obesity.

List of Figures

DEPICTS THE COMPLETED GASTRIC BANDING WITH IMBRICATION PROCEDURE.

FIGURE 10.
NUMBER OF WEIGHT-LOSS PROCEDURES BY YEAR.

FIGURE 11.
DEPICTS STAPLING TO CREATE THE SLEEVE.

FIGURE 12.
DEPICTS THE COMPLETED LAPAROSCOPIC SLEEVE GASTRECTOMY PROCEDURE.

FIGURE 13.
MINI-GASTRIC BYPASS.

FIGURE 14.
ROUX-EN-Y GASTRIC BYPASS.

FIGURE 15.
DEPICTS DUODENAL SWITCH PROCEDURE.

FIGURE 16.
SHOWS THE LRYGB PROCEDURE. THE ARROW INDICATES THE CONNECTION POINT THE SURGEON FORMS TO THE STOMACH POUCH.

Resources

Books

Doctor's Orders: 101 Medically-Proven Tips for Losing Weight by Kent Sasse, MD. (360 Publishing 2009) provides a summary of over 101 medically proven specific strategies and behaviors we can all do to lose weight and keep it off. The tips come from the medical literature and are translated into practices that everyone can implement.

Weight Loss Surgery for Dummies by Marina S. Kurian, Barbara Thompson and Brian K. Davidson (For Dummies, 2005; 2nd edition 2012). This guide is a well-written summary of many important considerations for someone undergoing a weight-loss operation. It includes perspectives from a surgeon, a psychologist and a patient. The diagrams and explanations are clear, and the issues discussed are relevant. It has recipes, interesting subsections and points to remember, as with all the Dummies guides. It offers a balanced and accurate view of the pros and cons of most types of surgery. While the fast-changing technology has made some sections outdated, this remains a helpful resource for anyone planning to undergo weight-loss surgery.

LAP-BAND® for Life by Ariel Ortiz Lagardere (LM Publishers, 2005; Venture Icon Media, 2011) offers insightful commentary from a surgeon knowledgeable about the LAP-BAND®. He covers many aspects of the process and offers one bariatric surgeon's perspective and advice on steps for patients to take.

Laparoscopic Adjustable Gastric Banding: Achieving Permanent Weight Loss with Minimally Invasive Surgery by Jessie H. Ahroni (iUniverse, 2004). This book describes the fundamental aspects of the adjustable gastric band and offers some coaching for patients.

The Success Habits of Weight-Loss Surgery Patients by Colleen Cook (Bariatric Support Centers Int, 2003; 3rd edition 2012) is a wonderful description of the habits that have proved successful for weight-loss operation patients. Ms. Cook is a patient who has researched this topic well, and she presents well-organized keys for patients undergoing weight-loss operations. She remains devoted to the field, her information is current, and she trains many support leaders throughout the country.

Life-Changing Weight Loss by Kent Sasse, M.D. (360 Publishing, 2010) offers a step-by-step guide to through a medically-supervised weight-loss program. The plan emphasizes the inspiration and psychology of personal change, and pairs those messages with a medically-based plan for losing weight and keeping it off.

Weight-Loss Surgery: Finding the Thin Person Hiding Inside You, Fourth Edition, by Barbara Thompson (Word Association Publishers; 4th edition, 2008) is also written by a successful gastric bypass patient who offers insightful details about her own personal journey and many helpful hints about the experience. Many readers find the information specific and valuable, told from the point of view of one who has "been there."

Web Resources

OBESITY RELATED SITES

Obesity Action Coalition (OAC): As a grassroots organization, OAC endeavors to bring together the individuals impacted by the life-changing disease of obesity. The OAC offers educational and advocacy information.

www.obesityaction.org/home/index.php

The Obesity Society: The Obesity Society promotes research, education and advocacy to better understand, prevent and treat obesity and improve the lives of those affected

www.obesity.org/

Obesity Prevention Foundation: The Obesity Prevention Foundation was established to provide communities with leadership and educational resources to combat the epidemic of childhood obesity.

www.obesitypreventionfoundation.org/

NATIONAL AND GOVERNMENT RESOURCES

CDC Division of Nutrition, Physical Activity, and Obesity: This website provides information regarding nutrition, physical activity, excessive weight and obesity, campaigns and programs, publications, recommendations, data and statistics, and training and tools.

www.cdc.gov/nccdphp/dnpa/

National Heart, Lung and Blood Institute: NHLBI of the National Institutes of Health launched the Obesity Education Initiative in January 1991. The overall purpose of the initiative is to help reduce the prevalence of excessive weight along with the prevalence of physical inactivity in order to reduce the risk of coronary

heart disease and overall morbidity and mortality from CHD.
www.nhlbi.nih.gov/

National Institutes of Health: The official website of the National Institutes of Health. NIH is one of the world's foremost medical research centers.
www.obesityresearch.nih.gov/

National Institute of Arthritis and Musculoskeletal and Skin Diseases: NIAMS offers roundtable Discussion on research career paths in rheumatic diseases and Molecular Pathway in Muscle.
www.niams.nih.gov/

American Heart Association: The American Heart Association is a nonprofit organization that fosters appropriate cardiac care in an effort to reduce disability and deaths caused by cardiovascular disease and stroke.
www.heart.org/HEARTORG/

American Cancer Society: The American Cancer Society is dedicated to eliminating cancer as a major health problem by preventing cancer, saving lives and diminishing suffering.
www.cancer.org/

National Cancer Institute: NCI offers accurate, up-to-date, comprehensive cancer information from the U.S. government's principal agency for cancer research.
www.cancer.gov/

Academy of Nutrition and Dietetics: The world's largest organization of food and nutrition professionals. The Academy is committed to improving the nation's health and advancing the profession of dietetics through research, education and advocacy.

www.eatright.org/

American Diabetes Association: The American Diabetes Association's mission is to prevent and cure diabetes and to improve the lives of all people affected by diabetes.

www.diabetes.org/

National Institute of Diabetes and Digestive and Kidney Diseases: This organization conducts and supports research on kidney, urologic, hematologic, digestive, metabolic and endocrine diseases, as well as on diabetes and nutrition.

www2.niddk.nih.gov/

BARIATRIC SURGERY

MedlinePlus: Weight Loss Surgery: a site describing research and clinical programs related to obesity.
www.nlm.nih.gov/medlineplus/weightlosssurgery.html

WebMD: a general medical site with a section on weight-loss surgery.
www.webmd.com/diet/weight-loss-surgery/gastric-bypass

Weight-Loss Surgery: a resource about weight-loss surgery from Allergan.
www.weightlosssurgeryoptions.com/

WIN - Bariatric Surgery for Severe Obesity: government publication on obesity.
win.niddk.nih.gov/publications/gastric.htm

The American Society for Metabolic and Bariatric Surgery (ASMBS): the professional society for weight-loss surgeons
www.asbs.org/

Obesity Help: helpful and complete information about weight-loss surgery:
www.obesityhelp.com/

WLS Lifestyles: a national publication and media outlet dedicated to providing inspiration, education and support for people struggling with obesity or maintaining a healthy weight:
www.wlslifestyles.com/

Bariatric Edge: a site maintained by Ethicon Endo-Surgery.
www.bariatricedge.com/

iMetabolic.com: a comprehensive weight loss site offering resources for medically supervised weight-loss programs, techniques and tools, nutritional supplements, BMI calculator, vitamins, protein shakes, diet plans and more.
www.imetabolic.com/

Sasse Guide: Dr. Sasse's personal website, with articles, books, information, resources and Dr. Sasse's blog all designed to be the best source of weight-loss information on the web.
www.sasseguide.com/

SasseSurgical.com: Dr. Sasse's surgical practice website, with testimonials, videos and descriptions of minimally invasive procedures he performs.

BARIATRIC SURGERY ARTICLES

Gastric Bypass Surgery Articles:
www.locateadoc.com/articles.cfm/1454
Sasse Guide articles and special reports
www.sasseguide.com/index.html#special
Gastric Banding Surgery Articles:
www.locateadoc.com/articles.cfm/1454
Mayo Clinic: bariatric surgery what can you expect:
www.mayoclinic.com/health/gastric-bypass/HQ01465
Long-term mortality after gastric bypass surgery:
http://www.nejm.org/doi/full/10.1056/NEJMoa066603
Laparoscopic gastric banding: a minimally invasive surgical treatment for morbid obesity: prospective study of 500 consecutive patients:
http://www.ncbi.nlm.nih.gov/pmc/articles/PMC1513972/

AUDIO PROGRAMS

www.iMetabolic.com

Preparing for Weight Loss Surgery: An audio program outlining the essential steps to take in preparing for weight-loss surgery, beginning now and up to the morning of surgery.

An Overview of Weight-Loss Surgery: Covers all the types of weight-loss surgery and the pros and cons, risks and alternatives of each in a candid discussion from a national expert. If you are considering weight-loss surgery, then the program is a great place to start.

Diabetes and Your Future: An in-depth discussion of Diabetes, Pre-diabetes, and how to prevent it and treat it. This program focuses on the exciting recent data of successful treatment and prevention of diabetes with weight loss.

After Weight Loss Surgery: An essential how-to manual for successful weight loss after bariatric surgery.

State-of-the-Art Medical Weight Loss: An in-depth audio program discussion of what is currently the best scientifically-based medical weight-loss program available. Focuses on the data showing weight-loss success with non-surgical, medically-supervised programs and how you can take advantage of those principles for your own personal weight loss.

Vitamins and Weight Loss Surgery: This audio program covers the important topic of vitamins and vitamin deficiencies after weight-loss surgery. It outlines what the common vitamin deficiencies are before and after surgery, and how to prevent any nutritional imbalances after surgery.

Notes

1   Sumithran, P . Long term persistence of Adaptations to weight loss, NEJM 2011 365(17): 1597-604

2   Kaplan, L,. Myths Associated with Obesity and Bariatric Surgery, Bariatric Times 2012 9(4): 12-13

3   Fleisher, L.A., Pasternak, L.R., Herbert, R., Anderson, G.F. Inpatient hospital admission and death after outpatient surgery in elderly patients: importance of patient and system characteristics and location of care. Arch Surg. 2004 Jan;139(1):67-72

4   Karlsson. J., Taft, C., Rydén, A., Sjöström, L., Sullivan, M. Ten-year trends in health-related quality of life after surgical and conventional treatment for severe obesity: the SOS intervention study. Int J Obes (Lond). 2007 Aug;31(8):1248-61. Epub 2007 Mar 13

5   Mathus-Vliegen, E.M., de Wit, L.T., Health-related quality of life after gastric banding. Br J Surg. 2007 Apr;94(4):457-65

6   Mathus-Vliegen, E.M., de Weerd, S., de Wit, L.T. Health-related quality-of-life in patients with morbid obesity after gastric banding for surgically induced weight loss. Surgery. 2004 May;135(5):489-97

7   Sjöström, L, Narbro, K., Sjöström C.D., Karason, K., Larsson, B., Wedel, H., Lystig, T., Sullivan, M., Bouchard, C., Carlsson, B., Bengtsson, C., Dahlgren, S., Gummesson, A., Jacobson, P., Karlsson, J., Lindroos, A.K., Lönroth, H., Näslund,

I., Olbers, T., Stenlöf, K., Torgerson, J., Agren, G., Carlsson, L.M. Swedish obese subjects study. Effects of bariatric surgery on mortality in Swedish obese subjects. N Engl J Med. 2007 Aug 23;357(8):741-52

8 Adams, T.D., Gress, R.E., Smith, S.C., Halverson, R.C., Simper, S.C., Rosamond, W.D., Lamonte, M.J., Stroup, A.M., Hunt, S.C. Long-term mortality after gastric bypass surgery. N Engl J Med. 2007 Aug 23;357(8):753-61

9 O'Brien, P.E., Dixon, J.B., Brown, W., Schachter, L.M., Chapman, L., Burn, A.J., Dixon, M.E., Scheinkestel, C., Halket, C., Sutherland, L.J., Korin, A., Baquie, P. The laparoscopic adjustable gastric band (LAP-BAND): a prospective study of medium-term effects on weight, health and quality of life. Obes Surg. 2002 Oct;12(5):652-60

10 Bult, M.J., van Dalen, T., Muller, A.F. Surgical treatment of obesity. Eur J Endocrinol. 2008 Feb;158(2):135-45. Review

11 Perry, C.D., Hutter, M.M., Smith, D.B., Newhouse, J.P., McNeil, B.J. Survival and changes in comorbidities after bariatric surgery. Ann Surg. 2008 Jan;247(1):21-7

12 Sugerman, H.J., Wolfe, L.G., Sica, D.A., Clore, J.N. Diabetes and hypertension in severe obesity and effects of gastric bypass-induced weight loss. Ann Surg. 2003 Jun;237(6):751-6; discussion 757-8

13 Adams, T.D., Gress, R.E., Smith, S.C., Halverson, R.C., Simper, S.C., Rosamond, W.D., Lamonte, M.J., Stroup, A.M., Hunt, S.C. Long-term mortality after gastric bypass surgery. N Engl J Med. 2007 Aug 23;357(8):753-61

14 Dhabuwala, A., Cannan, R.J., Stubbs, R.S. Improvement in comorbidities following weight loss from gastric bypass surgery. Obes Surg. 2000 Oct;10(5):428-35

15 AHRQ Study Finds Weight-loss Surgeries Quadrupled in Five Years. Press Release, 2005, July 12. Agency for Healthcare Research and Quality, Rockville, MD. http://www.ahrq.gov/news/press/pr2005/wtlosspr.htm

16 Popularity of Weight-Loss Surgeries. Daily News Central. 2005, July 12.

http://health.dailynewscentral.com/content/view/1265/63

17   Powers, K., Rehrig, S., Jones, D. Financial impact of obesity and bariatric surgery. Medical Clinics of North America, Volume 91, Issue 3, Pages 321-338

18   Chohen, D. Not without its risks: Recent studies show that the incidence of bariatric surgery is growing rapidly, and that cost and safety are major concerns. 2005, Dec. http://www.psp-interactive.com/issues/articles/2005-12_06.asp

19   Harvard School of Public Health. Diabetes: nutrition source. http://www.hsph.harvard.edu/nutritionsource/diabetes.html

20   Zinzindohoue F, Chevallier JM, Douard R, Elian N, Ferraz JM, Blanche JP, Berta JL, Altman JJ, Safran D, Cugnenc PH. Laparoscopic gastric banding: a minimally invasive surgical treatment for morbid obesity: prospective study of 500 consecutive patients. Ann Surg. 2003 Jan;237(1):1-9

21   O'Brien, P.E. The LAP-ABND AP system: The platform advances. Bariatric Times. 2007. 5(5). Retrieved in Aug: http://bariatrictimes.com/2007/06/02/the-lap-band-ap%e2%84%a2-system-the-platform-advances

22   O'Brien, P.E., McPhail, T., Chaston, T.B., Dixon, J.B. Systematic review of medium-term weight loss after bariatric operations. Obes Surg. 2006 Aug;16(8):1032-40

23   DeMaria EJ, Pate V, Warthen M, Winegar DA. Baseline Data from American Society for Metabolic and Bariatric Surgery – designated Bariatric Surgery Centers of Excellence using the Bariatric Outcomes Longitudinal Database. Surg Obes Relat Dis 2010(6):347-355

24   Maggard, M.A., Shugarman, L.R., Suttorp, M., Maglione, M., Sugerman, H.J., Livingston, E.H., Nguyen, N.T., Li, Z., Mojica, W.A., Hilton, L., Rhodes, S., Morton, S.C., Shekelle, P.G. Meta-analysis: surgical treatment of obesity. Ann Intern Med. 2005 Apr 5;142(7):547-59

25   Hakala, K., Stenius-Aarniala, B., Sovijärvi, A. Effects of weight loss on peak flow variability, airways obstruction, and lung volumes in obese patients with asthma. Chest. 2000 Nov;118(5):1315-21

26   Dixon, J.B., Schachter, L.M., O'Brien, P.E.. Sleep disturbance and obesity: changes following surgically induced weight loss. Arch Intern Med. 2001 Jan 8;161(1):102-6

27   Dhabuwala, A., Cannan, R.J., Stubbs, R.S. Improvement in comorbidities following weight loss from gastric bypass surgery. Obes Surg. 2000 Oct;10(5):428-35

28   Buchwald, H., Avidor, Y., Braunwald, E., Jensen, M.D., Pories, W., Fahrbach, K., Schoelles, K.. Bariatric surgery: a systematic review and meta-analysis. JAMA. 2004 Oct 13;292(14):1724-37. Review. Erratum in: JAMA. 2005 Apr 13;293(14):1728

29   Bacci, V., Basso, M.S., Greco, F., Lamberti, R., Elmore, U., Restuccia, A., Perrotta, N., Silecchia, G., Bucci, A. Modifications of metabolic and cardiovascular risk factors after weight loss induced by laparoscopic gastric banding. Obes Surg. 2002 Feb;12(1):77-82

30   Flum DR, Dellinger EP. Impact of gastric bypass operation on survival: a population-based analysis. J Am Coll Surg. 2004 Oct;199(4):543-51

31   Pories WJ, Swanson MS, MacDonald KG, Long SB, Morris PG, Brown BM, Barakat HA, deRamon RA, Israel G, Dolezal JM, et al. Who would have thought it? An operation proves to be the most effective therapy for adult-onset diabetes mellitus. Ann Surg. 1995 Sep;222(3):339-50; discussion 350-2

32   Schauer PR, Kashyap SR, Wolski K, Brethauer SA, Kirwan JP, Pothier CE, Thomas S, Abood B, Nissen SE, and Bhat DL Bariatric Surgery versus Intensive Medical Therapy in Obese Patients with Diabetes. N Engl J Med. 2012; Apr 366:1567-1576 DOI: 0.1056/NEJMoa1200225

33.   Mingrone G, Panunzi S, De Gaetano A, Guidone C, Iaconelli A, Leccesi L, Nanni G, Pomp A, Castagneto M, Ghirlanda G, and Rubino F Bariatric Surgery versus Conventional Medical Therapy for Type 2 Diabetes. N Engl J Med. 2012; Apr 366:1577-1585 DOI: 10.1056/NEJMoa1200111

34   Stratopoulos, C., Papakonstantinou, A., Terzis, I., Spiliadi, C., Dimitriades,

G., Komesidou, V., Kitsanta, P., Argyrakos, T., Hadjiyannakis, E. Changes in liver histology accompanying massive weight loss after gastroplasty for morbid obesity. Obes Surg. 2005 Sep;15(8):1154-60

35   Furuya, C.K., Jr, de Oliveira, C.P., de Mello, E.S., Faintuch, J., Raskovski, A., Matsuda, M., Vezozzo, D.C., Halpern, A., Garrido, A.B., Jr, Alves, V.A., Carrilho, F.J. Effects of bariatric surgery on nonalcoholic fatty liver disease: preliminary findings after two years. J Gastroenterol Hepatol. 2007 Apr;22(4):510-4

36   Luyckx, F.H., Desaive, C., Thiry, A., Dewé, W., Scheen, A.J., Gielen, J.E., Lefèbvre, P.J. Liver abnormalities in severely obese subjects: effect of drastic weight loss after gastroplasty. Int J Obes Relat Metab Disord. 1998 Mar;22(3):222-6

37   Dixon, J.B., O'Brien, P.E. Changes in comorbidities and improvements in quality of life after LAP-BAND placement. Am J Surg. 2002 Dec;184(6B):51S-54S. Review

38   Dixon, J.B., Dixon, M.E., O'Brien, P.E. Depression in association with severe obesity: changes with weight loss. Arch Intern Med. 2003 Sep 22;163(17):2058-65

39   Schok, M., Geenen, R., van Antwerpen, T., de Wit, P., Brand, N., van Ramshorst, B. Quality of life after laparoscopic adjustable gastric banding for severe obesity: postoperative and retrospective preoperative evaluations. Obes Surg. 2000 Dec;10(6):502-8

40   Weiner, R., Datz, M., Wagner, D., Bockhorn, H. Quality-of-life outcome after laparoscopic adjustable gastric banding for morbid obesity. Obes Surg. 1999 Dec;9(6):539-45

41   Christou, N.V., Sampalis, J.S., Liberman, M., Look, D., Auger, S., McLean, A.P., MacLean, L.D., Surgery decreases long-term mortality, morbidity, and health care use in morbidly obese patients. Ann Surg. 2004 Sep;240(3):416-23; discussion 423-4

42   Totty, P., Gastric Bypass Surgery Could Be Key to Reversing Diabetes in Non-Obese Patients. Diabetes Health, 2010 Mar.

43   Colles, S.L., Dixon, J.B., O'Brien, P.E. Grazing and loss of control related to

eating: two high-risk factors following bariatric surgery. Nature Publishing Group. Obesity Journal 2008 March 16(3) :615-22.

44   Klem, M.L., Wing, R.R., Chang, C.C., Lang, W., McGuire, M.T., Sugerman, H.J., Hutchison, S.L., Makovich, A.L., Hill, J.O. A case-control study of successful maintenance of a substantial weight loss: individuals who lost weight through surgery versus those who lost weight through nonsurgical means. Int J Obes Relat Metab Disord. 2000 May;24(5):573-9

45   Busetto, L., Mirabelli, D., Petroni, M.L., Mazza, M., Favretti, F., Segato, G., Chiusolo, M., Merletti, F., Balzola, F., Enzi, G. Comparative long-term mortality after laparoscopic adjustable gastric banding versus nonsurgical controls. Surg Obes Relat Dis. 2007 Sep-Oct;3(5):496-502; discussion 502

46   Belachew, M., Belva, P.H., Desaive, C. Long-term results of laparoscopic adjustable gastric banding for the treatment of morbid obesity. Obesity surgery. 2002, Aug 29; 12(4):564-68

47   Becker, S. Pa. Report: ASCs save medicare $464 million annually. Jan 18, 2008. Becker's ASC review retrieved on 28th March, 2008: http://www.beckersasc.com/ambulatory-surgery-center/surgery-center-education/pa.-report-ascs-save-medicare-464-million-annually.html

48   Helzner, J., ASCs vs hospitals: Struggling over a flawed system. Ophthalmology Management. 2004: November. http://www.ophmanagement.com/article.aspx?article=86225

49   Outpatient Departments. Healthcare Economist. Retrieved on March 28, 2008: http://healthcare-economist.com/2008/01/07/a-study-in-quality-ambulatory-surgery-centers-vs-hospital-outpatient-departments/http://content.healthaffairs.org/cgi/content/full/22/6/68

50   Brechner, R.J., Farris, C., Harrison, S., Tillman, K., Salive, M., Phurrough, S. A graded, evidence-based summary of evidence for bariatric surgery. Surg Obes Relat Dis. 2005 Jul-Aug;1(4):430-41. Review

51   Ebell, M.H. Predicting mortality risk in patients undergoing bariatric

surgery. Am Fam Physician. 2008 Jan 15;77(2):220-1

52   Morino, M., Toppino, M., Forestieri, P., Angrisani, L., Allaix, M.E., Scopinaro, N. Mortality after bariatric surgery: analysis of 13,871 morbidly obese patients from a national registry. Ann Surg. 2007 Dec;246(6):1002-7; discussion 1007-9

53   Fernandez, A.Z., Jr, Demaria, E.J., Tichansky, D.S., Kellum, J.M., Wolfe, L.G., Meador, J., Sugerman, H.J. Multivariate analysis of risk factors for death following gastric bypass for treatment of morbid obesity. Ann Surg. 2004 May;239(5):698-702; discussion 702-3

54   Roux-en-Y Gastric Bypass (RYGB) is another bariatric procedure endorsed by the NIH Consensus Report on surgical treatment of severe clinical obesity. http://www.annecollins.com/lose_weight/roux-en-y-gastric-bypass.htm

55   Rutledge, R., Continued excellent results with the Mini-Gastric Bypass: Six year study in 2,410 patients. Obes. Surg. 2005;15:1304-8

56   Wang, W., Short term results of Laparoscopic Mini-Gastric Bypass. Obes. Surg. 2005;15: 648-654

57   Chakhtoura, G., Primary results of Laparoscopic Mini-Gastric Bypass in a French obesity surgery specialized university hospital. Obes. Surg. 2008; 18: 1130-3

58   Lee, W.J., Laparoscopic Rouz-en-Y vs. Mini-Gastric Bypass for the treatment of morbid obesity: A prospective randomized controlled clinical trial. Obes. Surg. 2005; 242(1):20-8

59   Peraglie, C., Laparoscopic Mini-Gastric Bypass in the super, super obese: Outcomes in sixteen patients. Obes. Surg. 2008; 18: 1126-9

60   Loffredo, A., Cappuccio, M., De Luca, M., de Werra, C., Galloro, G., Naddeo, M., Forestieri, P. Three years experience with the new intragastric balloon, and a preoperative test for success with restrictive surgery. Obes Surg. 2001 Jun;11(3):330-3

61   Genco, A., Bruni, T., Doldi, S.B., Forestieri, P., Marino, M., Busetto, L.,

Giardiello, C., Angrisani, L., Pecchioli, L., Stornelli, P., Puglisi, F., Alkilani, M., Nigri, A., Di Lorenzo, N., Furbetta, F., Cascardo, A., Cipriano, M., Lorenzo M., Basso, N. BioEnterics Intragastric Balloon: The Italian Experience with 2,515 Patients. Obes Surg. 2005 Sep;15(8):1161-4

62   Angrisani, L., Lorenzo, M., Borrelli, V., Giuffré, M., Fonderico, C., Capece, G. Is bariatric surgery necessary after intragastric balloon treatment? Obes Surg. 2006 Sep;16(9):1135-7

63   Favretti, F., De Luca, M., Segato, G., Busetto, L., Ceoloni, A., Magon, A., Enzi, G. Treatment of morbid obesity with the transcend implantable gastric stimulator (IGS): a prospective survey. Obes Surg. 2004 May;14(5):666-70

64   De Luca, M., Segato, G., Busetto, L., Favretti, F., Aigner, F., Weiss, H., de Gheldere, C., Gaggiotti, G., Himpens, J., Limao, J., Scheyer, M., Toppino, M., Zurmeyer, E.L., Bottani, G., Penthaler, H., Progress in implantable gastric stimulation: summary of results of the European multi-center study. Obes Surg. 2004 Sep;14 Suppl 1:S33-9

65   Cigaina, V. Long-term follow-up of gastric stimulation for obesity: the Mestre eight-year experience. Obes Surg. 2004 Sep;14 Suppl 1:S14-22

66   Brolin, R.L., Robertson, L.B., Kenler, H.A., Cody, R.P. Weight loss and dietary intake after vertical banded gastroplasty and Roux-en-Y gastric bypass. Ann Surg. 1994 Dec;220(6):782-90

67   Balsiger, B.M., Poggio, J.L., Mai, J., Kelly, K.A., Sarr, M.G. Ten and more years after vertical banded gastroplasty as primary operation for morbid obesity. J Gastrointest Surg. 2000 Nov-Dec;4(6):598-605

68   Trus, T.L., Pope, G.D., Finlayson, S.R. National trends in utilization and outcomes of bariatric surgery. Surg Endosc. 2005 May;19(5):616-20

69   Santry, H.P., Gillen, D.L., Lauderdale, D.S. Trends in bariatric surgical procedures. JAMA. 2005 Oct 19;294(15):1909-17

70   Nguyen, N.T., Paya, M., Stevens, C.M., Mavandadi, S., Zainabadi, K., Wilson, S.E. The relationship between hospital volume and outcome in bariatric

surgery at academic medical centers. Ann Surg. 2004 Oct;240(4):586-93; discussion 593-4

71   Flum, D.R., Salem, L., Elrod, J.A., Dellinger, E.P., Cheadle, A., Chan, L., Early mortality among Medicare beneficiaries undergoing bariatric surgical procedures. JAMA. 2005 Oct 19;294(15):1903-8

72   Liu, J.H., Zingmond, D., Etzioni, D.A., O'Connell, J.B., Maggard, M.A., Livingston, E.H., Liu, C.D., Ko, C.Y. Characterizing the performance and outcomes of obesity surgery in California. Am Surg. 2003 Oct;69(10):823-8

73   O'Brien, P.E., Dixon, J.B. LAP-BAND: outcomes and results. J Laparoendosc Adv Surg Tech A. 2003 Aug;13(4):265-70

74   Chapman, A.E., Kiroff, G., Game, P., Foster, B., O'Brien, P., Ham, J., Maddern, G.J. Laparoscopic adjustable gastric banding in the treatment of obesity: a systematic literature review. Surgery. 2004 Mar;135(3):326-51. Review

75   Adams, K.F., Schatzkin, A., Harris, T.B., Kipnis, V., Mouw, T., Ballard-Barbash, R., Hollenbeck, A., Leitzmann, M.F. Overweight, obesity, and mortality in a large prospective cohort of persons 50 to 71 years old. N Engl J Med. 2006 Aug 24;355(8):763-78. Epub 2006 Aug 22

76   Calle, E.E., Thun, M.J., Petrelli, J.M., Rodriguez, C., Heath, C.W., Jr. Body-mass index and mortality in a prospective cohort of U.S. adults. N Engl J Med. 1999 Oct 7;341(15):1097-105

77   Damiani, G., Pinnarelli, L., Sammarco, A., Sommella, L., Francucci, M., Ricciardi, W. Postoperative pulmonary function in open versus laparoscopic cholecystectomy: A meta-analysis of the Tiffenau Index. Dig Surg. 2008 Jan 30;25(1):1-7

78   Karayiannakis, A.J., Makri, G.G., Mantzioka, A., Karousos, D., Karatzas, G. Postoperative pulmonary function after laparoscopic and open cholecystectomy. Br J Anaesth. 1996 Oct;77(4):448-52

79   Zacks, S.L., Sandler, R.S., Rutledge, R., Brown, R.S., Jr. A population-based cohort study comparing laparoscopic cholecystectomy and open cholecystectomy.

Am J Gastroenterol. 2002 Feb;97(2):334-40

80   Staph infections are more common because of the impaired blood supply through the extensive subcutaneous fat. The infection-fighting and prevention cells of the body have to travel to the skin to prevent infections, and obesity make that travel more difficult.

81   Suter, M., Giusti, V., Héraief, E., Calmes, J.M. Band erosion after laparoscopic gastric banding: occurrence and results after conversion to Roux-en-Y gastric bypass. Obes Surg. 2004 Mar;14(3):381-6

82   Suter, M., Calmes, J.M., Paroz, A., Giusti, V. A 10-year experience with laparoscopic gastric banding for morbid obesity: high long-term complication and failure rates. Obes Surg. 2006 Jul;16(7):829-35

83   Weiner, R., Blanco-Engert, R., Weiner, S., Matkowitz, R., Schaefer, L., Pomhoff, I. Outcome after laparoscopic adjustable gastric banding – eight years experience. Obes Surg. 2003 Jun;13(3):427-34

84   Weiner, R.A., Weiner, S., Pomhoff, I., Jacobi, C., Makarewicz, W., Weigand, G. Laparoscopic sleeve gastrectomy – influence of sleeve size and resected gastric volume. Obes Surg. 2007 Oct;17(10):1297-305

85   Mognol, P., Chosidow, D., Marmuse, J.P. Laparoscopic sleeve gastrectomy (LSG): review of a new bariatric procedure and initial results. Surg Technol Int. 2006;15:47-52. Review

86   Cottam, D., Qureshi, F.G., Mattar, S.G., Sharma, S., Holover, S., Bonanomi, G., Ramanathan, R., Schauer, P. Laparoscopic sleeve gastrectomy as an initial weight-loss procedure for high-risk patients with morbid obesity. Surg Endosc. 2006 Jun;20(6):859-63. Epub 2006 Apr 22

87   Braghetto, I., Korn, O., Valladares, H., Gutiérrez, L., Csendes, A., Debandi, A., Castillo, J., Rodríguez, A., Burgos, A.M., Brunet, L. Laparoscopic sleeve gastrectomy: surgical technique, indications and clinical results. Obes Surg. 2007 Nov;17(11):1442-50

88   Garcia, V.F., DeMaria, E.J., Adolescent bariatric surgery: treatment

delayed, treatment denied, a crisis invited. Obes Surg. 2006 Jan;16(1):1-4

89   Sugerman, H.J., Sugerman, E.L., DeMaria, E.J., Kellum, J.M., Kennedy, C., Mowery, Y., Wolfe, L.G. Bariatric surgery for severely obese adolescents. J Gastrointest Surg. 2003 Jan;7(1):102-7; discussion 107-8

90   Collins, J., Mattar, S., Qureshi, F., Warman, J., Ramanathan, R., Schauer, P., Eid, G. Initial outcomes of laparoscopic Roux-en-Y gastric bypass in morbidly obese adolescents. Surg Obes Relat Dis. 2007 Mar-Apr;3(2):147-52

91   Dillard, B.E. III, Gorodner, V., Galvani, C., Holterman, M., Browne, A., Gallo, A., Horgan, S., Le Holterman, A.X. Initial experience with the adjustable gastric band in morbidly obese U.S. adolescents and recommendations for further investigation. J Pediatr Gastroenterol Nutr. 2007 Aug;45(2):240-6

92   Summary of Clinical Measures And Data

Measurements at baseline (one to six months before surgery) and at approximately one month, three months, six months, nine months and twelve months after surgery, and then annually thereafter:

      ii.   Weight

      iii.   BMI (Body Mass Index)

      iv.   Resolution/development of comorbid conditions

Height

Total weight loss

Percent weight loss

      Participants

      Number of Subjects: The study population will consist of 25-50 adolescent (15-18 years old) patients who are undergoing or have undergone laparoscopic adjustable gastric band operation performed by a bariatric surgeon at Western Bariatric Institute (WBI).

      Inclusion Criteria: The subject may be enrolled if he/she meets all the following criteria:

Male or female subject 15-18 years old and is scheduled to have laparoscopic adjustable gastric band procedure.

The subject meets criteria for gastric bypass surgery as outlined by National Institutes for Health (NIH).

The subject has completed a bariatric surgery screening visit with a physician at WBI.

The subject has a physician's referral for a preoperative nutrition evaluation and postoperative fellow-up visit.

The subject is given written informed consent prior to enrolling in the study.

The subject has the physical, motivational, and intellectual ability to understand and follow all aspects of study requirement.

Exclusion Criteria: Subjects will be excluded from the study for any of the following reasons:

The subject does not meet the criteria for bariatric surgery as outlined by the National Institutes for Health.

The subject is not physically, motivationally and intellectually able to understand and follow all aspects of study requirement.

The subject is not willing to participate in both the nutrition evaluation and postoperative follow-up visit.

The subject has not completed a bariatric surgery screening visit with a physician at WBI.

The subject does not have a physician's referral for a preoperative nutrition evaluation and postoperative follow-up visit.

The subject is not willing to consent to release of data.

93   Busetto, L., Angrisani, L., Basso, N., Favretti, F., Furbetta, F., Lorenzo, M.; Italian Group for LAP-BAND. Safety and efficacy of laparoscopic adjustable gastric banding in the elderly. Obesity (Silver Spring). 2008 Feb;16(2):334-8

94   Taylor, C.J., Layani, L., Laparoscopic adjustable gastric banding in patients > or =60 years old: is it worthwhile? Obes Surg. 2006 Dec;16(12):1579-83

95   Sugerman, H.J., DeMaria, E.J., Kellum, J. Sugerman, E.L., Meador,

J.G., Wolfe, L.G. Effects of bariatric surgery on older patients. Annals of Surgery. 240(2):243-247, August 2004

96   Papasavas, P.K., Gagné, D.J., Kelly, J., Caushaj, P.F., Laparoscopic Roux-En-Y gastric bypass is a safe and effective operation for the treatment of morbid obesity in patients older than 55 years. Obes Surg. 2004 Sep;14(8):1056-61

97   HCUP Fact Book No. 9: Ambulatory Surgery in U.S. Hospitals, 2003 (continued) Part II: Detailed Statistics for Selected Procedures and Populations Procedures Influenced by Technological Advances. Retrieved on April 30, 2008 from: http://www.ahrq.gov/data/hcup/factbk9/factbk9c.htm

In 2003, only 3 percent of bariatric surgeries performed outpatient

Mean age for bariatric operation patients 42 years, inpatient or outpatient

Almost all bariatric surgeries performed outpatient in patients ages 18 to 64 (55.7 percent in patients ages 18 to 44 and 42.9 percent in patients ages 45 to 64)

Nearly 83 percent of outpatient bariatric surgeries performed on females

Private insurers billed for eight out of 10 outpatient bariatric operations. 5 percent of outpatient operations billed to government insurance programs (i.e., Medicare and Medicaid)

Rate of outpatient bariatric surgeries billed to uninsured patients was almost 5 times rate of inpatient bariatric surgeries billed to this group (11.6 percent versus 2.4 percent). This finding may reflect surgeries among patients who are otherwise insured, but opt to self-pay for outpatient bariatric surgery, which is often less expensive, when bariatric surgery is not a covered benefit.

98   Regi Schindler of BLIS, Inc., a company currently providing such insurance or warranty coverage, puts it this way: "If everyone pays a little bit more for the premium, then very few people will have to be exposed to financial hardship should a complication arise."

99   Sasse, KC, et al, Pre-Surgical Weight Loss Using Protein Meal Replacement Shakes is Associated with Durable Surgical Weight Loss Results at 3 years (Manuscript Submitted)

100   Dávila-Cervantes, A., Domínguez-Cherit, G., Borunda, D., Gamino, R., Vargas-Vorackova, F., González-Barranco, J., Herrera, M.F. Impact of surgically-induced weight loss on respiratory function: a prospective analysis. Obes Surg. 2004 Nov-Dec;14(10):1389-92

101   Thomas, P.S., Cowen, E.R., Hulands, G., Milledge, J.S. Respiratory function in the morbidly obese before and after weight loss. Thorax. 1989 May;44(5):382-6

102   Sabar, R., Kaye, A.D., Frost, E.A., Perioperative considerations for the patient on herbal medicines. Middle East J Anesthesiol. 2001 Oct;16(3):287-314. Review

103   Kaye, A.D., Kucera, I., Sabar, R.. Perioperative anesthesia clinical considerations of alternative medicines. Anesthesiol Clin North America. 2004 Mar;22(1):125-39. Review

104   Lee, et al. Overweight, Obesity and Mortality in a Large Prospective Cohort of Persons 50-71 Years Old. NEJM 2004; 103

Index

A

D

E

F

H

I

J

K

L

M

N

O

Q

R

S

T

U

V

W

Z

Other books in the
'A SasseGuide Series'

Check with *iMetabolic.com* or *Amazon* for availability and ordering

E-Books Available

Weight-Loss Surgery: Which One is Right for You? (SasseGuide) (360 Publishing, 2009)

After Weight Loss Surgery (SasseGuide) (360 Publishing, 2009)

Available in Paperback

Doctor's Orders: 101 Medically Proven Tips for Losing Weight (SasseGuide) (360 Publishing, 2009)

Life-Changing Weight Loss: Feel More Energetic and Live a More Active Life with a Proven, Medically Based Weight-Loss Program (SasseGuide) (360 Publishing, 2010)